THE INTELLIGENCE MEN: Makers of the IQ Controversy

ALSO BY RAYMOND E. FANCHER

Psychoanalytic Psychology: The Development of Freud's Thought
Pioneers of Psychology

THE INTELLIGENCE MEN: Makers of the IQ Controversy

Raymond E. Fancher

W·W·NORTON & COMPANY · New York · London

Published simultaneously in Canada by Penguin Books Canada Ltd., 2801 John Street, Markham, Ontario L3R 1B4.
Printed in the United States of America.

The text of this book is composed in 10/12 Baskerville, with display type set in Windsor Light Condensed. Composition and manufacturing by The Maple-Vail Book Manufacturing Group.
Book design by Nancy Dale Muldoon.

First published as a Norton paperback 1987.

Library of Congress Cataloging in Publication Data

Fancher, Raymond E.
    The intelligence men: Makers of the IQ controversy.

    Bibliography: p.
    Includes index.
    1. Intellect.   2. Intelligence tests—History.
    I. Title.
BF431.F27   1985   153.9   84-27381

ISBN 0-393-95525-7

W. W. Norton & Company, Inc., 500 Fifth Avenue, New York, N.Y. 10110
W. W. Norton & Company Ltd., 37 Great Russell Street, London WC1B 3NU

2 3 4 5 6 7 8 9 0

In memoriam

Bernard Norton

Contents

List of Portraits

Preface

Few scientific issues arouse as much public interest, emotional heat, or general confusion as the so-called "IQ controversy." Indeed, those who have ventured to express opinions about the meanings or causes of individual differences in intelligence test scores have sometimes found themselves embroiled in disputes considerably more violent than they bargained for. Consider, for example, the experience of Harvard psychologist Richard Herrnstein, who in 1971 attempted to summarize some basic facts about IQ tests in an article for the popular *Atlantic Monthly* magazine.[1]

Here, Herrnstein argued that IQ scores have proven to be reasonably accurate predictors of people's occupational levels, and thus of differences in social class. He also cited evidence which seemed to indicate that genetic factors are more important than environmental ones in producing different IQ scores, and hence differences in social class. Further, he warned that, ironically enough, this apparent prepotency of heredity over environment might become even greater if social progress were to be made toward the equalization of all people's environments. That is, if everyone has the same environmental advantages, then differences in their *innate* abilities will perhaps loom proportionately even larger than they do now.

Herrnstein did not *advocate* this as a *desirable* consequence of greater environmental equality, but simply pointed to it as a possibility that might have to be reckoned with in the future. More-over, he took pains to argue that the available genetic evidence had no bearing on the potentially explosive *racial* question, and did not rule out a completely environmentalist explanation for the somewhat lower average IQ scores obtained by black than by white Americans.

Herrnstein's article aroused a large but generally decorous response, both pro and con, from fellow scientists who flooded the *Atlantic* with letters to the editor.[2] In general, these represented the sort of thoughtful response he had hoped to stimulate. By raising the IQ issue in the popular press, however, Herrnstein also touched off a more irrational and disturbing public reaction.

In Boston, radical college students promptly distributed leaflets entitled "Fight Harvard Prof's Fascist Lies," and staged a demonstration outside the *Atlantic*'s editorial offices to protest the publication of Herrnstein's article.[3] Soon thereafter Harvard radicals initiated a "fall offensive" against Herrnstein by planting non-enrolled demonstrators in his lecture classes. "Wanted for Racism" posters bearing his photograph appeared on campus, accusing him of "misusing science" in support of "racial superiority, male supremacy, and unemployment." When he tried to deny these unwarranted and irresponsible charges at a public meeting, he was heckled from the floor as a "political reactionary," and as he left the hall a member of the audience threatened to stab him some night in the Harvard Yard.

Herrnstein's reputation with student radicals spread throughout the country, and even rose to plague him when he visited the University of Iowa to lecture on animal psychology, a topic far removed from the issue of intelligence testing. Activist groups there circulated slanderous leaflets like those in Boston, and packed the auditorium with demonstrators before his scheduled talk. As Herrnstein approached the lecture hall he heard some three hundred people inside rhythmically shouting "We want Herrnstein," and decided to follow police advice by departing in an unmarked car. Two weeks later, he felt compelled to cancel another scheduled talk on animal psychology, at Princeton University, because of threatened violence by demonstrators.

Herrnstein's persecution is not the only recent example of improper response to the IQ controversy, nor has all of the malfeasance been on the "radical" or anti-testing side. As the following pages will document more fully, some individuals have in fact done what Herrnstein was falsely accused of, by drawing unwarranted racist conclusions from ambiguous scientific evidence concerning the genetics of intelligence. In one of the more spectacular scientific news stories of the 1970s, an eminent supporter of IQ testing whose studies were widely accepted as providing the best available evidence in favor of the genetic factor was found guilty of fraudulently fabricating his data. In short, culpability and virtue have been confusingly mixed among the participants in the IQ controversy, just as the scientific evidence regarding it has been mixed.

Any attempt to deal rationally with the IQ controversy must recognize that it entails two logically distinct but practically interrelated disputes. First is the so-called "nature-nurture" question, which asks the degree to which individual differences in intelligence are attributable to hereditary and congenital factors ("nature") on the one hand, or to environmental factors ("nurture") on the other. Nearly all scientists agree that both factors play some role, but they differ as to the relative importance which should be assigned to each. Inasmuch as differing opinions on this question point logically to differing social policies for improving the overall levels of intelligence in society, the debate can become hotly politicized, as it was made by Herrnstein's radical antagonists.

The second disputed issue concerns the validity of the *tests* actually used to measure intellectual ability. "Intelligence" is not a simple quantity, susceptible to straightforward measurement in the way that height and weight are. Any measure of it inevitably entails a complex series of assumptions about what intelligence is and how it manifests itself. And while all of the currently most popular tests have demonstrated a certain degree of practical usefulness, at least in some situations, disagreement still exists over exactly what it is they measure, and whether they measure the same thing for all populations of subjects. Some strongly question the propriety, for example, of using a test that was originally developed for a basically white, middle-class population to estimate the intelligence of children from cultural minorities. When differing opinions on questions like this are compounded by the differing possible attitudes toward the nature-nurture issue, a bewildering array of final positions on the general IQ controversy emerges.

This book attempts to ease if not remove the bewilderment by examining the two aspects of the IQ controversy from a biographical and historical perspective. Questions concerning intelligence and its origins inevitably strike close to some of the deepest questions people may have about themselves—about what their "true" abilities may be, for example, or about what they would have turned out like had they had different parentages or upbringings. Biographies of the protagonists in the IQ controversy often reveal life circumstances which led them to consider these kinds of questions particularly seriously, and to favor certain kinds of answers over others. Thus a biographical approach helps show how disparate but equally sincerely held attitudes toward the IQ controversy can be adopted by generally reasonable people.

This book's historical perspective will show that the recent IQ controversy is but the latest phase of a debate which has been going on for a very long time now. Attempts to resolve the nature-nurture question today still rely on basic techniques and arguments that were developed over a century ago, and, despite innumerable refinements of method and conception, many of today's pronouncements are really echoes of much older voices. Moreover, historical analysis shows that modern intelligence tests are the complex outgrowth of at least two separate research programs—their having been originally *conceived of* as potential devices for detecting inheritable genius in young adults, but first *successfully developed* as measures of mental retardation in children. Many of the ambiguities and disputes surrounding intelligence tests today derive from a confusion of the aims and ideas of these two programs. By understanding these and other historical factors, we are granted a clearer view of the complexities underlying the present IQ controversy.

The chapters of this book follow a roughly chronological sequence, with Chapter 1 introducing the general nature-nurture controversy through the biographies of John Stuart Mill (1806–1874) and Francis Galton (1822–1911). These two English child prodigies grew up to develop diametrically opposed theories to account for their own—and everyone else's—intellectual abilities. Galton, the proponent of hereditary explanations, first popularized the very phrase "nature and nurture," and invented many of the experimental techniques still used to try to distinguish between the effects of the two factors.

Galton also originated the *idea* of the intelligence test, and Chapter 2 opens with an account of his generally unsuccessful attempts to develop workable tests. The main part of the chapter is devoted to the life and work of Alfred Binet (1857–1911), the French psychologist who succeeded where Galton had failed. Starting with aims and assumptions more like Mill's than Galton's, Binet pioneered the approach to intelligence test construction that is still generally followed today.

Binet died before he could fully develop or perfect his tests, however, and Chapters 3 and 4 describe the men and ideas primarily responsible for the evolution of intelligence testing following his death. Chapter 3 tells how Binet's immediate successors adopted his testing methods but promoted an interpretation of test results more in line with Galton's basic philosophy. Chapter 4 describes the three American psychologists who made intelligence testing the influential and nearly ubiquitous industry it remains today.

Chapter 5 returns to the nature-nurture question, with an account of how twin studies (another idea of Galton's) have recently been used—and misused—in attempts to sort out the separate influences of heredity and environment on IQ test scores. Arthur Jensen and Leon Kamin, two outspoken and opposing voices of recent years, are shown to be the modern counterparts of Galton and Mill, respectively. The conclusion offers a personal assessment of the current state of the IQ controversy.

Research for this book was both begun and ended in England, with the generous support of Leave Fellowships from the Canada Council in 1976–77, and from the Social Sciences and Humanities Research Council of Canada in 1983–84. In between, two small research grants from York University's Faculty of Arts helped a great deal.

Professors Arthur Jensen and Leon Kamin were extremely gracious in providing information about themselves and their work for Chapter 5. Norman Endler and Theta Wolf commented helpfully on parts of the manuscript, and the editorial staff at Norton—Mary Cunnane, Donald Fusting, Debra Makay, and Katie Nelson—offered their customary invaluable services. Seth Fancher assisted ably with the proofreading.

My special thanks go to Michael Sokal, who went beyond the call of duty and friendship alike in providing a detailed and always constructive commentary on the entire manuscript. He did his best to make a historian out of a psychologist—not always the easiest of tasks.

My interest in many of the figures discussed in this book was stimulated and maintained through contacts with my friend Bernard Norton. To the immense sadness of all who knew him, and to the great loss of British history of science, Bernard died in December of 1984. This book is dedicated to his memory.

THE INTELLIGENCE MEN: Makers of the IQ Controversy

1 | The Nature-Nurture Controversy

In 1760, the musician Leopold Mozart was astounded when his four-year-old son wrote out a "concerto" for harpsichord, ink-bespattered and too difficult for anyone to play, but completely correct musically. This was but one of several signs that convinced Leopold that God had entrusted him with the care and upbringing of an extraordinary genius. He abandoned his own serious professional ambitions to devote himself instead to the musical education of his son, and to the promotion of his son's career. In due course, Wolfgang Amadeus Mozart (1756–1791) became not only the most celebrated child prodigy in Europe, but also the greatest composer of his time.

More than a century later, the linguist and college professor Leo Wiener became unhappy with the formal educational opportunities available for *his* young son, who had already learned to read at home at the age of three. Leo undertook to educate the boy himself, communicating his own broad knowledge and interests during breaks from his work. When finally released into the ordinary academic world, Norbert Wiener (1894–1964) was admitted to Tufts College at age eleven, and then gained national recognition as a fourteen-year-old graduate student at Harvard. As a man, he became internationally famous as a mathematician and originator of the science of cybernetics.

These two cases followed a similar pattern: children who showed early sparks of ability, which were detected by knowledgeable parents who followed up with specialized training. Despite the similarity, however, Leopold Mozart and Leo Wiener arrived at very different explanations for their sons' successes. Leopold Mozart had no doubt that his son had been born with an unparalleled degree of musical ability, the flowering of which was merely facilitated somewhat by his careful nurture. Leo Wiener, asked by a reporter to account for *his* son's accomplishments, replied, "It is nonsense to say, as some people do, that Norbert [and his sisters] are unusually gifted children. They are nothing of the sort. If they know more than other children of their age, it is because they have been trained differently."[1]

Neither of these explanations is unassailable, of course. On the one hand, Leopold Mozart provided his son with a stimulating environment in a musical household from birth onward, and it may be argued that he grossly underestimated the influence of that environment and the specialized instruction he was so unusually qualified to give. On the other hand, the elder Wiener may well have underestimated his son's native gifts. Norbert Wiener himself, while acknowledging the influence of his father's teaching, came to believe that he had been born with greater than average ability, which made him particularly responsive to his father's tutelage. He pointed to the failure of his younger brother to respond as well as he had to his father's training as one indicator of the insufficiency of education alone.[2]

Such are some of the complexities of the "nature-nurture controversy" as it pertains to the origins of human abilities. In virtually all documented cases of child prodigies, some early sign of ability (indicating the child's "nature") has been accompanied by a program of specialized and intense training (the "nurture"). Further, modern psychologists and experts on child development continue to disagree about the relative importance of these two factors, much as the Mozart and Wiener fathers did. In the summer of 1981, for example, two psychologists were asked to comment on Ruth Lawrence, a ten-year-old mathematical prodigy in England. Taught completely at home by her computer-expert father, she had received the top marks in England's national mathematics examinations, designed for students some six years older than she. One of the experts emphasized her special training, as compared to normal educational programs: "What she did is unusual only because we [normally] damage our children so badly from the start. We repress their initial ability; children are taught things as if they are incompetent, or that things are difficult and can't be done." The second expert emphasized the inability of training to transcend the limits set by natural ability: "I think that most of the evidence points to the fact that genius is an inborn phenomenon. You can train someone in a particular skill, but that doesn't constitute genius."[3] These two comments are not entirely irreconcilable, of course, but they do represent the contrasting viewpoints of two modern protagonists in the nature-nurture controversy.

As it happens, most of the scientific terms, techniques, and lines of argument which characterize the modern nature-nurture controversy were laid out more than a century ago by a pair of Englishmen who had both been impressive child prodigies themselves. Both had intellectually eminent forebears, pointing to a possible genetic factor in their own abilities, and both received the intensive early training common to most prodigies. Yet one, John Stuart Mill (1806–1874), came to believe passionately in the preeminent power of environment and circumstance to produce all of the major differences between people in ability and character; while the other, Francis Galton (1822–1911), was just as fervent on the opposite side.

Advocate of an *associationistic psychology* which emphasized the experiential basis of all human knowledge, Mill was openly contemptuous of the nativist argument, writing, "Of all vulgar modes of escaping from the consideration of the social and moral influences on the human mind, the most vulgar is that attributing the diversities of human conduct and character to inherent original natural differences."[4] Consistent with these beliefs, Mill argued that the greatest differences between races and sexes, as well as between individuals, are due to environmental and circumstantial factors. Sometimes called "the patron saint of liberty," Mill and his arguments are still widely cited by supporters of the nurture side in the nature-nurture controversy.

Galton came to a diametrically opposed explanation of differences in human ability, whether between races, sexes, or individuals. His contempt for the environmentalist view matched that of Mill for the nativist:

> I have no patience with the hypothesis occasionally expressed, and often implied, especially in tales written to teach children to be good, that babies are born pretty much alike. . . . It is in the most unqualified way that I object to pretensions of natural equality. The experiences of the nursery, the school, the University, and of professional careers, are a chain of proofs to the contrary.[5]

The first person to argue strenuously that the major psychological characteristics are *inherited* as well as innate, Galton first popularized the expression "nature and nurture," and developed many research techniques still used by behavior geneticists today in his attempts to demonstrate the great influence of the former. He originated and named the *eugenics* movement, whose purpose is to improve the hereditary quality of the human race by following selective breeding practices. In the service of eugenics, he also originated the basic idea for the intelligence test, which he envisioned as a tool for selecting the most able young men and women for eugenic breeding.

Examination of the early lives of Mill and Galton shows that they were led by their experiences to respond very differently to their own precocity, and in ways that clearly foreshadowed their mature views. Thus their childhood biographies serve as excellent prefaces to a discussion of the fundamental issues in the nature-nurture controversy, and also help to explain how two very able people can sincerely come to disagree so sharply on those issues.

John Stuart Mill (1806–1874) *(National Portrait Gallery, London)*

JOHN STUART MILL: THE MAKING OF AN ENVIRONMENTALIST

John Stuart Mill was deliberately reared to be a monument to the power of education, by a father with attitudes similar to Leo Wiener's. James Mill (1773–1836) was not only an outstanding scholar, but also the principal spokesman for the so-called "utilitarian" or "philsophical radical" school founded by his mentor Jeremy Bentham (1748–1832). To achieve their goal of bringing "the greatest good to the greatest number," Mill and

Bentham wished to make government more responsive to the interests of the great masses of people. Ultimately and ideally this would require extending them the right to vote—restricted at the time in Britain to landowners. First, however, the masses would have to be educated to assume power responsibly. The recent bloody excesses of mob rule in the French Revolution seemed evidence to many of the total unsuitability of the poor for political responsibility. To make their case, the Benthamites would have to prove the power of education. Accordingly, they strongly supported experimental educational programs of many kinds. As a demonstration of the extent to which learning could potentially be accelerated, James Mill personally undertook the tutelage of his eldest child John.

Beginning at an age before John could remember, he and his father worked at the same table, while James conducted lessons during breaks from his own voluminous writing. Training in Greek began at age three, with John memorizing the English definitions of Greek words that had been written on cards—thus indicating that he already could read English. He quickly proceeded to translating actual Greek classics, beginning with Aesop's *Fables.* By the age of eight, John's reading had included the original Greek versions of the whole of Herodotus, much of Xenophon, and the first six dialogues of Plato (though he later candidly confessed that he had not quite *understood* some of the Plato on first reading). At age eight he started on Latin, which he was required not only to learn himself but also to teach to his younger sister. By twelve, he had both read and taught the major Latin classics, and in after-dinner lessons had learned mathematics through the differential calculus.

James Mill was an exacting taskmaster; an otherwise admiring friend once called him "excessively severe" and noted that "no fault, however trivial, escapes his notice; none goes without reprehension or punishment."[6] But at the same time James tried to ensure that his training was *useful,* and involved more than the mere exercise of memory. He always discussed the *meaning* of the classics with his son, and saw to it that formal study was augmented by ample reading in English books John chose himself. Writing was also encouraged, and throughout his child-hood John produced a series of historical sketches, culminating in a book-length "History of the Roman Government" when he was twelve. He also dabbled in the writing of verse—a literary form not much esteemed by his practical father, but which he permitted for the characteristic reason that "people in general attached more value to verse than it deserved, and the power of writing it was, on this account, worth acquiring."[7] *

James Mill gave further practical emphasis to John's educa-tion by engaging him at an early age as an assistant in his own professional scholarship. When James Mill's massive *History of India* was being readied for publication in 1817, eleven-year-old John read the manuscript aloud as James corrected the galley proofs. A much more remarkable collaboration occurred two years later, as James Mill wished to produce a readable account of the theory contained in his friend David Ricardo's classic but mon-umentally obscure writings on economics. Each day, on a walk with John, James would lecture on some aspect of this difficult subject. The next day, John would produce a written account of the lecture, which, he noted, "[my father] made me rewrite over and over again until it was clear, precise, and tolerably com-plete."[8] In due course, James used the collection of his son's accounts as the basis of his own popular book, *Elements of Political Economy.* The subject of logic was worked through in a similar way, but here the written accounts would later serve as the start-ing point for *John*'s first published book, *A System of Logic,* com-pleted in 1843. When James wrote his psychology textbook,

---

* James Mill was notorious for an unsentimental practicality, which extended well beyond his disdain for poetry. The *Oxford Book of Literary Anecdotes* (New York: Simon and Schuster, 1975, p. 184) provides an amusing if somewhat macabre example. Bentham had willed his body for scientific dissection, and shortly after his death Mill told a friend of a rumor that a virtually unfreezable oil had been synthesized from Bentham's head. Mill conjectured that such a substance might prove useful for the oiling of chronometers in ships exploring the arctic. His friend quashed this plan by replying "The less you say about that, Mill, the better it will be for *you;* because if the fact once becomes known, just as we see now in the newspapers that a fine bear is to be killed for his grease, we shall be having advertisements to the effect that a fine philosopher is to be killed for his oil."

Analysis of the Phenomena of the Human Mind, he proudly reported that sixteen-year-old John had been his only constructive critic.

In general, John Mill received a supremely powerful and useful academic education. At age seventeen he was entreated by a professor friend to enroll at the prestigious Trinity College, Cambridge—the college of Isaac Newton and, later on, Francis Galton—where he could mingle with the nation's intellectual and social elite. The Mills politely declined, however, because of the difficulty the agnostic John would have had in subscribing to the articles of the Church of England (then required of all matriculated students at Cambridge and Oxford) and because he was already the academic superior of most university graduates. James Mill had in fact succeeded in turning out an intellectual prodigy. In assessing the effect of his education from the perspective of middle age, John concluded: "Through the early training bestowed on me by my father, I started, I may fairly say, with an advantage of a quarter of a century over my contemporaries."[9]

John Mill's education also had some drawbacks, however. His father assiduously kept him away from the intellectually contaminating influence of ordinary schoolboys, so John grew up without benefit of the rough and tumble activities which help most boys to acquire a practical and social knowledge of the world. He grew up in a strictly intellectualized atmosphere, where he learned, as he put it, much more how "to *know* than to *do*."[10] It took him much longer than normal to learn to dress himself or tie a knot, and when he visited France at age fourteen his hostess was astonished to discover that he could not yet brush his own hair. A lack of practical ability continued to plague him throughout his life, as he was always heavily dependent upon his mother, wife, or stepdaughter for meeting the everyday necessities.

Unsurprisingly, John also grew up socially maladroit. The wife of a colleague of James Mill left one vivid description of John as a child:

> Little Mill makes more observations than almost any child I ever saw who was crammed, but they are always in slow measured tones, and delivered with the air of a person who is conscious of his superiority, and if you

> hazard an observation in return you are perhaps assured
> that "the *authorities* will not bear you out in what you
> have asserted."[11]

It was ironic that "Little Mill" left such a priggish impression, for in truth he held a very modest impression of his own abilities. His father, for fear that he might develop the reprehensible habit of "self-conceit," never allowed John to be praised for his accomplishments, or even to hear himself compared with others his age. Of course, this also meant that young John lacked any information to help him assess the impression he made on others or to guide him in tailoring his social behavior.

One of the most memorable passages in Mill's autobiography—and a key to his entire adult personality and outlook—tells how his father finally gave him his first inkling of his true intellectual status:

> I remember the very place in Hyde Park where, in my
> fourteenth year, on the eve of leaving my father's house
> for a long absence, he told me that I should find, as I
> got acquainted with new people, that I had been taught
> things which youths of my age did not commonly know;
> and that many persons would be disposed to talk to me
> of this, and to compliment me upon it. What other things
> he said on this topic I remember very imperfectly; but
> he wound up by saying, that whatever I knew more
> than others, could not be ascribed to any merit in me,
> but to the very unusual advantage which had fallen to
> my lot, of having a father who was able to teach me,
> and willing to give the necessary trouble and time; that
> it was no matter of praise to me, if I knew more than
> those who had not had a similar advantage. . . . I felt
> that what my father had said respecting my peculiar
> advantages was exactly the truth and common sense of
> the matter, and it fixed my opinion and feeling from
> that time forward.[12]

Thus John Mill came to see his father's educational experiment as a great success, at least in the intellectual realm. He believed he was living proof that virtually anyone could be taught virtually anything, given ideal conditions. Even as an eminent adult he argued, with complete sincerity, that natural gifts had had little to do with his success, because he had few such gifts: "If I had been by nature extremely quick of apprehension, or had possessed a very accurate and retentive memory, the trial would not have been conclusive; but in all these natural gifts I am rather below than above par. What I could do, could assuredly be done by any boy or girl of average capacity and healthy physical constitution."[13]

Similarly, however, Mill attributed his weaknesses to failures in his education and upbringing: he blamed his clumsiness on a lack of practical exercise, for example, and his early social ineptitude (which he later took pains to correct) on a lack of outside company. When he experienced a painful "mental crisis" in young manhood, and worked his own recovery partly through his discovery of Romantic poetry, he blamed his breakdown on the fact that he had never been trained to cultivate the feelings along with the intellect.

From an outside perspective, of course, one may question the accuracy of John Mill's self-assessment—noting that his very lack of experience with other young people made it impossible for him to judge whether he was comparatively "below par" or not. One may also note, like Norbert Wiener, that Mill's younger sisters and brothers, who received educations similar in many ways to his own, never reached his own level of accomplishment. The important point, however, was that Mill himself believed he was primarily the product of his environment and training, and he generalized this into a view of *all* people as creatures of circumstance, potentially almost indefinitely malleable to early environmental influences. This view was clearly echoed in the associationistic psychology Mill espoused as an adult, and which underlay his many influential social and political writings.

MILL'S ASSOCIATIONISTIC PSYCHOLOGY

John Stuart Mill prescribed what he saw as the essentials for a science of psychology in his first published book, *A System of Logic*, in 1843. He continued to comment on psychology in seven revisions of the *Logic*, and in a series of other works throughout his life.[14] His starting point, as it had been for his father and for many other English philosophers over the preceding 150 years, was the *associationism* of John Locke (1632–1704). Locke had assumed that the human mind at birth is like a tabula rasa, or blank slate, with the capacity for receiving and recording permanent impressions of the events which it experiences. Mill expressed this capacity as follows:

> Whenever any state of consciousness has once been excited in us, no matter by what cause; an inferior degree of the same state of consciousness, a state of consciousness resembling the former, but inferior in intensity, is capable of being reproduced in us, without the presence of any such cause as excited it at first. Thus, if we have once seen or touched an object, we can afterwards think of the object though it is absent from sight or from touch.[15]

As Mill summarized, "every mental *impression* has its *idea*," and the idea may be called to consciousness as a memory, independently of the original impression which produced it.

The major subject of Mill's psychology was the flow of impressions and ideas through consciousness, which he argued was determined by the manner in which individual ideas have become interconnected, or *associated* with one another. A particular impression may give rise to a whole chain of ideas or associations that have become connected with its idea, according to just three basic laws of association:

> The first [law] is, that similar ideas tend to excite one another. The second is, that when two impressions have been frequently experienced (or even thought of) either simultaneously or in immediate succession, then whenever one of these impressions, or the idea of it, recurs, it tends to excite the idea of the other. The third law is, that greater intensity in either or both of the impressions, is equivalent, in rendering them excitable by one another, to a greater frequency of conjunction.[16]

Thus, according to the first law, commonly called the law of *association by similarity,* the idea of one kind of a flower, such as a rose, tends to arouse that of another, such as an orchid. The second law, *association by contiguity,* dictates that the smell of a rose, experienced by itself, will tend to call up a memory of the sight of a rose, since the sight and smell have been frequently experienced together in the past. The third law, that of *intensity,* concerns the speed and strength with which associations are formed by similarity or contiguity. If the first roses one experiences are particularly bright-colored and odiferous, the association between their smell and sight will become established more quickly and strongly than if the original impressions are milder.

To this point, Mill's psychology was no more than a recapitulation of the views of his predecessors. He introduced some original theorizing of his own, however, when he considered a class of mental phenomena known as *complex ideas.* Complex ideas supposedly occur when two or more simple, original ideas become so closely associated as to act as a single unit. Earlier theorists, most notably Mill's father, had tended to think of the coalescence as the simple sum of its individual constituents; the complex idea of a "house," for example, was seen as simply the sum of all the ideas of brick, mortar, planks, glass, and so on which form the constituent parts of a house. John Mill believed this was not enough, that complex ideas could be and often were something more than just the sum of their constituents. The idea of a house includes meanings quite above and beyond those of its individual physical components, such as "a place to live."

Thus, according to John Mill, a process he called *mental chemistry* often occurs: "When many impressions or ideas are operating in the mind together, there sometimes takes place a process of a similar kind to chemical combination."[17] When mental chemistry occurs, a complex idea may emerge which has new properties independent of its individual components, just as water has properties very different from those of the hydrogen and oxygen which compose it.

Mill believed that the workings of mental chemistry complicate the task of a psychologist greatly, because the emergent

THE NATURE-NURTURE CONTROVERSY 13

properties of complex ideas are not easily deducible in advance, but can only be determined by actual experiment and observation. A great deal of experimental work on the actual fusion and compounding of myriad simple ideas therefore had to be done, before psychologists could have a reasonably complete inventory of the products and processes of association.

Thus Mill regarded associationistic psychology as incomplete, requiring much further time and effort to determine for certain how far it could *ultimately* go in explaining mental life. The question of its ultimate range of applicability arose in two forms. First was the issue of the extent to which the contents of a person's consciousness are the results of experience and association, as opposed to being "innate ideas" or other inborn responses. Second was the question of the role of experience and association, as opposed to innate or constitutional factors, in determining psychological differences among people. In neither case could Mill provide an unequivocal, proven answer. Consistent with his upbringing, however, he believed that associationism could ultimately go very far—much farther than most people thought. He offered several lines of argument to support, if not to prove, his contention.

Mill argued, for example, that associationism could adequately account for many of the ideas traditionally regarded by philosophers as innate and independent of experience, such as "infinity." Apparently a necessary aspect of our concepts of space and time, "infinity" is never immediately experienced as an entity. Thus, many philosophers believed the notion of infinity to be part of the inborn contents of the mind. Mill, however, explained infinity as "an ordinary manifestation of the laws of association of ideas," since we never actually experience any point in time or space without having others beyond it. Thus we develop extremely powerful associations between the ideas of *any* points in space or time, and the ideas of other points still more remote. In fact, it becomes impossible to think of any point as not being followed by others, because we have never experienced one that was not. For Mill, this experiential and associationistic base seemed completely adequate to account for the notion of "infinity."[18]

Another class of mental contents sometimes believed to be innate or instinctive were a sense of conscience and the moral sentiments. Mill thought it much more likely, however, that these complicated feelings were actually the acquired products of mental chemistry. The sense of "moral reprobation" which one experiences after committing a dishonest act, for example, could be explained as a complex associational fusion of the idea of "pain" and the idea of committing the act, resulting from punishments received in childhood.

Mill did not deny the existence of innate factors altogether, admitting that animals have instincts (such as for nest building in birds), and that there must exist a "portion of human nature which corresponds to those instincts."[19] Nevertheless, he noted that even these "innate" instincts were capable of substantial modification or suppression through learning. Further, and more important, Mill asserted that psychology's first task—even for those who believed in the existence of many innate mental contents—*had to be* the extension of associational theorizing just as far as it could go. On purely logical grounds, Mill argued, any evidence for ultimate factors must always be negative; thus there can be no positive proof that oxygen is a simple substance, but only evidence of failure to decompose it into anything simpler.* Similarly, "Nothing can possibly prove that any particular one of the constituents of the mind is ultimate. We can only presume it to be such from the ill success of every attempt to resolve it into simpler elements." So the first question the psychologist must answer is, "How much of the furniture of the mind will experience and association account for? The residuum which cannot be so explained, must provisionally be set down as ultimate."[20] Mill felt confident that when such analyses were pursued vigorously by people expert in the laws and phenomena of associationistic psychology, the "residuum" would turn out to be much smaller than most people expected.

---

*Mill was writing here before the atomic theory was developed, and showed that even "elements" such as oxygen could in fact be broken down into more basic, subatomic particles. Had he known of it, he could have cited that development as confirming his point that it is dangerous to assume that any level of analysis is the "ultimate" one.

Mill's argument with respect to individual differences among people in ability and character was very similar. He did not deny that innate differences in people's physical makeup could lead to certain differences in their mental character; such was "the opinion of all physiologists, confirmed by common experience."[21] But Mill was also convinced that constitutional explanations were all too often facile rationalizations offered by people unsophisticated in the application of psychological analysis. The difference between people of artistic and scientific temperament, for example, was often "explained" in terms of a supposed difference in their innate faculties, presumably based on differences in the structure and functioning of their brains. Mill, however, offered an alternative associationistic explanation. He argued that particularly intense experiences in childhood should lead to the formation of especially strong connections among ideas occurring *synchronously* with the intense ones, whereas milder intensities of experience should relatively favor the formation of associations among *successive* experiences. The synchronous associations constitute knowledge about *things* or *objects;* the successive ones knowledge of *events.* Thus people with many intense childhood experiences are likely to grow up with a keen interest in objects, while their counterparts become involved in the analysis of events and processes. Such might well be the basis of the difference between the artistic and scientific temperaments. Mill could not prove that this was the case, but it was another example of the sort of experiential explanation that had to be ruled out before any nativistic hypothesis could logically be accepted.

Mill developed this theme further in his *Logic,* when he proposed the development of a new science to be called *ethology,**
whose purpose would be the explanation of individual differences in people's character on the basis of associationistic psychology. The future ethologist would be thoroughly familiar with the circumstances under which various character types are

---

* Mill derived this name from the Greek *ethos,* or "character." Sometime before this, naturalists in France had begun using the term *éthologie* to denote a completely different science, namely, the study of animals in their natural habitats. Over time the French usage has prevailed, and "ethology" is seldom used in Mill's sense now, except in historical writing.

formed, and then would use associationistic psychology "to explain and account for the characteristics of the type, by the peculiarities of the circumstances: the residuum alone, when there proves to be any, being set down to the account of congenital predispositions."[22]

As with the study of mental contents, the "residuum" left after a thorough associational analysis is all that should be attributed to innate factors. And here again, Mill felt certain that the residuum would be small: "It is certain that, in human beings at least, differences in eduation and outward circumstances are capable of affording an adequate explanation of by far the greatest portion of character."[23]

Mill believed his ethology could make a special contribution by offering environmental explanations of differences between nations and sexes. "National character," as well as a person's "masculine" or "feminine" character, were often thought of as genetically or constitutionally fixed. Mill, however, argued that environment was much more important:

> The French people had, or were supposed to have, a certain national character: but they drive out their royal family and aristocracy, alter their institutions, pass through a series of extraordinary events for the greater part of a century, and at the end of that time their character is found to have undergone important changes. A long list of mental and moral differences are observed, or supposed, to exist between men and women: but at some future, and, it may be hoped, not distant period, equal freedom and an equally independent social position come to be possessed by both, and their differences of character are either removed or totally altered.[24]

As his reference to sexual equality implies, Mill believed that environmental explanations ought to take precedence on *moral* as well as logical grounds, a view echoed by environmentalist social critics to the present day. Mill expressed this view most energetically in his *Autobiography:*

> The prevailing tendency to regard all the marked dis-
> tinctions of human nature as innate, and in the main
> indelible, and to ignore the irresistible proofs that by
> far the greater part of those differences, whether
> between individuals, races, or sexes, are such as not only
> might, but naturally would be produced by differences
> in circumstances, is one of the chief hindrances to the
> rational treatment of great social questions, and one of
> the greatest stumbling blocks to human improve-
> ment.[25]

If people in power believe that the poor and disadvantaged occupy
their lowly positions in life because of an innate and "natural"
inferiority, they will see little reason for even trying to improve
the environments of the poor. Thus politicians have a moral
obligation to accept the environmentalist explanation, at least as
a working hypothesis.

In sum, Mill did not deny that individuals and groups vary
considerably in the quality of their character and intellect, nor
did he altogether deny the possibility that some part of the variation was innate. His own upbringing had impressed upon him
the great power and pervasiveness of environmental factors,
however, and so he argued that it was the logical scientific duty
of the psychologist or ethologist, and the ethical obligation of
the politician, to thoroughly test out environmental hypotheses
before anything else. He had little doubt that many of these
hypotheses would prove true, and that the final "residuum" left
over to be attributed to innate differences would be relatively
small.

When Mill first published his *Logic* in 1843, he believed that
his next major project would be the actual working out of his
ethology, within the framework he had prescribed. This was not
to be, however, for he soon found his attention increasingly drawn
to much more immediate practical and social questions, which
preempted his time and energy. His ethology, like his associationistic psychology, remained an incompleted program which
he hoped would be brought to fulfillment by others.

Nevertheless, throughout his subsequent career as a social critic

and member of the British Parliament, Mill continually brought
to bear on the great social issues of his day the same environmentalist principles which had underlain his psychology and
ethology. In his 1848 book, *Principles of Political Economy*, for
example, he blamed the degradation of Irish peasants on the
unfair land-tenure laws imposed on them by their English land-
lords, and argued that land reform would produce a great change
for the better in their character. In a heated published exchange
on "The Negro Question" with Thomas Carlyle the next year,
Mill castigated Carlyle's scurrilous caricature of the typical West
Indian black as the congenitally indolent "Black Quashee," and
cited numerous environmental explanations for the recently freed
slave's un-European behavior.[26] During the American Civil War,
Mill was among the most active British supporters of the northern and abolitionist cause, and as a Member of Parliament he
led the fight to prosecute Edward Eyre for his brutal suppression of blacks while governor of Jamaica. A lifelong believer in
the fundamental equality of the sexes, Mill abjured his legal pro-
prietary rights over his wife when he married, introduced Britain's first women's suffrage bill into Parliament in 1866, and in
1869 published *The Subjection of Women*, still regarded as a classic
argument in favor of sexual equality.

Indeed, most of Mill's writings continue to be read and studied today. Even though his conception of psychology soon came
to be seen as too limited, and even though he never really defined
"intelligence" beyond the notion of a general mental ability susceptible to great molding by circumstances, environmentalist
participants in the IQ controversy today continue to re-state his
basic views. Before discussing these more recent developments,
however, we must consider the genesis of a highly contrasting
point of view, in the early life of Francis Galton.

Francis Galton: The Making of a Hereditarian

Francis Galton was the seventh and last child in a
wealthy and distinguished English family. His mother was the
daughter of Erasmus Darwin (1732–1802)—the famous poet,

Francis Galton (1822–1911) *(National Portrait Gallery London)*

physician, and early evolutionary theorist—by Darwin's second wife. Charles Darwin, whose father was the son of Erasmus's *first* wife, was thus an older half-cousin. Galton's paternal line extended back to the founders of the Quaker religion, though his great-grandfather Galton had become rich through the distinctly un-Quakerish occupation of manufacturing guns. By his father's generation the family money had been invested more respectably in banking, and his father had joined the Church of England.

As the youngest child in a large family, young Francis was

pampered and doted upon, particularly by his sister Adele, twelve years older than he. A chronic invalid from a "spinal weakness" that was probably hysterical or psychosomatic in origin, Adele conspired to have Francis's cradle moved into her room, and devoted all of her free time to his care and upbringing. Though formally untrained herself, she tutored him enthusiastically and with great success. At age two and a half he was reading children's books and printing his name with tolerable neatness. At three he was writing simple letters, and at four learning some Latin and French, which Adele had had to teach herself first. Just before his fifth birthday he summarized his accomplishments in a remarkable letter to his tutor:

> My dear Adele,
>   I am four years old and I can read any English book. I can say all the Latin Substantives and Adjectives and active verbs besides 52 lines of Latin poetry. I can cast up any Sum in addition and can multiply by 2, 3, 4, 5, 6, 7, 8, , 10, .* I can also say the pence table. I read French a little and I know the Clock.[27]

The precocious development continued. At six, Francis amazed a visitor to the Galton home by his ability to read Shakespeare's and Pope's poetry, repeat pages of text by heart after reading them over twice, do long division, and recite much of the Latin grammar. At eight, he could discourse learnedly to his family on the construction of Saxon ships, or demonstrate his entomological sophistication by chastizing his mother for confusing locusts, which belong to the order Neuroptera, with cockchafers, of the order Coleoptera.

All of these accomplishments won Francis great acclaim from his family, who recorded them proudly in diaries, and formally "witnessed" his childish letters and literary productions as evidence of his precocity.[28] Indeed, family records make it clear that Francis Galton was cast firmly and solely in the role of fam-

---

*Francis had originally written a 9 and an 11 into the sequence. Apparently realizing he had claimed too much, he scratched out the one numeral with a penknife, and pasted over the other with a blank piece of paper.

ily intellectual and academic from earliest childhood onward. He is virtually *never* mentioned in family diaries except in the context of his education or intellectual exploits. The family nurtured great hopes that he would become the first in his line of Galtons to have a distinguished university career—his father and earlier generations having been barred from the universities for religious reasons, his older brothers opting for farming or military careers, and his sisters being disqualified from the unversities because of their sex. Young Francis avidly adopted these hopes as his own, for at age four he began saving his pennies "to buy honours at the University;" and shortly after, when asked by his father what he would most like to have in the world he replied, "Why, University honours to be sure.[29]

Thus young Francis Galton grew up with a very different self-image from that of John Mill, for Mill was assiduously prevented from knowing how advanced he was, while Galton was constantly reminded of that fact, and made to believe it was his role in life to continue as a prodigy. While James Mill disdained academic honors for his son, and discouraged him from attending university, the Galton family held the attainment of orthodox academic prizes to be among the most important of goals. Francis Galton early developed a strong sense of his own precocity, and a powerful motive to excel in academic competition.

Unfortunately, however, he was not really prepared by his early training for the ultimate achievement of these goals. His early education was not nearly as professional or substantial as Mill's, and impressive as his boyish academic credentials may have been for show, they actually were *not* particularly well suited to win success in the British educational establishment of the time. That system, from the schools through the universities, emphasized the acquisition of "discipline" in thinking, especially through rigorous study of the classics. Classes were run on a severely competitive basis, with all students carefully and publicly ranked from first to last on the basis of all-important examination results. Young Francis Galton was clearly a bright, curious, and enthusiastic child—but his early training did not fully prepare him to meet these rigors and competitions. His first education had been at the hand of an enthusiastic amateur who had to teach herself before she could teach him, and for all the talk of Latin and the classics, had been mainly in English. Years later, Galton wrote that Adele's idea of education had been, simply, "to teach the Bible as a verbally inspired book, to cultivate memory, to make me learn the merest rudiments of Latin, and above all a great deal of English verse."[30]

This training did not prove particularly useful when Francis, at age eight, was abruptly removed from the benign influence of his sister and sent to the first of a series of distant boarding schools. In this "real world" of British education, his accelerated early development proved to be of scant advantage. The great curiosity and intellectual restlessness which characterized him throughout his life were distracting and negative qualities here. Though initially placed in a class with boys older than himself, he could not keep up in Latin and was quickly sent back a class. For the rest of his academic career he remained a mediocre classical scholar, and his diaries and letters reflected a dreary sequence of punitive assignments and feeble excuses for his failure to excel. He never stood a chance of achieving classical honors.

Nevertheless, Galton retained an exceptionally strong desire to excel in other academic fields, and always sized up his "competition" with great calculation and care. Before a school mathematics examination, he wrote his father, "A boy who is doing trigonometry will be counted of my class so he will be certain of the prize, but . . . there are three others very equal, myself and two other boys. They know what they do more perfectly than I do but then I have learnt many more proofs . . . so it is very doubtful."[31] At the end of a two-year spell of medical training between the ages of sixteen and eighteen, he led his family as well as himself to believe that he would finish first in the forensic medicine examination. He was bitterly disappointed, however, to finish second and win a Certificate of Honour instead of a book prize. He explained to his father: "I am much vexed at not being first but there was more competition than usual. One of the men (I am above him) got a Certificate of Honour in For. Med. *last year*."[32] In his autobiography, written almost seventy years after the event, Galton incorrectly recalled that he had actually *won* the prize—a wish-fulfilling slip that betrayed the intensity of his youthful ambition.

At age eighteen Galton enrolled at Trinity College Cambridge—the college Mill had declined to enter—where he hoped to fulfill his childhood wish by winning high honors in mathematics. He clearly bore his family's hopes on his shoulders along with his own, for within the first week a sister wrote to say, "Father is building castles in the air that you will turn out so clever that you will have enough to spare for [your brothers] also."[33] Cambridge was a brutally competitive university, with many of England's brightest youths among its students. Galton did just well enough in the minor examinations of his first year to keep his hopes alive.

At the same time, he became highly interested in the nature of examinations themselves, disparaging those which did not sharply differentiate students at the top from the rest of the pack. Galton approved very highly of that year's honors examination for seniors, in which the first and second "Wranglers"* scored more than 1000 marks above the third, while it took a score of only 500 marks altogether to be a Wrangler at all.[34] He had come to believe that the very top people stood head and shoulders above everyone else—virtually in a class by themselves—and that examination scores ought to reflect that superiority. He also nurtured hopes, of course, that *he* would shortly prove to be one of those mathematical superstars himself.

During his second year Galton studied hard and enthusiastically for the "Little Go," an important examination, though not yet for honors. When the results were announced he learned he had done creditably and finished in the second class—roughly, a B+ performance at one of the most competitive universities in the world. While most students would have been satisfied with such a result, Galton was shattered. Several of his friends, with classes and tutoring identical to his, had taken firsts. The results indicated to Galton that he could never hope to be one of those

---

*"Wrangler" was the term applied at Cambridge to the top 35 or 40 scorers in each year's mathematics honors examination.

top Wranglers, far above the crowd. Within a week of learning his results, he withdrew from a forthcoming scholarship examination because he believed he had no chance of winning. Shortly after that he underwent a severe emotional breakdown, which prevented him from studying mathematics altogether. The symptoms persisted into the next year, forcing him to withdraw from honors competition altogether to take an ordinary or "poll" degree. At his disappointed father's urging he returned to medical training, but in a desultory way. When his father died in 1844 and left him a substantial inheritance, Galton abandoned medical study completely. His formal academic career was now over, and far from having proved himself as a genius, he had failed to meet the high goals he and his family had set.

There followed an unhappy period of several years' drifting, as Galton lived the life of the idle rich. Unhappy with himself, and perhaps from desperation, he finally consulted a professional phrenologist for reading of his character based on the shape of his head. The phrenologist had more to go on than just Galton's skull, of course, and from some combination of cues emerged with a shrewd assessment which said, "The intellectual capacities are not distinguished by much spontaneous activity in relation to scholastic affairs. Men so organized do not . . . distinguish themselves in universities." Another course seemed desirable instead: "There is much enduring power in a mind such as this—much that qualifies a man for 'roughing it'. . . . It is only when rough work has to be done, that all the energies and capacities of minds of this class are brought to light."[35]

At just this time, reports of exciting geographical explorations in southern Africa were much in the English news. With his new insight into his presumably "natural" aptitude for rough work, and with a liking for travel and an income sufficient to support an expedition of his own, Galton resolved to become an African explorer himself. Between 1850 and 1852 he led an expedition through much of southwest Africa—the present-day troubled country of Namibia—producing the first accurate map of the region and earning his spurs as a geographer. Upon his return he was greeted as a man of accomplishment, and welcomed into the governing establishment of the Royal Geographical Society.

At this point in his life, Galton had not yet explicitly formulated his nativistic psychological theories, but he had had many crucial experiences to predispose him in that direction. He had been brought up to believe in the existence and importance of large individual differences in people's intellectual abilities. His early experiences had led him to hope that he himself would turn out to be one of the geniuses at the top of the ability distribution, but his academic career had suggested otherwise, as he was always being surpassed by at least a few of his competitors. Coming from a privileged family background, and having been sent to what were supposedly the best schools, he could not easily account for his relative failure on an environmental basis. When the phrenologist accounted for his scholastic deficiency on the basis of his inappropriately shaped head and brain, it must have come as almost a relief to accept the idea that he had failed because he lacked the innate gifts necessary for academic success.

Years later, when he wrote his book *Hereditary Genius,* Galton elaborated upon his belief in natural inequality in a passage we can now recognize as poignantly autobiographical. Immediately following his unqualified objection to "pretensions of natural equality," quoted at the beginning of this chapter, he went on to elaborate. Training and education certainly can influence the development of talent, he admitted, but only to the same degree that *physical* training can improve physical ability. And with physical ability, there is always a limit beyond which improvement ceases, no matter how strenuous the training. The trained athlete's top performance always becomes "a rigidly determinate quantity" as "he learns to an inch how high or how far he can jump." And so it is with mental ability as well:

> This is precisely analogous to the experience that every student has had of the working of his mental powers. The eager boy, when he first goes to school and confronts intellectual difficulties, is astonished at his progress. He glories in his newly developed mental grip and

growing capacity for application, and, it may be, fondly believes it to be within his reach to become one of the heroes who have left their mark upon the history of the world. The years go by; he competes in the examinations of school and college, over and over again with his fellows, and soon finds his place among them. He knows that he can beat such and such of his competitors; that there are some with whom he runs on equal terms, and others whose intellectual feats he cannot even approach.[36]

Thus Galton did not completely deny the effects of environmental or educational influences, just as Mill did not altogether deny innate ones. Galton's experiences, however, led him to place much greater emphasis on the differences which still remained among people after presumably similar environmental effects had occurred. Preoccupied as he was with the upper end of the ability continuum, and with a group of "competitors" from roughly equal and highly privileged backgrounds, these presumably innate differences seemed particularly large. Quite naturally, he went on to grant them a major role in the psychological theories he constructed in mid-life.

GALTON'S NATIVISTIC PSYCHOLOGY

Following his return from Africa, Galton made a name for himself with a popular account of his explorations (*Tropical South Africa*, 1853), and a delightfully informative how-to book for other travelers in the wild, entitled *The Art of Travel; or, Shifts and Contrivances Available in Wild Countries* (1855).* He then concerned himself with meteorology—a subject naturally of much interest to travelers—and had the happy idea of plotting simultaneous weather information from many places on a single map. This invention of the now-commonplace weather

---

*Among the diverse topics discussed here were how to avoid the charge of an enraged beast, the "management of savages," pitching a tent in the sand, and rolling up one's sleeves so they do not come unrolled. (The trick, he says, is to roll them up on the *inside* rather than the outside.)

map, and the subsequent discovery of alternating high- and low-pressure weather systems, earned Galton a permanent place in the history of meteorology.

While working on these projects, Galton also found his attention increasingly drawn to a subject which he called "the human side of geography." As a recently returned African explorer, he was sometimes called upon to advise missionary groups about how and where they might best expend their efforts to spread Christianity and civilization to Africa. Sharing the ethnocentricity common to many (but not all) Victorian explorers, Galton argued that most Africans were intellectually and morally incapable of responding positively to Western influence, and were best left to the Arabs. Nevertheless, he had also been impressed by the enormous diversity of character among differing African groups—those he had encountered personally as well as those described by other explorers.[37] In the early 1860s, Galton's conviction of ethnic diversity interacted with a startling new scientific theory to produce several major ideas that continue today at the heart of the nature-nurture and IQ controversies.

In December of 1859, Galton, like the intellectual world in general, had been aroused by the publication of Charles Darwin's *On the Origin of Species,* announcing the theory of evolution by natural selection. Galton had never been much interested in biology before, and had had no inkling that his half-cousin was preparing this major work. Nonetheless, he was immediately struck by the ingenuity and power of evolutionary theory, and soon began applying it to his own interests in human psychological diversity. Gradually, he developed a new set of ideas which took on literally a religious significance for him, and whose promulgation dominated the rest of his long life.

Darwin had hypothesized that different species were not the products of separate creations, but had evolved from common ancestors over millions of years, through the mechanism of natural selection. Within particular breeding populations, small, inheritable variations which were favorable to survival and procreation tended inevitably to increase in frequency over generations, while unfavorable variations decreased. Since different

characteristics were favorable or unfavorable in different environments, originally similar breeding groups in different environments diverged from each other increasingly, until eventually
they became different species. By this unceasing process of
adaptation and differentiation, all of the varieties of life came
into being, and new ones were presumably still developing.

In *Origin of Species,* Darwin dealt primarily with the evolution
of physical characteristics in animal species. The idea which excited
Galton so much was that human, psychological differences might
be inheritable too, based on small variations in the brain and
nervous system. He already believed differences in ability and
character to be innate, and recognized that with the added
assumption of inheritability they took on tremendous theoretical
and practical significance. Psychological differences among individuals and ethnic groups could potentially be explained on
hereditary grounds, and, even more important, such variations
could be recognized as the basis from which the human race will
evolve in the future. Further, Galton believed it should theoretically be possible to intervene intentionally in the process of evolution, speeding up the process of natural selection and producing
a superior breed of human being in much the same way that an
animal breeder creates a particularly desirable breed of dogs.
Here was the inspiration for *eugenics,* which Galton later named
and defined as "the science of improving [human] stock, . . . which
takes cognisance of all influences that in however remote a degree
give to the more suitable races or strains of blood a better chance
of prevailing over the less suitable than they otherwise would
have had."[38]

The Case for Mental Heredity

Before an effective eugenics program could come
into being, of course, Galton had to provide concrete support
for its underlying premise that intellectual ability and other
desirable psychological qualities are inherited. Among the first
lines of presumptive evidence to occur to him were "the mental
peculiarities of different races,"[39] which were apparently transmitted from generation to generation with impressive regular-

ity. In a 1865 paper, "Hereditary Talent and Genius," Galton relied on a few, characteristically ethnocentric Victorian sources to contrast the "typical West African Negro" with the American Indian, and to conclude that these two characters were even more dissimilar mentally than physically. The Indian, according to Galton, had "great patience, great reticence, great dignity, . . . no passion, [and] the minimum of affectionate and social qualities compatible with the continuance of their race." The African, by contrast, supposedly had "strong impulsive passions, and neither patience, nor reticence, nor dignity. . . . He is eminently gregarious, for he is always jabbering, quarrelling, tom-tom-ing, or dancing. He is remarkably domestic, and he is endowed with such constitutional vigour, and is so prolific, that his race is irrepressible."[40]

Moving on from these long-established "national characters" to a new one in the making, Galton also considered Americans, whom he saw as developing according to perfectly comprehensible hereditary principles:

> Whenever, during the last ten or twelve generations, a political or religious party has suffered defeat, its prominent members, whether they were the best, or only the noisiest, have been apt to emigrate to America, as a refuge from persecution. Men fled to America for conscience' sake, and for that of unappreciated patriotism. Every scheming knave, and every brutal ruffian, who feared the arm of the law, also turned his eyes in the same direction. . . . If we estimate the moral nature of Americans from their present social state, we shall find it to be just what we might have expected from such a parentage. They are enterprising, defiant, and touchy; impatient of authority; furious politicians; very tolerant of fraud and violence; possessing much high and generous spirit, and some true religious feeling, but strongly addicted to cant.[41]

Galton argued that the open educational system of America, offering intellectual opportunity to a much broader segment of the population than the restrictive and exclusive British system, had failed to turn out very many people of genuine intellectual distinction: "America most certainly does not beat us in first-class works of literature, philosophy, or art. . . . The Americans have an immense amount of the newspaper-article-writer or of the member-of-congress stamp of ability; but the number of their really eminent authors is more limited even than with us."[42] In sum, the American character seemed just about what one would expect on a strong hereditarian hypothesis: highly similar to that of the first forebears, largely impervious to environmental or educational manipulation, and on its way to becoming as distinctive and stable as that of the black African, the red Indian, or any other established ethnic group.

A second line of support for the hereditarian hypothesis occurred to Galton, he recalled, "when the fact, that characteristics cling to families, was so frequently forced on my notice as to induce me to pay special attention to that branch of the subject. I began by thinking over the dispositions and achievements of my contemporaries at school, at college, and in after life, and was surprised to find how frequently ability seemed to go by descent."[43] Probably the first such instance to strike Galton was the sudden emergence of Charles Darwin as a great scientist, even surpassing in importance his (and Galton's) celebrated grandfather Erasmus Darwin. As other cases of intellectual eminence within the same families came to mind, Galton introduced one of his most influential innovations by making a *statistical study* of the issue. His first results, published in the paper "Hereditary Talent and Character" (1865) and expanded in the book *Hereditary Genius* (1869), seemed to him compelling evidence in favor of his hypothesis.

First, Galton selected a representative sample of people who had achieved sufficient eminence in their lives to be listed in biographical dictionaries (somewhat like the *Who's Who* volumes of today). After eliminating those who were notable only for their parentage, such as members of the hereditary aristocracy, he believed he was left with a group of people who had shown unusual talent in their lives. According to his calculations, they represented a proportion of about one person in four thousand from the normal population.

Next, Galton checked the family trees of these talented individuals, and found that approximately 10 percent of them had at least one close relative sufficiently eminent to be listed in a biographical dictionary as well. Though representing an absolute minority of cases, this proportion was still enormously higher than would have been expected by chance.

In *Hereditary Genius*, Galton presented a list of almost one thousand of these eminent relatives, drawn from three hundred different families, and subclassified according to type of relationship and the general field in which eminence was achieved. Close relatives such as fathers, sons, or brothers appeared much more frequently than distant ones such as cousins or great-grandfathers and great-grandsons. Galton also noted an imperfect but strong tendency for related individuals to achieve eminence in the same or similar fields. Among his cases was the father-and-son team of James and John Stuart Mill, classified alike as "literary men." Taken as a whole, Galton's data provided undeniable evidence of the statistical tendency for eminence, and the particularized abilities which presumably underlay it, to run in families. Though far from perfect, and predictively useful only in a general statistical sense, this tendency seemed on a par with that for unusual physical variables, such as extreme height or weight, which were already known to be influenced by heredity. The general pattern of results was thus completely consistent with Galton's hypothesis that differences in ability are inherited.

But while *consistent with* the genetic hypothesis, these results alone could not *prove* it. Families tend to share environmental circumstances as well as genes, and one can argue that eminence runs in some families because they provide their members with the material and psychological conditions particularly favorable to the development of their particular kinds of talent. Galton noted these factors but doubted their great importance, writing: "There is no favour [in coming from an eminent family] beyond the advantage of a good education. Whatever spur may be given by the desire to maintain the family fame, and whatever oppor-

tunities are provided by abundant leisure, are more than neu-
tralised by those influences which commonly lead the heirs of
fortune to idleness and dillettantism."[44] In his own experience,
the "advantage of a good education" had seemed slight, and he
was inclined to minimize it. Nevertheless, Galton realized the
desirability of having some real data to support his view. To that
end, he introduced two research techniques to help sort out the
relative contributions of nature and nurture.

In *Hereditary Genius,* Galton presented the prototype for what
has since been called the *adoptive family method.* He noted that it
was once common for Roman Catholic popes to "adopt" young
boys and bring them up in their own households as "nephews,"
who thus shared the environmental but not the genetic advantages of eminent families. Galton tried to determine if these boys
went on to attain eminence themselves in anything like the proportion that would be expected of the natural sons of eminent
fathers:

> I do not profess to have worked out the kinships of the
> Italians with any special care, but I have seen amply
> enough of them, to justify me in saying that . . . the
> very common combination of an able son and an emi-
> nent parent, is not matched, in the case of high Romish
> ecclesiastics, by an eminent nephew and an eminent
> uncle. The social helps are the same, but hereditary
> gifts are wanting in the latter case.[45]

Galton clearly did not lavish the same statistical care on this
analysis that he did on his compilation of positive hereditary
relationships, and a critic could rightly argue that his test sample
was small and highly unrepresentative. Few objective observers
would agree with Galton that this study conclusively ruled out
any major influence for environment in the production of eminence. Nevertheless, the basic method underlying the study was
sound. Adopted children do provide a potentially useful comparison group in studies of familial similarity. As we shall see in
Chapter 5, later generations of researchers have employed the

adoptive family method with increasing degrees of sophistication, if still with somewhat inconclusive results.

Another technique for separating the effects of heredity and environment on mental development occurred to Galton in the early 1870s, when he became interested in *twins*. He learned that, biologically speaking, there are two different kinds of twins: those who develop from the separate (though nearly simultaneous) fertilization of two ova by two sperm; and those who result after a single fertilized ovum splits in two, and the two halves develop into separate individuals. The first type, now referred to as *fraternal* or *dizygotic twins*, bear the same genetic similarity to each other as ordinary siblings; the second type, *identical* or *monozygotic twins*, are genetically identical. Galton's attention may originally have been drawn to the issue because he himself had a pair of nephews who were identical twins, and an aunt and uncle who were a fraternal pair. In any case, he believed that a comparison of the similarities between co-twins of the two types could throw light on the nature-nurture question, because while both types share similar environments, only the identical twins have exactly the same heredity. Here was the basic idea for the *twin-study method*, which Galton introduced in his 1875 paper, "The History of Twins, as a Criterion of the Relative Powers of Nature and Nurture."

In this original study, Galton solicited case histories of as many twins as he could locate, and discerned two striking categories. Some twins, including his nephews, went through life showing remarkable similarity to each other in both physical and psychological qualities, sometimes in spite of having experienced quite different life circumstances. Others, in contrast, went through life very differently from each other, showing markedly divergent characters, sometimes in spite of having been deliberately treated as similarly as possible by their families. Galton lacked direct evidence on the matter, but reasoned that the twins with highly similar character must have been monozygotic, their psychological similarity deriving from their genetic identity. The dissimilar twins he presumed to be dizygotic, differing in the same degree that ordinary siblings are known to do. He confidently summarized: "There is no escape from the conclusion that nature prevails enormously over nurture when the differences of nurture do not exceed what is commonly to be found among persons of the same rank in society and in the same country."[46]

His results were not actually as conclusive as he thought, of course. He had no proof that the similar twins were in fact monozygotic—and even if they were it was possible that their more similar, genetically given physical appearance had led them to be *treated* as more alike, and thus to experience greater environmental similarity than their dizygotic counterparts. As shall be seen in Chapter 5, the interpretation of *all* twin studies—from Galton's to the present day—is complicated by many factors such as these. Debates about the proper interpretation of twin studies lie close to the heart of the current IQ controversy. Nevertheless, the twin-study method has yielded some important and interesting findings, and Galton deserves credit for originating, if not perfecting, it.

In summary, Galton made a plausible but not unassailable case for the hereditarian explanation of psychological differences, much as Mill had made the opposing argument. He developed several ingenious techniques for investigating hereditary influence, and collected considerable data that were consistent with his convictions. After him, the hypothesis that intelligence and other mental qualities are strongly inherited had to be taken very seriously.

Eugenics and the First "Intelligence Tests"

Galton himself regarded the hereditarian hypothesis as sufficiently proved that he could push forward with his eugenics program. Convinced that educational and environmental reform would have little effect in raising the overall intellectual caliber of society, he tried to envision ways for improving the genetic stock of humankind. Two goals seemed paramount: first, the development of an intellectually and psychologically superior "breed" of human beings who would be able to transmit their genetic virtues to their offspring; and second, the institution of customs and laws to ensure that this superior breed proliferates at a faster rate than the common run, and thus comes to dominate society numerically as well as qualitatively.

The founding parents of a eugenic society, Galton believed, should be people like those he studied in *Hereditary Genius*: talented individuals who became eminent because of their positive contributions to society. A major problem arises, however, because such eminence customarily does not arrive until middle age. Galton wanted a means of identifying potentially eminent people earlier, while they were still at prime childbearing age. Thus he imagined the development of a series of examinations for young adults' "natural ability," capable of predicting which among them were likely to make eminent contributions later on. High-scoring men and women would be encouraged to intermarry, somewhat as in the following whimsical scene from "Hereditary Talent and Character":

> Let us then, give reins to our fancy, and imagine a Utopia . . . in which a system of competitive examinations . . . had been so developed as to embrace every important quality of mind and body, and where a considerable sum was allotted to the endowment of such marriages as promised to yield children who would grow into eminent servants of the State. We may picture to ourselves an annual ceremony in that Utopia, in which the Senior Trustee of the Endowment Fund would address ten deeply-blushing young men, all of twenty-five years old, in the following terms:—"Gentlemen, I have to announce the results of a public examination, conducted on established princples; which show that you occupy the foremost places in your year, in respect to those qualities of talent, character, and bodily vigour which are proved, on the whole, to do most honour and best service to our race. An examination has also been conducted on established principles among all the young ladies of this country who are now of the age of twenty-one, and I need hardly remind you, that this examination takes note of grace, beauty, health, good-temper, accomplished housewifery, and disengaged

affections, in addition to the noble qualities of heart and brain. By a careful investigation of the marks you have severally obtained, . . . we have been enabled to select ten of [the young ladies'] names with special reference to your individual qualities. It appears that marriages between you and these ten ladies, according to the list I hold in my hand, would offer the probability of unusual happiness to yourselves, and, what is of paramount interest to the State, would probably result in an extraordinarily talented issue. Under these circumstances, if any or all of these marriages should be agreed upon, the Sovereign herself will give away the brides, at a high and solemn festival, six months hence, in Westminister Abbey. We, on our part, are prepared, in each case, to assign 5,000£ as a wedding-present, and to defray the cost of maintaining and educating your children, out of the ample funds entrusted to our disposal by the State.[47]

In this fancifully stated but seriously intended passage, Galton introduced the idea (though not the name) of the *intelligence test* to the world. Thus the intelligence test was seen as a measure of people's differing hereditary worth from its very inception; it is no mere coincidence that questions of genetics and intelligence testing have been inextricably intertwined ever since.

Of course, it was one thing for Galton to introduce the *idea* for tests of hereditary ability, and quite another again actually to develop the "established principles" mentioned by his Senior Trustee. In 1865, neither Galton nor anyone else could be sure how to go about measuring so elusive a quality as hereditary intelligence or "natural ability" in the young. Galton had just a few general notions, based on the assumption that inheritable intelligence must be based on measurable differences in people's brains and nervous systems. He finally went so far as to devise a series of tests measuring reaction time, sensory acuity, and physical energy, which he hoped would indicate differences in neurological efficiency, and hence of natural intelligence. In the mid-1880s he assembled the apparatus for these tests together in an

"Anthropometric Laboratory" at London's South Kensington Museum, and assessed the capacities of several thousand people curious enough to pay three pence apiece to undergo the experience. The Anthropometric Laboratory established "mental testing" as a new and interesting area of research. The specific tests Galton devised never worked out properly, however, as their results failed to correlate with any independent signs of accomplishment or intelligence: people with fast reactions or acute senses did not turn out to be unusually talented in other areas. Details of this failure, and of the more successful development of intelligence tests by a man whose first psychological mentor had been John Stuart Mill, will be given in the next chapter. For the moment, it suffices to note that Galton introduced the *idea* of the intelligence test as a eugenic screening device, and made its actual development a major research problem for the future.

In the meantime—never doubting that accurate tests would ultimately be available—Galton went on to imagine schemes for the social implementation of eugenics. It would be necessary first to encourage the ablest young men and women to intermarry and have many children, thus *concentrating* their hereditary gifts in the next generation rather than diluting them through "mongrelization." State support, such as he had imagined when he introduced the idea of the intelligence test, would be invaluable here to help ensure that the young prodigies cast their eyes in each other's direction. On a still larger scale, Galton hoped that eventually the government would sponsor the creation of a "national register," or a "golden book of natural nobility," listing all of the superintelligent and marriageable people in the country. People on the register would be treated with special respect, and be granted special opportunities, so that a sense of "caste" would develop among them, and they would naturally look among themselves for marriage partners.

A complementary eugenic goal was the *dis*couragement of excessive childbearing among ordinary, and especially unfit, people. Galton calculated that a relatively small breeding advantage for the superior group could have a large cumulative effect in just a few generations, so he hoped that educational measures would suffice. As the facts of mental heredity became more widely known and accepted, Galton thought, people who tested as non-superior might voluntarily practice birth control, and perhaps even divert some of their money toward the gifted in a new and better form of "charity." This new form of charity, he noted, would be "quite another thing to patronising paupers, and doing what are commonly spoken of as 'charitable' actions, which, however devoted they may be to a holy cause, have a notorious tendency to demoralise the recipient, and to increase the extent of the very evils they are intended to cure."[48] The infirm and the unfit—the traditional recipients of charity—should continue to receive help, but only on the condition that they contribute to the betterment of future society by practicing birth control. Since Galton believed their infirmities were largely hereditary, he argued that after a few generations such people would cease to exist as a major problem.

Thus for Galton the adoption of eugenics became a matter of moral and civic obligation—just as the adoption of environmentalist views had been for Mill—and he spent the last forty years of his long life vigorously promoting eugenics as a virtual personal religion. In the process, he contributed incidentally but greatly to many different fields.

Galton monumentally enriched the field of statistics, for example, with his invention of the basic mathematical ideas underlying the *correlation coefficient*. Until Galton, scientists had had no way of precisely stating the degree of relationship between two variables that were associated with each other in less than perfect ways. Such relationships were particularly common in the field of genetics which so interested Galton. The heights of fathers and their grown sons *tended* to be similar, for example, but were seldom identical. Galton sought a means of describing the degree of similarity with mathematical precision, so it could be compared with other hereditary combinations such as brother-brother or grandfather-grandson. Correlation coefficients express these relationships with numbers ranging from a high of $+1.0$, representing perfect agreement between the two variables, to a low of -1.0, representing perfect disagreement; the middle value of 0 indicates no systematic relationship between the two values at all. Moderate degrees of relationship are expressed by intermediate figures; a typical correlation between the heights of fathers and sons might be about +.50, for example, or +.25 between grandfathers and grandsons. Galton's basic mathematical ideas for correlation were elaborated and perfected by his younger friend and disciple, Karl Pearson (1857–1936), and have proven invaluable in many diverse fields of science. And as we shall see in later chapters of this book, calculated correlation coefficients between the intelligence test scores of varying kinds of kinship pairs are among the most important data bearing on the modern IQ controversy.

Among his other diverse contributions, Galton originated a theory of heredity which ruled out the inheritance of acquired characteristics (believed in by most of Galton's contemporaries, including Darwin), and anticipated the germ plasm theory which is generally accepted by biologists today. For future psychologists, he originated the self-report questionnaire and the word association test, and pioneered in the study of imagery. One of the first investigators of fingerprints, he developed the classification system which was originally adopted by Scotland Yard, and which remains the basis of fingerprint detection systems today. The unifying feature behind these multifaceted activities was Galton's constant effort to demonstrate the existence and importance of hereditary relationships. Thus, while he is remembered today as an important explorer, geographer, meteorologist, biologist, statistician, criminologist, and psychologist, his most important achievement in his own mind was the creation of the new "science" of eugenics.

Ironically, however, Galton's *personal* attempts to live eugenically suffered a setback. In 1853 he married Louisa Butler, whose father was a noted ecclesiastic and former first Wrangler at Cambridge, and whose brother had been the top scholar in classics there. In the absence of valid tests of natural ability, she must have seemed an ideal eugenic match, with family genes for precisely the sorts of ability Galton had wished so much for himself as a young man. Hopes for offspring to fulfill his childhood dreams gradually faded, however, as it became evident that his marriage would remain childless.

Mill, too, had been childless, and so when they died neither of these great antagonists left direct biological descendants behind. Both left powerful *intellectual* legacies, however, and found no dearth of people pleased to be regarded as their intellectual heirs. As the following chapters will show, the opposing ideas of Mill and Galton have continued to reverberate among parties to the IQ controversy, up to the present day.

Suggested Readings

John Stuart Mill himself describes his education, and gives a succinct summary of his life work, in his classic *Autobiography* (Boston: Houghton Mifflin, 1969). Michael St. John Packe's delightful *The Life of John Stuart Mill* (New York: Macmillan, 1954) gives many further details. Mill's psychological views are most systematically expounded in Book Six ("On the Logic of the Moral Sciences") of his massive *A System of Logic, Ratiocinative and Inductive* (Toronto: University of Toronto Press, 1973).

Francis Galton too wrote an informative and entertaining autobiography, *Memories of My Life* (London: Methuen, 1908). A detailed and often hero-worshipful account of his life is provided in Karl Pearson's three-volume *The Life, Letters and Labours of Francis Galton* (Cambridge, England: The University Press, 1914–1930). A good briefer biography is D. W. Forrest's *Francis Galton: The Life and Work of a Victorian Genius* (London: Elek, 1974). For an appreciation of Galton's many and diverse contributions to psychology see Chapter 7 of the author's own *Pioneers of Psychology* (New York: Norton, 1979). Galton's *Hereditary Genius,* expressing the essence of his hereditarian theories, is available in a reprint edition (Gloucester, MA: Peter Smith, 1972).

2 | The Invention of Intelligence Tests

In 1884, visitors to the International Health Exhibition at London's South Kensington Museum
were invited to pay three pence each and enter
Francis Galton's "Anthropometric Laboratory." To
tempt them, Galton afforded a partial view of the goings-on inside
through a trellised wall. Outside observers could see that each
paying customer manipulated a variety of interesting-looking
contrivances, while an attendant wrote down something about
each performance on two cards. The customer received one of
these cards as he or she left, while the attendant carefully filed
the other one away. By the exhibition's end, more than nine
thousand men and women had been enticed into visiting the
Laboratory. Without knowing it, these people constituted the first
large sample to take what were intended as *intelligence tests*, though
that term was not then used, and a modern observer would find
scant similarity between the "tests" they took and the ones in
common use today.

Galton's Anthropometric Laboratory represented a step toward
realizing the dream he had introduced in 1865—for a series of
examinations "on established principles" which could accurately
predict the innate and inheritable "natural ability" of young
adults.* The principles had yet to be established, of course, so

*See Chapter 1, pp. 34 ff.

Galton had to proceed on the basis of tentative working assumptions as he designed his Anthropometric Laboratory. The most important of these was that natural ability must be dependent upon inheritable qualities of the brain and the nervous system. People with large brains, for example, might be expected to show high intellectual ability. Galton's personal experience seemed to show this, since many of the eminent men he knew or saw appeared to have large heads. Further, it was established that women, on the average, had slightly smaller heads than men. Like many of his Victorian contemporaries, Galton was certain that women were also less intelligent than men, so here was one more example of an apparent correlation between brain size and intelligence. Accordingly, the first "tests" which Galton included in his Anthropometric Laboratory were devices for measuring head sizes, as estimates of the different brain masses lying within.*

Galton recognized that brain size alone was an imperfect indicator of ability, however, perhaps in part because he himself had an unusually small head. He thought that brain size must interact with the overall efficiency of the nervous system to produce intelligence, in the same way that body size and muscular coordination interact to produce variations in physical or athletic ability. One obvious measure of neurological efficiency seemed to be the *reaction time*—the fraction of a second required between the time a stimulus occurs and a muscular act is initiated in response. Physiologists of Galton's time had related this delay to the time required for electrochemical impulses to traverse the sensory and motor nerves of the body, and it had also been known for some time that certain individuals were consistently quicker than others in responding to split-second stimuli. Thus, tests of

---

*When relating intelligence to brain size across different species of animals, most scientists now believe that the *ratio* of brain weight to body weight provides a better index of relative intelligence than does brain weight per se. Thus elephants, with larger brains but presumably lesser intelligence than human beings, have a lower brain weight to body weight ratio. When this same correction is introduced into the male-female comparison for humans, women come out slightly higher than men. So far, however, all attempts to correlate brain-size variables with intelligence *within* the human species have turned up negligible relationships.

reaction time promised reliable, measurable differences among people in a task involving neurological efficiency. Galton included them in his laboratory, assuming that people with shorter reaction times would prove to have more natural ability.

Most of Galton's other devices measured *sensory acuity*, since intelligence presumably involved the interplay of ideas, and ideas in turn were based on sensory experience. As Galton stated the case, "The only information that reaches us concerning outward events appears to pass through the avenue of our senses; and the more perceptible our senses are of difference, the larger the field upon which our judgment and intellect can act."[1] As with his brain-size hypothesis, he culled some questionable anecdotal evidence to support this theory. Men, he was certain, were more sensorily acute than women. Why else would there be a total lack of women in jobs requiring fine sensory discrimination, such as wine or tea tasting, or wool sorting? Further, "Ladies rarely distinguish the merits of wine at the dinner-table, and though custom allows them to preside at the breakfast-table, men think them on the whole to be far from successful makers of tea and coffee."[2] Yet another example of the presumed association between low intelligence and low sensory acuity was provided by the mentally retarded:

> The discriminative faculty of idiots is curiously low; they hardly distinguish between heat and cold, and their sense of pain is so obtuse that some of the more idiotic seem hardly to know what it is. In their dull lives, such pain as can be excited in them may literally be accepted with a welcome surprise.[3]

Thus Galton's tests also included measures of keenness of sight and hearing, color sense, and eye judgment in bisecting a line.

Galton's nine thousand paying subjects all received their own results for these measures on their cards, while the duplicate copies were retained for statistical analysis. Galton and Karl Pearson had not yet developed the techniques for calculating correlation coefficients when he collected these data, so he had no way of precisely measuring the degrees of interrelationship among his separate measures. He merely sought at this time to obtain overall impressions of the states of varying segments of the British population, which could be compared with each other or, potentially, with similar measures from other national groups. The plan for using such tests in individualized eugenics assessments remained a utopian hope in the 1880s. Nevertheless, Galton's Anthropometric Laboratory brought the *idea* of the tests very much to the forefront, and while Galton himself would go little further, others would soon take up the project. Among the most important of these was the young American psychologist James McKeen Cattell (1860–1944).

JAMES MCKEEN CATTELL AND "MENTAL TESTS"

Son of the president of Pennsylvania's Lafayette College, James Cattell was graduated from that institution in 1880 and, like an increasing number of his generation, set off for graduate training in Germany. After starting out in philosophy, he became one of the first American students in Wilhelm Wundt's (1832–1920) Institute at Leipzig University—the only place in the world at that time where one could receive specialized, Ph.D. training in experimental psychology. During five years in Leipzig, Cattell became Wundt's assistant and prize student, conducting a brilliant series of doctoral studies on reaction time. Using just himself and one other student as subjects, Cattell took thousands of reaction-time measurements under varying conditions of concentration and awareness, precisely assessing the fractions of seconds presumably required for varying kinds of mental reactions. He also noted in passing small but consistent differences between his own times and those of his colleague, and proposed a further study to Professor Wundt, one aspect of which would be an investigation of individual differences in reaction time. Wundt was much more interested in the *general* features of the mind, however, and offered no support for this aspect of Cattell's proposal. Cattell put the idea on a back burner, and proceeded to finish his degree in a manner more acceptable to his mentor.

James McKeen Cattell (1860–1944) *(Archives of the History of Amerian Psychology, University of Akron)*

But the idea remained alive, for just as Cattell was proposing it to Wundt he learned about Galton's Anthropometric Laboratory in London. Cattell was interested to compare Galton's techniques for measuring reaction time with his own, and began a friendly correspondence. He soon became very interested in the entire issue of testing individual differences, and arranged to get a two year research fellowship for himself at England's Cambridge University after finishing his degree with Wundt. At Cambridge he established an anthropometry laboratory similar to Galton's, got to know Galton personally, and made tentative arrangements to collaborate with him in the writing of a laboratory manual covering the use of the apparatus. The manual was never completed and the Cambridge laboratory faded away soon after Cattell's return to the United States in 1888, but his enthusiasm for testing remained. As a psychology professor at Columbia University, Cattell became a highly effective exponent of the new psychology of individual differences.

Cattell published the details of his research program, and introduced the catchy term "mental test" into the psychologist's lexicon, in an 1890 article entitled "Mental Tests and Measurements." Here he described a basic set of ten "mental tests," which he proposed for use with the general public, as well as a longer series of fifty to be completed by university students. His basic ten tests, which he acknowledged owed much to Galton's previous work, were as follows:

1. Dynamometer pressure, the strength of one's hand squeeze. Cattell allowed that this measure "may be thought by many to be a purely physiological quantity," but added that "it is impossible to separate bodily from mental energy."[4] Thus he thought dynamometer pressure, as a general index of energy, reflected one's degree of *mental* power as well.
2. Rate of movement of the hand through a distance of 50 centimeters, when started from rest. The rationale for this was similar to that for dynamometer pressure.
3. Sensation areas, the so-called "two-point threshold." A pair of variably separated rubber-tipped compass points was applied to the back of a subject's hand, out of sight, to determine the minimum separations which could be reliably detected as two separate points. (When the tips were very close together, they were perceived as a single point of pressure.) Presumably, those who could detect the smallest separations had the most sensitive and efficient nervous systems.
4. Pressure causing pain. A hard rubber tip was pressed against the subject's forehead with increasing force, until the subject reported or showed signs of pain. Galton, of course, had

related pain sensitivity to intelligence in his discussion of the mentally defective.

5. Weight differentiation. The subject was required to differentiate the relative weights of identical-looking boxes, varying by 1-gram differences from 100 to 110 grams. Here was another test of the fineness of the subject's sensory discrimination.

6. Reaction time for sound. This standard measure of reaction time was similar to that used in Galton's laboratory, or Cattell's Ph.D. research.

7. Time for naming colors. Randomly ordered patches of red, yellow, green, and blue were pasted on strips. The subject had to name the colors in order, as fast as possible, while being timed with a stopwatch.

8. Bisection of a 50-centimeter line. As in Galton's Anthropometric Laboratory, the subject was required to place a sliding line as close as possible to the exact middle of an unmarked, 50-centimeter-long strip of wood.

9. Judgment of ten seconds of time. After demonstrating one ten-second interval, the experimenter tapped on the table and asked the subject to signal the end of another ten seconds. The accuracy of the estimate was measured with a stopwatch.

10. Number of letters repeated on one hearing. Lists of random consonants were read to the subject, who was required to repeat them from memory.

Such were the basic tests. The more comprehensive series of fifty included more complicated and intricate measures, but their general domain was the same. Thirty-eight measured different forms of sensory acuity, and another seven examined different reaction times. Obviously, these "mental tests" had a very strong sensory and physiological bias, consistent with the Galtonian theory of mental ability.

During the decade of the 1890s the cause of mental testing was enthusiastically taken up by an increasing number of investigators in several different countries. Gradually, however, it became evident that there was something seriously wrong with the tests, which did not really seem to measure useful differences in "mental" functions, as they had been designed to do. The crowning blow was struck in 1901 by Clark Wissler, one of Cattell's own graduate students, who obtained both mental test scores and records of academic grades from more than 300 Columbia University and Barnard College students. Wissler also learned the techniques for computing correlation coefficients, just recently perfected by Karl Pearson, and so was able to estimate with mathematical precision the exact interrelationships between the various mental tests, and independent measures of intellectual achievement.

Wissler's devastating results[5] indicated that the "mental tests" showed virtually *no* tendency to correlate with academic achievement; for example, class standing correlated −.02 with reaction time, +.02 with color naming, − .08 with dynamometer strength, and +.16 with memory for number lists. This last modest figure was the highest single correlation between academic achievement and a mental test. Almost as damaging, the mental tests showed little greater tendency to intercorrelate among themselves; for example, reaction time and color naming correlated −.15, color naming and hand movement speed +.19. Some head measurements were thrown in for good measure, and in general they fared no better than did the mental tests. The only substantial correlations in Wissler's study were those between grades in individual academic subjects, which ranged from a low of +.30 (between Rhetoric and French) to a high of +.75 (between Latin and Greek). These were much more of the order of magnitude to be expected when dealing with an underlying general ability. Obviously the mental tests, which did not even tend to agree among themselves, were not good measures of anything like intelligence or Galton's "natural ability."

Wissler's results greatly disappointed psychologists. Perhaps realizing what his research had done to psychology, Wissler shortly switched fields to become an anthropologist and one of the ear-

liest American supporters of the environmentalist "culture concept" explanation for differences between ethnic groups. Cattell
remained a psychologist, but lost much of his enthusiasm for the
Galtonian approach to mental testing, and gradually turned his
primary attention to scientific administration and the editing of
journals. Other psychologists lost enthusiasm too, and for a while
intelligence testing seemed like a dying issue.

   This situation did not last long, however, for in 1905 a very
different approach to intelligence testing was introduced by the
French psychologist Alfred Binet (1857–1911). With a background and attitudes quite different from Galton's or Cattell's,
Binet achieved the "breakthrough" that finally made possible the
measurement of meaningful individual differences in intelligence, and which properly qualifies Binet for the title of "father"
of the modern intelligence test.

   Binet's development of the first successful intelligence test in
1905 was the capstone of his distinguished career as France's
leading experimental psychologist. His path to psychological
eminence had not been easy, however, as he lacked formal academic training in the field and received much of his education
in the proverbial school of hard knocks. He suffered severe
embarrassment and disappointment early in his career, but
managed to turn the experience into a valuable object lesson.
The story of Binet's success thus begins with failure, many years
before he directly confronted the issue of intelligence testing per
se.

ALFRED BINET: THE MAKING OF A PSYCHOLOGIST

   Alfred Binet was born in Nice, France, on July
11, 1857, the only child of a physician father and an amateur
artist mother. His wealthy parents separated when he was very
young, and he was raised primarily by his mother. This was just
as well for Alfred, who remembered his father as a stern and
uncompromising man who once tried to cure him of timidity by

Alfred Binet (1857–1911) *(Archives of the History of American Psychology, University of Akron)*

forcing him to touch a cadaver. The memory of that horrible experience remained vivid for life, and permanently darkened Binet's view of the world.

As a youth Binet attended private schools in Nice and Paris, where he did well and won prizes in French composition. Then he earned a *licence,* or first degree, in law, but developed no desire to practice and dropped out of the field completely. Years later he would describe law as "the career of men who have not yet chosen a vocation."[6] Next came a brief try at medical school, where the horrors of the operating theater apparently aroused old conflicts associated with his father and his childhood trauma.

He suffered an emotional breakdown and left medical school prematurely, requiring complete rest for his recovery.

Soon the dispirited and emotionally exhausted twenty-two-year-old started going to Paris's great library, the Bibliothèque Nationale, to pass the time quietly and work his recovery. Following some vague inclination, he began browsing in books on psychology, became fascinated, and sensed correctly that he had at last found his vocation. As his enthusiasm mounted, he could not resist trying out for himself some of the experimental procedures he read about, and writing articles about the many new ideas they aroused.

The first experiments to catch his fancy involved the two-point threshold: the simultaneous stimulation of the skin by two compass points, and the determination of the conditions under which they were perceived as one or recognized as two. This procedure had already been the subject of much experimental investigation, and early psychologists had learned that the separation of points required to produce a sensation of "twoness" varies greatly with the part of the body stimulated—for example, it is some thirty times greater for the small of the back than for the tip of the index finger. (For this reason Cattell, when he included the two-point threshold among his basic mental tests, specified that it was the back of the hand which was always to be stimulated in his test.) Several theories had been proposed to account for these variations, focusing on the presumably varying distribution of nerves in different parts of the body.

Binet conducted a few simple two-point threshold experiments on himself and some friends, and concluded that the theories he had read about were wrong in some of their details. He quickly wrote an article describing his experiments and offering a "corrected" theory. Always a graceful and persuasive writer, he succeeded in getting this published.[7] Any pleasure at seeing his words in print was soon curtailed, however, because his article caught the critical attention of one Joseph Delboeuf (1831–1896), a Belgian physiologist who had done some important work on the two-point threshold which had been overlooked by Binet. Delboeuf published a critique stating that his own much more systematic experiments did not agree with several of Binet's findings, and showing that he had already published a much more sophisticated version of Binet's theory long before.[8] Binet had obviously rushed prematurely into print, and Delboeuf publicly humiliated him for it.

Even Delboeuf's attack could not diminish Binet's ardor for psychology, however, and his next passion became the associationist psychology of John Stuart Mill, whom he would later call "my only master in psychology."[9] Binet was persuaded by Mill's arguments about the potentially unlimited explanatory power of associationism, and said as much in his second venture into psychological publication. This 1883 article, entitled "Reasoning in Perception," asserted: "The operations of the intelligence are nothing but diverse forms of the laws of association: all psychological phenomena revert to these forms, be they apparently simple, or recognized as complex. Explanation in psychology, in the most scientific form, consists in showing that each mental fact is only a particular case of these general laws."[10] John Mill himself could not have put the case more unreservedly.

Yet Binet was once again treading upon dangerous ground. Associationism as a psychological doctrine clearly had its merits, but by 1883 much evidence had already accumulated to show that it could not stand as a *complete* explanation of mental phenomena, even after any possible innate factors were placed aside. In particular, associationism was ill equipped to account for varying *motivational influences* on thought, or for many of the *unconscious phenomena* that were coming to increasing attention at that time. Thus the laws of association were hard pressed to explain, by themselves, why a particular starting thought can lead to totally different trains of associations, depending on the motivational state of the individual. Phenomena such as *post-hypnotic amnesia* posed another difficulty for exclusively associationistic theory. When a recently hypnotized subject was asked what happened while he was hypnotized and failed to remember, he provided an example of *dis*-association of ideas. The stimulus of the question failed to bring in its train the associated ideas and memories, including the answer, which one would normally expect.

Mill's laws of association had nothing to say about how ideas could become disconnected, or "dissociated," from each other.

This time Binet recognized the deficiencies in his psychology without help from a Delboeuf, and took steps to remedy them. But even though he was soon to *augment* his associationism, he never lost respect for its great though incomplete explanatory power. Years later, when he attacked the problem of assessing intelligence, he would not be restricted, as Galton and Cattell had been, to the consideration of presumably innate factors such as sensory acuity or neurological efficiency. Instead, Binet would argue that "intelligence"—whatever else it was—could never be isolated from the actual experiences, circumstances, and personal associations of the individual in question.

Charcot and the Salpêtrière

The broadening of Binet's psychology began in 1883, as he found a teacher in precisely those subjects associationism was least able to deal with. Jean Martin Charcot (1825–1893), director of the Salpêtrière Hospital and one of the most famous neurologists in the world, had recently turned his attention to the study of *hysteria* and *hypnosis*—two conditions in which the questions of motivation and unconscious psychological effects were strongly raised. Binet went to work for Charcot as a volunteer researcher.

Charcot had become interested in hysteria because its symptoms often *mimicked* those of ordinary neurological conditions, but lacked obvious neurological cause. Some patients complained of paralyses, anesthesias (losses of feeling), or amnesias (losses of memory), for example, but neurological examination showed no underlying pathology of the nervous system. Most physicians were suspicious of hysterical symptoms, regarding them as deliberate malingering and simulation. Charcot recognized the subjective reality of the symptoms to the patients themselves, however, and took hysteria seriously.

Hypnosis posed many obvious similarities to hysteria, as paralyses, anesthesias, selective amnesias, and virtually all other hysterical symptoms could easily be reproduced in a good hypnotic subject simply upon suggestion. Like true hysterical symptoms, these suggested hypnotic effects had a strong subjective reality for the subject, in spite of the absence of immediately obvious neurological causes. So close did these parallels seem that Charcot concluded (erroneously, it would turn out) that the capacity for being hypnotized was really a symptom of underlying hysteria. The study of hypnosis became important to Charcot because it promised to throw light on the mechanisms of hysteria.

Charcot customarily used an unusual research technique, involving the very close study of small numbers of individual cases. He believed it was possible to identify a few patients who suffer from certain neurological diseases in pure or complete form, representing what Charcot called the "types" of the illnesses. The close study of these extreme cases would presumably be very useful in understanding the much more numerous incomplete or "blurred" forms of the condition, in the same way that knowledge about the spectacular, three-stage *grand mal* form of epilepsy had yielded useful information about the condition in general, including the much more common *petit mal* forms.

Charcot had found a small number of patients who exhibited particularly striking patterns of hysterical and hypnotic effects, which he believed to represent the types for these conditions, and which he labeled "major hysteria" *("grande hystérie")* and "major hypnotism" *("grand hypnotisme"),* respectively. Binet's assignment was to investigate the hypnotic responses of one of these, an attractive young woman named Blanche Wittmann, whose flamboyant symptoms and haughty attitude toward other patients had led her to be called "Queen of the Hysterics." When being hypnotized she characteristically passed through three stages which Charcot believed to define major hypnotism. In the first "cataleptic stage" she became muscularly relaxed and apparently insensitive to all stimulation except the voice of the hypnotist. In the second "lethargic stage" her muscles became completely flaccid, as she collapsed into the arms of the hypnotist or an assistant. Finally in the "somnambulistic stage" she could carry out complex automatic behaviors on command from the hypnotist, including the paralytic, anesthetic, and amnesic responses that seemed so hysteria-like to Charcot. Charcot and Binet believed that this elaborate three-stage sequence revealed some fundamental features of the nervous system, though we now know that it really represented only the following of implicit *suggestions* administered by the hypnotist.

When Binet and a young doctor named Charles Feré began to work with "Wit" (as she was named in their published studies), she put on amazing performances for them. Perhaps thinking back to the days when hypnotism was called "animal magnetism," Binet and Feré discovered that a hypnotic effect such as a paralysis, which had been produced on one side of her body, could be transferred to the other side simply by reversing the polarity of a magnet in her presence. Emotional states could be similarly reversed. After suggesting to the hypnotized Wit that she felt very sad, for example, a flick of the magnet transformed her piteous sobs into joyful laughter. Binet and Feré believed that they had discovered a method here for identifying "complementary emotions," analogous to the well-known pairs of "complementary colors" which produce white or gray when mixed together.

Never shy about getting into print, Binet and Feré published their hypnotic findings in four articles during 1884 and 1885. Admitting that some results seemed implausible, they still assured their readers that the effects had been "entirely unexpected," and had therefore "issued from nature herself, . . . showing an inflexible logic."[11] Unsurprisingly, these amazing reports aroused the interest of Binet's old nemesis, Joseph Delboeuf, who had maintained a side interest in hypnotism for many years. Though inclined to accept Charcot's theory of major hypnotism because of his great prestige, Delboeuf found the magnetic results utterly improbable; with Binet's name on them, they seemed doubly suspect. "One fine morning I could contain myself no longer," Delboeuf later recalled,[12] so he went to the Salpêtrière to see for himself:

> I will never forget those delicious hours. M. Feré and Binet are both young, both tall; M. Feré more reflec-

> tive, it seems to me, and more accessible to objections
> raised; M. Binet more adventurous and more affirma-
> tive; . . . with fine features and mischievous expression.
> Between them sat . . . the placid and "appetizing" Alsa-
> cienne Wit . . . not only wearing a complacent look, but
> finding visible pleasure in getting ready to do anything
> that should be asked of her.

Delboeuf saw at once that Feré, the principal hypnotist, had an
extraordinary degree of rapport with Wit, playing her "as if
playing upon a piano. . . . A light touch on any muscle—or even
pointing to it without touching—made Wit . . . contract any muscle, even in her ear."[13] The magnet which produced such amazing effects was of the large horseshoe variety, wielded and
reversed openly before Wit during the demonstration. Binet and
Feré spoke openly about Wit's anticipated responses as if she
were not there. When asked why they did not take common-
sense precautions to disguise their expectations, they explained
that according to Charcot's theory Wit was unable to compre-
hend things normally while in the somnambulistic stage of major
hypnotism.

The skeptical Delboeuf returned to Belgium and repeated the
Salpêtrière experiments, but with proper precautions against
simulation by his subjects. He concluded that not only the Binet-
Feré findings, but also Charcot's entire theory of major hypnosis
were false, the result of conscious or unconscious simulation by
the subjects. At first Binet objected that Delboeuf had failed to
find genuine cases of major hypnotism on which to experiment,
but slowly and gradually the terrible truth dawned. He finally
realized that he had put too much faith in Charcot's name and
prestige, and had accepted the reality of "grand hypnotism"
without sufficient question. He recanted publicly in 1891:

> One can see for oneself that these studies present a great
> many loopholes for error, which very often perverts
> the results in spite of the precautions of the most care-
> ful experimenter; no one can boast that he has never
> failed. One of the chief and constant causes of mis-

takes, we know, is found in suggestion—that is to say,
in the influence the operator exerts by his words, ges-
tures, attitudes, even by his silences, on the subtle and
alert intelligence of the person he has put in the somnambulistic state.[14]

Ever afterward Binet was acutely aware of the power of uninten-
tional suggestion—which he called "that cholera of psychology,"[15]—to contaminate experiments.

Following his humiliation, Binet was understandably ready to
find a new base of operations. Just as understandably, prospec-
tive employers did not come flocking to his door. In 1891 his
situation finally resolved itself at a chance meeting in a railway
station with Henri Beaunis (1830–1921), a physiologist and the
director of the newly created Laboratory of Physiological Psychology at the Sorbonne. Beaunis had publicly opposed Binet
during the hypnotism controversy and must have seemed an
unlikely ally, but Binet summoned his courage and asked if he
could come to work, without pay, in the Laboratory. Beaunis,
appreciative of the fact that Binet was wealthy enough to work
for nothing, agreed, and got one of the best bargains in the history of psychology. Binet had now learned his lesson, and though
he would remain an enthusiastic and prolific writer, he would
never again trust unauthenticated authority, or go out on a limb
in support of a position he had not thoroughly tested himself.
In sum, he had learned the hard way to be a model experimenter.

He had gained some other things from the Salpêtrière as well.
For one, he had learned the art of studying individual cases.
Though it was dangerous to generalize prematurely from small
numbers of individuals, as both he and Charcot had done in
studying hypnosis, the case-study approach nevertheless helped
one to appreciate the individuality and complexity of real people. Binet's practice with the case-study method helped him to
appreciate that any abstract psychological variable—including
"intelligence"—was neither unitary nor simple of measurement,
and that any attempt to measure it must take into account its

complexity and diversity of manifestation. The case-study approach, of course, was very different from that of Galton and Cattell, who preferred to assess large numbers of people rather superficially, on simple and one-dimensional scales.*

Further, Binet had truly succeeded at the Salpêtrière in broadening and deepening his naive associationistic psychology. He had investigated other things besides hypnosis while there, and produced three books and more than twenty articles on subjects as diverse as sexual fetishism, illusions of movement, and child psychology. He continued to appreciate the importance of environment and circumstance, but now recognized the importance of other factors as well. In a paper on the origins of sexual fetishism (a phenomenon which he named), for example, he called attention to the roles of both chance circumstances occurring in childhood, and an innate and presumably hereditary predisposition.[16]

Binet also came to recognize the inability of pure associationism to account for the vagaries of *attention* which occurred so strikingly in hypnosis and hysteria, and also played a major role in "normal" conscious states. Associationistic psychology, he now wrote, tended to reduce the mind too much to "a sort of passive automatism, ... to a *spectator*-me rather than to an *actor*-me." Attention was the most important process of the mind for asserting its active nature, *guiding* association but itself being unexplainable by association.[17] As shall be seen, attention came to play an important role in Binet's analysis of human intelligence.

In general, then, it was a highly competent and broadly educated psychologist whom Beaunis took on as his assistant at the Sorbonne Laboratory in the autumn of 1891. He never regretted his decision, as Binet became his successor as director in 1894 and remained in that position—though always unpaid—for the rest of his life. In short order, Binet became the outstanding

*Another young student of Charcot's, who overlapped with Binet, was Sigmund Freud. Though Freud, like Binet, ultimately rejected most of Charcot's specific theory, he also always credited him with a profound influence on his own clinical technique. More than coincidentally, Freud's major psychoanalytic writings commenced with a brilliant series of case studies, in his *Studies on Hysteria*.

experimental psychologist in France, and leader of a new program which he called "individual psychology."

BINET'S INDIVIDUAL PSYCHOLOGY

Even as Binet was winding up his affairs at the Salpêtrière, he was conducting a small series of experiments at home which markedly influenced his later career. He had developed the habit of trying out all sorts of tests and puzzles on his young daughters Madeleine and Alice, born in 1885 and 1887, respectively. These early home experiments culminated in three short articles published in 1890.[18] While belonging chronologically to the end of his Salpêtrière period, these papers marked the logical beginnings of his new career as an experimental child psychologist and "individual psychologist."

Several of the tests and tasks in these early experiments were derived from the Galton and Cattell series, assessing reaction time and various forms of sensory acuity. Binet found that his daughters and their small friends had *average* reaction times about three times longer than typical adults', but with much greater variability. On some trials the children responded just as quickly as adults, but on others they were much slower. Since the children could *sometimes* match the adult speed, Binet concluded that the crucial factor differentiating children from adults was not reaction time per se, but rather the ability to sustain *attention* to the task. When children paid attention they responded like adults, but on those frequent occasions when their attention wandered, their reaction times increased drastically. This finding reinforced Binet's conviction of the importance of attention in mental life, and he would continue throughout his career to emphasize its importance in the development of adult intelligence.

Binet's investigations of sensory acuity showed that children's senses were often much sharper than commonly believed. For example, Madeleine's ability to judge the relative lengths of parallel lines, or the relative sizes of pairs of angles, actually exceeded that of many adults.

Tests of "color sense" like those in Cattell's battery, which required subjects to *name* color patches as quickly as possible, generally revealed a large superiority of adults over children. Binet discovered, however, that tests requiring subjects to *match* colors showed very much smaller differences. This indicated that the children's *perceptual* and *sensory* abilities of color discrimination were really very good. Their major inferiority to adults was *linguistic*, residing in their slowness to assign proper names to their color perceptions.

On another test requiring language use—this one very different from anything in the Galton or Cattell batteries—Binet found even more striking differences between children and adults. He simply asked his young subjects to define a series of everyday objects, and discovered that their thoughts immediately leapt to the *uses* of the objects inquired about, or to the actions habitually taken with or toward them. Thus a knife was simply "to cut meat"; a box "means put candies inside"; and a snail was, emphatically, "Squash it!" The young girls did not and indeed *could* not "define" the concepts as an adult would:

> It is clear that a little girl is incapable of defining. When you say "definition" you imply a certain work of reflection, of comparison, of elimination, etc. The little children that we studied responded immediately without thinking, and their replies express very simply the first images which were evoked by the name of a certain well-known object.[19]

Binet's discovery of this "functional" or "utilitarian" nature of young children's thought, as compared to the much greater abstraction of adults, led him to recognize the increasing capacity for abstraction as one of the hallmarks of increasing intelligence.

These early experiments generally led Binet to doubt the usefulness of sensory or neurological tests for making psychological or intellectual discriminations among people. When young children with obviously undeveloped intellects could approach or match the performance of adults, then those tests did not seem very promising discriminators of adult levels of intellectual ability. Those tests which did discriminate children from adults required the application of higher and more complex faculties than simple acuity or reaction speed, such as sustained attention and the sophisticated use of language. Thus, while Binet was not yet concerned with defining the nature of "intelligence" per se, he came away from his studies convinced that there are important differences between mature and immature intellects, measurable only by tests requiring higher, *complex* mental operations.

An equally important insight followed Binet's observation of the marked stylistic and temperamental differences between his two girls. As they learned to walk, for example, he observed:

> Standing on her feet, holding on to a solid object, a chair or a table, [Madeleine] risked abandoning that support only when she had visually selected another object a short distance away which would offer new support; she directed herself very slowly towards the second object, paying great attention to the movements of her legs. These movements were executed with great seriousness in perfect silence. [Alice, on the other hand], was a laughing, turbulent child; when put on her legs, she remained immobile for some moments and then was suddenly pushed forward by a desire to progress. It was evident that she never anticipated which object could furnish support, because she advanced without the slightest hesitation to the middle of an empty part of the room. She cried out, she gestured, she was very amusing to watch; she advanced staggering like a drunken man, and could not take four or five steps without falling.[20]

Other aspects of the girls' behavior showed similar differences. Madeleine was consistently thoughtful and deliberate while Alice remained distractable and impulsive. Binet would continue to be impressed with such characteristic differences, not only between his daughters but among people in general. He recognized that individual differences in style were just as important as differences in level—that two equally intelligent people, for example, could go about solving the same problem in entirely different ways.

Studies of Suggestibility

The themes introduced in Binet's early studies of his daughters developed during his first years at the Sorbonne. He remained interested in children, and used the authority of his new position to gain access to schools for subjects. With this larger sample he immediately began to study memory and "that cholera of psychology," suggestibility. The memory task required a child to remember the length of a straight line, choosing the one of the same length from a pair of unequal lines presented afterward. The tests of suggestibility used a similar task, but attempted to influence the choices with suggestive statements from the experimenter ("Are you sure? Isn't it the next line?"); with suggestive responses from "leaders" among the subjects themselves; and by the establishment of "preconceived ideas" (e.g., for several consecutive trials the correct line would be above the incorrect one, and then on the crucial trial placed below).

Binet found that accuracy in memory steadily increased, and susceptibility to suggestion steadily decreased, with the ages of his seven- to thirteen-year-old subjects. He did not yet appreciate its full significance, but this was one of his first hints as to the role of *age* in the development of children's mental faculties, and of its potential usefulness as a measuring stick for varying degrees of intelligence.[21]

Binet's first studies of memory and suggestibility reported only the average results, for large numbers of different subjects. He recalled his training at the Salpêtrière, however, and explicitly recognized that these average figures inevitably obscured the richness and complexity of the actual responses of individual people. In 1900, when summarizing several years of work on suggestibility, he issued a stern warning about the limitations of statistical results:

> Mere numbers cannot bring out ... the intimate essence of the experiment. This conviction comes nat-

urally when one watches a subject at work. . . . What
things can happen! What reflections, what remarks, what
feelings, or, on the other hand, what blind automatism,
what absence of ideas! . . . The experimenter judges
what may be going on in [the subject's] mind, and certainly feels difficulty in expressing all the oscillations of
a thought in a simple, brutal number, which can have
only a deceptive precision. How, in fact, *could* it sum up
what would need several pages of description!

We feel it necessary to insist that the suggestibility of
a person cannot be expressed entirely in a number, even
if the latter should correspond exactly to his degree of
suggestibility. It is necessary to complete this number
by a description of all the little facts that complete the
physiognomy of the experiment.[22]

Binet retained this attitude toward quantified data for the rest
of his life, in investigations of intelligence as well as of suggestibility. While recognizing the usefulness of averages and other
conglomerate data for expressing general trends, he also was
acutely aware of their limitations. Unlike Francis Galton and many
of his followers in the mental testing field, who believed that
precise scores and numbers could capture the real essence of
psychological characteristics, and moreover were *necessary* if their
work was to be truly "scientific," Binet never came close to being
a worshipper of "mere numbers."

Case Studies

From the outset of his Sorbonne career, Binet also
kept his individualistic faith by regularly conducting in-depth
case studies. First, he examined a small group of people with
unusual mental abilities: chess players who could play (and win)
several simultaneous games while blindfolded, and two "calculating prodigies" who could solve complicated mathematical
problems rapidly and entirely in their heads.[23] Two surprising
facts emerged. First, these people showed no particularly keen
mental abilities apart from their special talents. The chess players had keen memories for the "lines of force" surrounding the

various pieces on the board, and the calculators had unusually good memories for numbers, but their memories in other areas were not unusual. The second surprise was the diversity of ways in which these people went about their specialized tasks. One calculator, for example, used exclusively auditory imagery as he worked, always hearing but never seeing the numbers in his imagination; for another, the reverse was true. Here was a fine example of different mental operations being used to solve the same kinds of problems, by people equally extraordinary in their special abilities.

This same general finding emerged when Binet attempted to investigate the wellsprings of literary creativity. Through interviews and questionnaires, Binet studied the working habits of several of France's leading authors.[24] If he had hoped to uncover some secret technique common to all creative authors he was disappointed, for he found great variability in their approaches. The dramatist François de Curel, for example, did his best work when he felt under the influence of "spontaneous inspirations" and he seemed merely "the vessel through which his characters spoke." Inspiration for Curel came especially frequently in early morning, as if produced by unremembered dreams. Several other successful authors, however, worked much more systematically and deliberately, at all hours of the day or night, and felt that their writing turned out to be equally effective regardless of whether they felt "inspired" or were doggedly forcing themselves to write. For Binet, here was more impressive evidence of great complexity and lack of uniformity in the operation of the highest mental functions.

Binet's most important case studies were of his two daughters. As they grew up, he continued to test them with a wide variety of experimental tasks, including the two-point threshold, measures of memory and judgment, and imaginative exercises in word association, inkblot interpretation, or story telling. He gave the results from twenty of these different tests in his 1903 book, *L'Étude Experimentale de l'Intelligence (The Experimental Study of Intelligence)*, regarded by some psychologists as his most creative work.

Though this book's title contained the word "intelligence," it primarily dealt with qualitative differences in personality or mental functioning in general. Binet had continued to be impressed with the temperamental and stylistic differences between his daughters as they grew up, and had characterized the deliberate and down-to-earth Madeleine as "the observer" *("l'observateur"),* and the impulsive, fanciful Alice as "the imaginer" *("l'imaginitif").* The book was replete with ingenious illustrations of their differences, including a test which required them to write descriptions of objects such as a coin, a feather, a chestnut leaf, or a question mark drawn on a sheet of paper. Here were the two teenaged girls' responses to the chestnut leaf:

> *Madeleine:* The leaf I am looking at is a chestnut leaf gathered in the autumn, because the folioles are all almost yellow except for two, and one is half green and yellow. This leaf is composed of several folioles joined at a center which ends at the stem called a petiole, which supports the leaf on the tree. The folioles are not of the same size; out of the 7, 4 are much smaller than the 3 others. The chestnut tree is a docotyledon, as one can tell by looking at the leaf, which has ramified nervures.

> *Alice:* This is a chestnut tree leaf which has just fallen languidly in the autumn wind. . . . Poor leaf, destined now to fly along the streets, then to rot, heaped up with the others. It is dead today, and it was alive yesterday! Yesterday, hanging from the branch it awaited the fatal flow of wind that would carry it off, like a dying person who awaits his final agony. But the leaf did not sense its danger, and it fell softly in the sun.[25]

Binet's experience of testing his daughters in so many different ways proved invaluable later on, when he tried to measure different *levels* of intelligence. And in the meantime, it strongly reinforced his conviction that "intelligence" could appear in highly diverse manifestations, even among approximately equally able members of the same family.

Tests for "Individual Psychology"

Even as he appreciated the richness which only individualized and detailed case studies could provide, Binet also recognized the desirability of establishing some *standard* dimensions along which individuals could be quickly and easily compared. Psychologists might not always have the hours or days to spare for in-depth case study, but still might want to make comparative judgments about the psychological functioning of different people. To this end, Binet devised a research program which he called "Individual Psychology," and which he described in a paper of that title written with his assistant Victor Henri in 1896. This new field contrasted sharply with the standard "general psychology" pursued in most laboratories:

> General psychology studies the general properties of psychological processes, which are by consequence common to all individuals; individual psychology, to the contrary, studies those properties of psychological processes which vary from one individual to another. It must determine those variable processes, and then study to what degree and how they vary across individuals.[26]

In other words, individual psychology had to define the basic dimensions of human psychological variation, and then show how those dimensions interrelated both across and within individual people.

The immediate practical problem for individual psychology, as Binet saw it, was to develop the series of tests which could be given in less than two hours, and which would adequately sample the major variables in psychological functioning. But what were the variables, and how were they to be assessed? This was (and indeed still remains) the basic question for individual psychology.

Binet and Henri reviewed the work of Cattell and the other mental testers, finding it much too heavy in emphasis on elementary sensory or physiological processes. Binet voiced his suspicion that any measure which fails to discriminate well between adults and children cannot be a very useful index of psychological or intellectual differences. Sensations and reaction times might be easy to measure, he admitted, but their variability was too small to enable worthwhile comparisons. The *higher* processes were more difficult to measure precisely, but they alone showed sufficient variation for the job of individual psychology. "It thus results," Binet and Henri concluded, "that if one wishes to study the differences existing between two individuals it is necessary to begin with the most intellectual and complicated processes, and it is only as a second line that one must consider the simple and elementary processes; it is, however, just the opposite which is done by the great majority of authors who have taken up this question."[27] Written five years before Wissler's study highlighted the general irrelevance of sensory and physiological measures, Binet's suspicions were prophetic.

As Galton and others had learned before, however, it was one thing to *imagine* a program of successful testing and quite another again actually to develop it. In 1896, Binet and Henri had only some rather vague ideas about what kinds of tests to employ. They tentatively suggested that tests of ten different "faculties" might reasonably sample the range of individual differences. These were (1) *memory;* (2) *imagery* (the capacity to imagine things in the various sense modalities); (3) *imagination* (to be assessed by measures such as an inkblot test); (4) *attention;* (5) *comprehension* (for example, the ability to observe and understand the sequence of movements in devices like sewing machines); (6) *suggestibility;* (7) *aesthetic sentiment* (tested by comparing the subjects' preferences for pictures and designs with those of established artists); (8) *moral sentiment* (assessed by recording the subjects' reactions to pictures of people committing various antisocial acts); (9) *muscular strength and willpower* (involving comparisons of a subject's dynamometer strength under neutral and highly motivated conditions, as when a male subject is observed by a woman); and (10) *motor ability and hand-eye coordination.* Only the last two of these ten suggested tests bore much similarity to the standard "mental tests" of the time. The rest were all notable for the degree to which higher, complex, and obviously learned abilities were involved.

Sad to say, however, Binet and Henri's ambitious goal for individual psychology was never really achieved. As they and other workers tried out tests of the ten faculties on real subjects, the results did not fall into coherent patterns. In an influential study in 1899, Cornell graduate student Stella Sharp gave the Binet-Henri tests to seven of her fellow students in psychology, and found little meaningful interrelation among them—even between subtests supposedly measuring the same basic faculty.[28] Binet and Henri themselves obtained similarly disappointing results. In 1904 they reported on eight years of effort to develop a test battery for schoolchildren, and concluded "that it is premature to look for tests permitting a diagnosis during a very limited time (one or two hours), and that, much to the contrary, it is necessary to study individual psychology without limiting the time—especially by studying outstanding personalities."[29] At about the same time Binet published a sixty-page case study of the dramatist Paul Hervieu, based on many hours of systematic interviews with the subject, and detailed observation of his work and working habits. Here Binet reluctantly concluded that such extensive and time-consuming analyses were the only valid approaches yet open to the individual psychologist.[30]

In fact, the major goal of Binet's individual psychology has proven chimerical even to the present day. Psychologists have yet to develop tests comprehensive and efficient enough to permit reasonably complete psychological assessments of individuals in two hours' time. Nevertheless, Binet's technically unsuccessful foray into individual psychology was not entirely wasted. His experience confirmed his belief that a psychologist should deal directly with the higher and more complex mental functions, in situations that closely simulate real life. He had experimented extensively with many different varieties of such tests, and this experience proved invaluable when he turned his attention in 1904 to a much more specific task than that of individual psychology—namely, the development of a test for identifying and diagnosing mentally retarded children.

THE BINET-SIMON INTELLIGENCE SCALES

Two events in 1899 had helped turn Binet's interest toward the problem of mental subnormality, or retardation.* First, an able young physician named Theodore Simon (1873–1961) applied to do doctoral research under Binet's supervision. As an intern at a large institution for the mentally subnormal, Simon could provide access to this new kind of subject for Binet's innumerable experiments. Binet was quick to take advantage of this opportunity, and began trying out his many tests on the retarded.

Also in 1899, Binet became a member of the Free Society for the Psychological Study of the Child (La Societé Libre pour l'Étude Psychologique de l'Enfant), a newly organized group interested in general educational problems and research. With his characteristic energy, Binet became the leader of the Society, founding a *Bulletin* for the publication of its members' research, and turning more and more of his own attention to educational aspects of experimental child psychology.

Mental subnormality was a subject of especially strong concern to French educators at that time. Recently enacted universal education laws now required that *all* French children be given several years of public education. Retarded children, who in earlier years would have dropped out early or never attended school at all, now had to be provided with special classes and programs. This suddenly visible problem group naturally aroused much official interest, so in 1904 the French government appointed a commission to investigate the state of the mentally subnormal in France. Binet, because of his position in the Society, was named a member.

As a commissioner, Binet discovered that the most pressing problem facing workers with the subnormal was the lack of a reliable and useful diagnostic system. A tradition of sorts subdi-

---

*The actual term "mental retardation" was not yet generally used at the turn of the century, since it connotes a point of view which became established largely as a *result* of Binet's work. The children he became involved with, however, were of a kind who today would be referred to as retarded.

vided the population into three groups: profoundly mentally deficient people called *idiots;* moderately deficient but still severely handicapped people called *imbeciles;* and a large number of people whose mental abilities approached the lower limits of the normal population. Binet referred to this group as *"débiles"* (literally, "weak ones"), a French word for which his American translators soon coined the less appropriate substitute, "morons" (from the Greek *moros,* meaning "dull"). While there was rough agreement as to the *existence* of these three general categories, Binet found appalling confusion when it came to assigning real people to them. Individual children were often placed in different categories by different diagnosticians, using highly impressionistic diagnostic criteria. Binet realized that the question of diagnosis was of particular moment in borderline cases. A truly subnormal child could waste much of his own and his class's time if placed in an ordinary school, and, more tragically, a truly normal child could be unfairly stigmatized for life if misdiagnosed and sent to special classes. As Binet observed, "It will never be a mark of distinction to have passed through a special school, and those who do not merit it must be spared the record."[31] Binet and Simon set out to resolve this important problem in 1904 by devising a series of psychological tests to differentiate clearly among the three grades of subnormal children, and the slowest group of children whose intelligence could be considered "normal."

The 1905 Tests

Since Binet and Simon had at first little theoretical conception of the nature of the "intelligence" they hoped to diagnose, they began their search inductively. That is, they identified groups of children who had been unequivocally diagnosed by teachers or doctors as mentally deficient or as normal, and then gave both groups a wide variety of different tests in hopes of finding some that would differentiate between them. They wished their final test to be "psychological" rather than "pedagogical" in nature, and so avoided problems which relied heavily on reading, writing, or other clearly school-related abilities for their completion. At the same time, Binet still believed the most useful tests would assess higher, complex functions in lifelike situations, and so did not hesitate to include items which assumed a basic familiarity with French life and culture—the sort of familiarity, he thought, that even a poor child might reasonably be expected to acquire. Binet and Simon realized that their tests would be valid only with children for whom this assumption was true—but these constituted the vast majority of the population they were concerned to diagnose.

At first, the task seemed hopeless, for while there were clear differences between the groups in *average* performance on many items, it proved impossible to find tasks that were almost always solved by all normal children, and almost never by the retarded ones. There was always some overlap between the groups, with subnormal children passing or normal children failing tasks that were intended to discriminate between them.

Gradually, however, a key insight developed—one which seemed perfectly obvious once recognized, but which nevertheless had previously eluded Binet and other investigators of intelligence. *Age* was a crucial factor to be considered: both subnormal and normal children might learn to pass the same tests, but normal children did so at a younger age. With a now characteristic caution Binet summarized his discovery as follows:

> We noted that it was almost always possible to equate [the subnormal children] with normal children very much younger. ... It is possible that certain differences remain hidden underneath the resemblances, and that we will one day succeed in differentiating them. ... But for the moment, what especially strikes us are the resemblances between very young normal children and subnormals considerably older. These resemblances are so numerous and so striking, that truly one was unable after reading the reactions of a child whose age was not given, to say whether it was normal or abnormal.[32]

With this basic insight, Binet and Simon developed a series of thirty tasks of increasing levels of difficulty. The simplest tasks presumably reflected the earliest glimmerings of intelligence in normal human infants, as well as the *upper* limits for the most severely retarded of any age. The most difficult tasks were beyond the reach of even the oldest and most capable of the subnormal children, but were easily passed by normal children of eleven or twelve. These thirty items, standardized on groups of about fifty normal children of varying ages and forty-five subnormals of varying degrees, constituted the famous first "Test" of intelligence, published by Binet and Simon in 1905.[33]

The easiest item on the test simply required subjects to follow the movement of a lighted match with their eyes, demonstrating the elementary capacity for *attention* which is necessary for all intelligent behavior. The next few items required the child to grasp a small object placed in the hand, to distinguish and eat a small piece of dark chocolate placed next to a piece of white wood, to unwrap and eat a piece of candy, and to shake hands with the tester and comply with a few very simple spoken or gestured requests. Normal children could complete all of these by the age of two, but the most profoundly retarded of *any* age failed on some or all of them. Binet argued that the last of these items, requiring the rudiments of social interaction and language, should be considered as defining the boundary between idiots and imbeciles. Idiots thus became defined as people whose maximum capacity was like that of a normal two-year-old, falling short of the ability to interact socially and linguistically with others.

The next, intermediate series of items required subjects to point to various named parts of the body; to identify a 4-centimeter line as longer than one of 3 centimeters; to repeat back correctly a spoken sequence of three random digits; to determine the heavier of two identical looking boxes weighing 6 and 15 grams; to recognize and give simple, "functional" definitions of the words "house," "fork," "horse," and "mama"; and to repeat back some simple sentences averaging fifteen words in length, such as "I get up in the morning, dine at noon, and go to bed at night."

These tasks, involving the ability to understand a basic vocabulary, and to communicate and comply with simple requests, were all routinely passed by normal five-year-old children. Binet suggested that the imbecile category be defined by the inability to progress further than this in the tests; that is, the imbecile's intelligence at full maturity was comparable to that of a normal child between two and five years of age.

The remaining items on the test, which defined the upper boundaries for the *débile* or moron group, could be passed by normal children between the ages of five and eleven. The easiest in this series required children to state the differences between pairs of things, such as paper and cardboard, or a fly and a butterfly. Slightly more difficult questions asked for the *similarities* between a fly and an ant; a poppy and blood; or a newspaper, a label, and a picture. The next six tests required subjects (1) to reproduce pen-and-ink designs from memory; (2) to arrange five identical-looking weights of 3, 6, 9, 12, and 15 grams in order, and to identify the gap by hand-weighing after one of the middle weights was secretly removed; (3) to provide rhymes to the French word *obéissance;* (4) to fill in the missing words in spoken sentences such as "The weather is clear and the sky is __?__ "; (5) to construct sentences which include three given words, such as "Paris," "river," and "fortune"; and (6) to answer a series of questions involving practical comprehension and social consciousness, such as "When someone has offended you and asks you to excuse him, what ought you to do?" The two most difficult items—not always passed even by the oldest of the normal children—asked subjects (1) to figure in their heads what time it would be if the large and small hands of the clock were reversed for various times (for example, twenty past six would become half past four); and (2) to *imagine* the design which would result if a piece of paper were folded in quarters, a triangular cut were made in it, and then the paper were unfolded.

Here at last was an intelligence test which seemed to work in making valid discriminations, but what exactly was the nature of the "intelligence" it measured? Binet was never able to offer a simple answer to this question, but in 1905 two general features seemed to stand out. First, the successful items entailed the use of a *wide variety* of separate mental functions: attention, memory, discrimination, imagination, and verbal fluency, to mention but a few. Second, tying together most of the items above the low imbecile range was the common requirement for a quality which Binet and Simon called *judgment,* and whose essence they attempted to convey as follows:

> There is in intelligence, it seems to us, a fundamental agency the lack or alteration of which has the greatest importance for practical life; that is judgement, otherwise known as good sense, practical sense, initiative, or the faculty of adapting oneself. To judge well, to understand well, to reason well—these are the essential wellsprings of intelligence. A person may be a *débile* or an imbecile if he lacks judgement; with good judgement, he will never be either. Compared to judgement, the rest of the psychology of the intellect seems of little importance.[34]

Thus Binet came to see "intelligence" as the exercise of multifarious psychological faculties in the real world, tied together by and always under the control of practical judgment. This somewhat loose and ever-practical conception remained at the heart of the two revised and improved intelligence scales that Binet presented in 1908 and 1911.

The 1908 and 1911 Revisions

Though they marked a genuine turning point in the history of psychology, the 1905 tests had a number of weaknesses and shortcomings. Developed with very small samples of normal and retarded children, they permitted only rough comparisons between retardates and normal children of varying specific ages. More than half of the items were geared to the very retarded and the very young, yet the majority of hard decisions to be made involved older children near the borderline of normality.

Binet soon realized that his basic technique could be considerably extended and refined with a larger pool of test items, each specifically "located" at the particular age where normal children first developed the ability to pass it. Thus an item located at the seven-year level would draw on abilities consistent with Binet's rough conception of intelligence, and be passed by a minority of six-year-olds, a majority of seven-year-olds, and an even larger majority of normal eight-year-olds. Between 1905 and 1911 Binet experimented with innumerable individual tasks, on larger samples of variously aged subjects. In 1908 he and Simon were able to publish a new "scale" consisting of fifty-eight items located at specific age levels between three and thirteen. In 1911, Binet alone further extended the scale to include fifteen-year-olds and an "adult" category, and to provide an even five items for each age level.[35] Some of the final scale's items were the following:

At *age three*, typical normal children could point at request to eyes, nose, and mouth; name common objects from a printed picture; repeat back correctly two spoken numbers; correctly repeat a six-syllable sentence; and give their last names.

At *age six*, they could distinguish in words between morning and evening; discriminate an attractive from an ugly face in a drawing; copy from memory a diamond-shaped design; count thirteen pennies; and give simple, "functional" definitions of words such as "horse," "fork," "table," or "mama."

At *age ten*, normal children could reproduce line drawings from memory; compose a sentence containing the three words "Paris," "fortune," and "stream"; place identical-looking weights of 6, 9, 12, 15, and 18 grams in proper order; and answer questions involving *social* judgment, such as "Why should one judge people by their acts rather than their words?" The ten-year-olds' series concluded with several statements containing absurdities which the children had to detect and explain: for example, "The body of an unfortunate girl was found, cut into 18 pieces. It is thought that she killed herself."*

---

*Still another macabre absurdity went: "Someone said that if I should ever go desperate and kill myself, I will not choose Friday, because Friday is an unlucky day and will bring unhappiness." When some American psychologists later com-

At *age fifteen* the average child could correctly repeat back seven digits; find three good rhymes for the French word *obéissance;* repeat back a sentence of 26 syllables; give appropriate interpretations of some pictured scenes of people; and solve such problems as "My neighbor has just been receiving strange visitors. He has received in turn a doctor, a lawyer, and then a priest. What is taking place?"

Children who took these tests almost never came out exactly at an age level—for example, by passing all of the items through the eight-year level, but none beyond. Instead, they tended gradually to taper off over several different age levels before reaching their limits. Further, very few children, even within the same age group, gave exactly identical patterns of right and wrong responses. Here was more evidence of the variability in intelligence which had impressed Binet for so long.

Nevertheless, Binet believed it was appropriate to impose a degree of standardization and quantification on the revised test results by calculating an "intellectual level" for each child according to a formula which allowed one-fifth of a year for each subtest passed:

> Here is the rule to follow: one takes as a starting point the age for which all tests are passed; beyond that, one counts as many fifths of a year as there are tests passed. For example, a child of eight years succeeds at all of the tests for six years, 2 for seven years, 3 for eight years, 2 for nine years, and 1 for ten years. He thus has the level of six years, plus the benefit of eight tests or eight-fifths years, that is, one and three-fifths years, for a level of seven and three-fifths years, or more simply, 7.6.

Binet recognized that he was treading on dangerous ground here, for not only were there multiplicities of different ways in

---

plained that their subjects found items such as these upsetting, Binet was amused and reported that French children usually found them funny. These different reactions may illustrate the way cultural factors can interact with measures of "intelligence."

which any given level could be achieved, but also the fractioni-
zation of year levels into fifths implied a misleading degree of
precision for the tests. Thus he immediately went on to warn,
"It must be well understood that these fractions in so delicate an
appreciation do not merit absolute confidence, because they will
vary noticeably from one examination to another.[36] Reflecting
his caution, Binet always used the rather general word "level"
(French *niveau*) to describe this final score; he never used the
more precise-sounding "mental age" which soon came to be substituted for "intellectual level" by his successors.

Despite his reservations about its imprecision, Binet still felt
that a child's intellectual level could be useful information in
diagnosing subnormality. He noted that children whose intellectual levels trailed their actual ages by *one* year or so were quite
common in the normal population, and they generally could cope
with standard school programs. Retardations of *two or more* years
occurred in less than 7 percent of the population, however, and
such children usually experienced great difficulty in ordinary
schools. Thus Binet offered a provisional rule of thumb: if a
child's calculated intellectual level trailed his actual age by more
than two years, *and* the assumptions of the test were met—that
is, the child was healthy and well motivated when he took the
test, and came from a reasonably ordinary French cultural background—then a diagnosis of genuine subnormality should be
seriously considered. This was as close as he ever came to reducing the results of his test to numbers.

For Binet, there were two strong reasons for not taking the
exact intellectual level scored by a child too seriously as an absolute measure of innate intelligence. First, there were sources of
unreliability and error in the tests themselves. Even though they
had been selected and standardized with care, the items were
few in number, and subject to some variation due to chance factors in the circumstances of the testing session. Second, and of
greater theoretical importance, Binet believed that "intelligence"
itself was liable to substantial change within an individual. While
he granted that there probably exists a relatively fixed upper
limit for each person's intelligence, he also believed that few people

ever actually approach that limit in real life. Thus there is almost always room for improvement, especially at the lower levels of intelligence which his tests were primarily designed to measure. "It must be understood that these diagnoses apply only to the present moment," he wrote in 1911. "One who is an imbecile today, may perhaps by the progress of age be able to reach the level of a *débile*, or on the contrary remain an imbecile all his life. One never knows; the prognosis is reserved."[37]

Mental Orthopedics

Consistent with his conviction that intellectual levels could change over time, Binet also believed that there were certain things one could deliberately do to improve the intelligence levels of retarded children. In his 1909 book, *Idées Modernes sur les Enfants (Modern Ideas about Children)*, Binet lashed out against the "brutal pessimism" and the "deplorable verdicts" of those who believe an individual's intelligence is a fixed quantity.[38] He elaborated:

> If one considers that intelligence is not a single indi-
> visible function with its own particular essence, but that
> it is formed by the harmonious combination of all the
> minor functions of discrimination, observation, reten-
> tion, etc., to which we have attributed plasticity and the
> capacity for growth, it will seem incontestable that . . .
> the intelligence of anyone is susceptible of develop-
> ment. With practice, enthusiasm, and especially with
> method one can succeed in increasing one's attention,
> memory, judgment, and in becoming literally more
> intelligent than one was before; and this process can go
> on until one reaches one's limit.[39]

Accordingly, Binet helped design a series of exercises which he called "mental orthopedics" to raise not only the intellectual levels but also the actual intelligence of retarded children. In particular, these exercises improved the children's ability to pay attention to things—the first requisite for any form of intelligent behavior. Retarded children, like very young normal children, were often excessively distractable, and unable to sit still long enough to pay attention to anything. Thus children in mental orthopedics were taught the game of "Statue," where the teacher gave a sudden signal for the children to "freeze" in their present positions until told to stop. Binet observed:

> On the first try, one obtained little good, and the whole class shook with foolish laughter. Then, little by little, things calmed down. . . . Self-regard became involved for those who could hold the attitude the longest. I saw turbulent, noisy, undisciplined children, who were the despair of their teacher, make a serious effort for the first time. . . . They were thus capable of attention, will power, and personal control.[40]

Another exercise developed memory along with attention. Each day, nine new objects were removed from a carton and revealed to the children for just five seconds' inspection before being re-hidden. The children had to remember as many objects as they could—and with practice they became surprisingly proficient:

> The adult who witnesses this exercise receives a great surprise. I remember when the deputies, at the time they voted on the law for the abnormal, visited our classes and assisted in this exercise. Some, intrigued, asked to try the experiment themselves; and they succeeded very much less well than the little patients—to the astonishment, laughs, mockeries of their colleagues, and all of the comments one can imagine. . . . In reality, in spite of the piquancy of the adventure, all could be explained. Our deputies had not taken account of the intensive training our students had received.[41]

Ever the pragmatist, and convinced that intelligence is something which manifests itself only in practical interaction with the circumstances of the real world, Binet saw no reason why those circumstances could not be so manipulated as to raise a person's general intellectual level.

Binet's Death

Only in his early fifties, Binet was at the height of his powers as he developed mental orthopedics and the revisions of his intelligence scale. Sadly, however, the events of his personal life failed to parallel his professional triumphs. It appears that his wife suffered from a progressively worsening psychiatric malady which inhibited his social life. Perhaps reflecting his own gloomy mood, Binet began collaborating with the dramatist André de Lorde, known popularly as "The Prince of Terror," in the writing of a series of plays dealing with macabre subjects such as a released mental patient turned murderer, or the ghoulish attempt of a scientist to restore his dead daughter to life. Finally, the ultimate tragedy occurred in real life, as Binet contracted a terminal disease whose exact nature is no longer known. With full and rueful knowledge of the unfinished work he was leaving behind, Alfred Binet died in 1911, at the age of 54.

BINET AND GALTON COMPARED

Binet had succeeded where Galton, Cattell, and the other early mental testers had failed—in developing a test which bore a significant relationship to manifestations of "intelligent" behavior in real life. To the present day, most successful intelligence tests, for subjects of all ages, have continued to use the kinds of items pioneered by Binet—requiring the play of many different mental functions on a wide variety of complex tasks.

It must not be forgotten, however, that Binet's purposes, procedures, and attitudes differed markedly from his predecessors', so that the "intelligence" which he successfully assessed was not necessarily identical to that which workers in the older tradition had sought to measure. Galton and his followers were primarily interested in measuring the intellectual potential of *young adults* at the *upper end* of the ability distribution; Binet's great success was to assess the intelligence of *children* at the *lower end*. Only because he worked with children whose intellectual abilities were naturally changing and developing over time was Binet able to appreciate the importance of age differences, and to use them as his standards for measuring degrees of intelligence. By the time children reached their middle to late teens, their performance on the Binet-type test items ceased to improve further. Thus if Binet had worked with older subjects, as Galton and Cattell had done, he would have missed out on one of his most important insights regarding the nature of intelligence. The question still remained, of course, whether the intelligence of children was like, or was even a valid predictor of, the intelligence of adults. This important question will be discussed in later chapters.

Binet noted in passing that some children achieved intellectual levels on his tests a year or more in advance of their actual ages. He also reported a tendency—though far from a perfect one—for these "advanced" children to come from higher class neighborhoods and to be somewhat accelerated in their schooling. This was a far cry, however, from proving that his tests measured high ability or "genius" as effectively as they did retardation. Binet's own earlier studies of exceptional and creative people had highlighted the great individuality and complexity of genius, as well as its *resistance* to analysis by standardized tests. In 1905 he had thought it perhaps *possible* that, in the future one could extend the scale "up to the normal adult, the normal intelligent, the hyperintelligent and measure, or try to measure, talent and genius."[42] By 1908 he had developed reservations about that idea, however; he now wrote, "We are of the opinion that the most valuable applications of our scale will not be for the normal subject, but instead for the inferior degrees of intelligence."[43] He did in fact extend his last scale to the level of the adult normal, but never attempted to reach the strata beyond. Thus the amalgam of attention, memory, discrimination, and judgment which presumably constituted "intelligence" on Binet's tests was really only proven to be something which *prevented* people from being retarded. The extent to which it overlapped with "genius" or the superior intellectual ability Galton wanted to measure was—and remains to some degree—a debatable question.

Binet differed further from Galton by conceptualizing intelligence as a fluid and highly individualized quality, shaped to a large extent by each person's environmental and cultural circumstances, and quantifiable only to a limited and tentative degree. The "intellectual level" yielded by one of Binet's tests was an estimate of a child's functioning in a particular society at a particular time; change in that level was to be naturally expected, as a function both of normal growth and of significantly altered circumstances. Galton, in contrast, was primarily interested in the upper limits of a person's ability—presumably innate, fixed by physiology rather than culture, and potentially expressible in numbers as precise as those defining a trained broad-jumper's maximum leap. Indeed, his dream of a valid, physiologically based test which would be relatively "culture free" in its assessment of intelligence—as Binet's tests manifestly were not—has never died out completely. Today, some investigators still try to find correlates of intelligence in patterns of brain waves recorded by the electroencephalograph, or in reaction-time measures more complex than those used by Galton and Cattell. The results of their work have been mixed and controversial, however, and to date all practically useful intelligence tests continue to rest on the more culturally involved assumptions of Binet.

By coincidence, Galton and Binet both died in 1911. Galton was then an old man whose active testing days were far behind him, but who had been able during his final years to arouse a great deal of enthusiasm for his eugenics program and basic hereditarian theory. Though Binet's death occurred when he was at the height of his personal creativity and power, he had cultivated few followers to carry on his work. Thus the next generation of intelligence testers tended to include more people favorable to Galton's philosophy than to Binet's. Seizing upon Binet's basic *technique* for assessing intelligence as the best one available, these people began interpreting its results in more "Galtonian" ways. They quantified Binet test scores into precise "Intelligence Quotients," for example, which many interpreted as fixed and innately given measures of superior as well as inferior mental ability. The story of these developments, many of which Binet would probably have resisted had he been able, begins in the next chapter.

SUGGESTED READINGS

Galton's sensory theory of intelligence is given in his *Inquiries into Human Faculty and Its Development* (New York: Dutton, 1907); accounts of his anthropometric laboratories are provided in the works by Forrest and Fancher, suggested at the end of the last chapter. A vivid account of Cattell's development as a psychologist, including his relations with Galton, is provided in the collection of his letters and journal entries edited by Michael Sokal under the title *An Education in Psychology* (Cambridge, MA: MIT Press, 1981).

An indispensable work for all students of Binet is Theta H. Wolf's *Alfred Binet* (Chicago: University of Chicago Press, 1973), which combines biographical detail with apt analyses of the full range of Binet's work. Much of Binet's important work remains untranslated, but a sampling of his papers is found in R. H. Pollack and M. W. Brenner (eds.), *The Experimental Psychology of Alfred Binet: Selected Papers* (New York: Springer, 1969). His articles introducing the 1905, 1908, and 1911 intelligence scales are translated in A. Binet and T. Simon, *The Development of Intelligence in Children (The Binet-Simon Scale)*, Reprint Edition (New York: Arno Press, 1973).

3 | Intelligence Redefined

Sometime around 1890, a young English army officer named Charles Spearman (1863–1945) started reading psychology textbooks in his spare time. The product of an English upper-class school, he had even as a boy masked a secret propensity for philosophical speculation beneath an aggressive and competitive exterior. Following school he had self-consciously decided to follow the example of the philosopher René Descartes by joining the army to see something of the practical world. As a member of the Royal Engineers, Spearman served and was decorated in the Burmese Wars of the 1880s, but even as his military career was thriving he continued to seek intellectual stimulation for his hidden philosophical side. Thus he began reading psychology books.

By chance, the first texts he found were by John Stuart Mill and other associationists, who argued that most if not all mental experiences could be explained through the various forms of the laws of association. As Spearman later recalled, he responded to these works very strongly:

> My reaction to all this view was intensely negative. The ideas and arguments appeared to me astonishingly crude, equivocal, and erroneous. But even so, my conviction was accompanied by an emotional heat which cannot . . . be explained on purely intellectual grounds.

The source of this heat I take to have been—little as I admitted this to myself at the time—of an *ethical* nature. Sensualism and associationism tend strongly to go with hedonism; and this latter was (and is) to me an abomination.[1]

Of course, we may question the literal accuracy of Spearman's judgment, and cite John Stuart Mill himself as at least one staunch associationist whose personal life was unmarked by excessive hedonism. But that is really beside the point. The important fact is that *Spearman* was morally offended by associationism, whether rightly or wrongly, and he has given us an unusually candid description of this emotional bias with which he began his psychological career. For his heated initial response ignited a more general interest in the field of psychology, and he soon found other psychological approaches much more to his taste. In 1897 Spearman decided that his army decision had been "the mistake of my life." At age thirty-four, he resigned his army post in order to seek a Ph.D. in experimental psychology with the renowned German professor Wilhelm Wundt (who had also been James McKeen Cattell's teacher) at the University of Leipzig.

Spearman's choice was not accidental, for Wundt propounded what he called "voluntaristic psychology," according to which events at the center of a person's consciousness are *not* completely and mechanically determined by prior associations, but are augmented and directed by internal and voluntary factors such as intentions or motives. When full conscious attention is focused on a group of ideas, they can be combined and related to one another in ways that have never been actually experienced before, in acts that Wundt labeled *creative syntheses*. While mechanical laws of association might be able to explain mental events occurring automatically at the periphery of consciousness, the voluntaristic creative syntheses were necessary to account for all "higher" intellectual activity. This view, of course, fitted perfectly with Spearman's anti-associationistic feelings.

It took Spearman seven years to complete his Ph.D. with Wundt, partly because he had to return to England for two years of home

Charles Spearman (1863–1945) *(British Psychological Society)*

duty during the Boer War of 1900–1902. Those years were hardly a complete loss, however, because during them he encountered a second major psychological influence, in the works of Francis Galton. Impressed by Galton's case for the importance of intelligence testing, Spearman started some small-scale experiments of his own in his spare time. The results of those experiments led him to postulate a new theory of *General Intelligence,* to the advancement of which he would devote the rest of his long career. Unsurprisingly, given Spearman's original anti-associationistic and pro-Galtonian attitudes, this theory differed considerably from Binet's—though he felt it was capable of accounting for the success of Binet-type intelligence tests. This theory marked the first stage of a major transformation in Binet's concept of intelligence, after which it became precisely quantified, and interpreted as a primarily hereditary characteristic. We shall first turn to Spearman's theory in some detail.

CHARLES SPEARMAN AND "GENERAL INTELLIGENCE"

The immediate inspiration for Spearman's first crucial experiments was Galton's belief that differences in intelligence should be reflected by corresponding differences in sensory acuity. As Spearman recalled in his autobiography:

> One day, inspired by Galton's *Human Faculty*, I started experimenting with a little village school nearby. The aim was to find out whether, as Galton had indicated, the abilities commonly taken to be "intellectual" had any correlation with each other or with sensory discrimination.[2]

In the village school, Spearman estimated the "intelligence" of twenty-four children in three ways: by having their teacher rank them for their "cleverness in school," and by having the two oldest children rank the members of their class for "sharpness and common sense out of school." Spearman also ranked the children's performances on three *sensory* tasks involving pitch, light, and weight discrimination. When he calculated the intercorrelations among these six measures, he found that the three "intellectual" variables correlated with *each other* at an average of +.55, while the corresponding average within the three sensory measures was +.25. For the crucial correlations between intellectual and sensory measures, the average was +.38.

This last value, of course, seemed to provide modest support for Galton's hypothesis, and was considerably higher than what Clark Wissler had obtained in his somewhat parallel study of "mental tests" with Columbia University students.* Spearman had not known of the Wissler study when he conducted his own, however, and when he finally did learn of it he was much troubled until an important insight occurred to him:

> Had I seen [Wissler's] work earlier, I should certainly have thought the matter disposed of and should never have started my own work in this direction. Since the conflicting results were there, however, they had at least to be explained. After much pondering over them, I had at last a happy thought which embodied itself in the concept of "attenuation."[3]

This "happy thought," which would have great consequences for Spearman's subsequent work, was his realization that any empirically observed correlation between two variables will underestimate the "true" degree of relationship, to the extent that there is inaccuracy or unreliability in the measurement of those two variables. Further, if the amount of unreliability is precisely known, it is possible to "correct" the attenuated observed correlation according to the formula (where r stands for the correlation coefficient)

$$r_{true} = \frac{r_{observed}}{\sqrt{\text{reliability of variable}_1 \times \text{reliability of variable}_2}}.$$

Consider a hypothetical example. A carnival estimator guesses both the heights and the weights of a group of people, and his two measures intercorrelate to the degree of $+.60$. Previous analyses have shown that his guesses of height correlate $+.80$ with true, tape-measured height, and his guesses of weight correlate $+.70$ with actual readings from a scale. Thus the guesses, while much more accurate than chance, are still less than perfect, and one effect of their inaccuracy is to reduce the observed height-weight correlation below what it would have been if perfectly accurate measures were available. Applying Spearman's correction formula to obtain this "true" value, we get

---

*See Chapter 2, pages 48–49, for an account of Wissler's study.

$$r_{\text{true}} = \frac{.60}{\sqrt{.80 \times .70}} = .80.$$

Thus one could conclude, on the basis of the estimator's imperfect guesses, that height and weight actually correlated to the degree of +.80.

Armed with this insight, Spearman argued that the chief source of the lowness of the correlations in Wissler's study had been the unreliability of his sensory discrimination measures. Scores had been obtained from subjects in groups and under apparently harried conditions, thus attenuating the observed correlations.[4] In Spearman's study discrimination had been assessed on individual subjects, presumably with greater accuracy. Wissler had made a good try, Spearman concluded, but his data had been so unreliable as to obscure the true relationships.

In fact, Spearman's own procedures were not beyond reproach, and were almost immediately questioned by some of his contemporaries. For the moment we shall defer criticism, however, and follow his theoretical arguments to their conclusion. After dismissing Wissler with the aid of the attenuation concept, he went on to apply the correction formula to *his own* data. Though Spearman did not doubt that these data were considerably better than Wissler's had been, he modestly allowed that they too had been less than perfectly reliable. He knew, for example, that his three "intelligence" ratings did not perfectly agree with each other, but intercorrelated at an average level of .55. The three sensory measures were even less consistent, intercorrelating at an average of only .25.

Spearman now put his correction formula to use, suggesting that one think of all three of the intellective measures *considered together* as an index of a hypothetical "General Intelligence," and the three sensory measures as an index of "General Sensory Discrimination." He proposed to take his observed Intelligence × Sensory Discrimination average of .38 as the observed correlation between General Intelligence and General Discrimination, and then to "correct" it by taking .55 and .25 as the "reliabilities" of the two general variables. Thus he calculated the "true" or theoretical relationship between General Intelligence and General Discrimination in the following equation[5]:

$$\frac{.38}{\sqrt{.55 \times .25}} = 1.01.$$

Correlations greater than 1.0 (which represents a perfect correspondence between the variables) are theoretically impossible, but Spearman attributed the slight excess in his calculated figure to random errors, and assumed that the "true" value was really the perfect 1.0.

Next, Spearman corroborated this striking finding with a second, somewhat parallel study of a group of boys from an "upper-class preparatory school." Here, however, his "intelligence" measures were obtained differently. They consisted of class ranks in the four subjects of Classics, French, English, and Mathematics, corrected to counteract the influence of age. Basically, his correction procedure involved the subtraction of each subject's rank in school from his rank in age, so if the fifteenth oldest student stood eleventh in Classics, he would receive a score of +4 in that subject; if the fourth oldest stood tenth, he would receive a −6; and so on. Spearman devised this technique shortly before Binet and Simon published *their* age-based tests, so he should be credited with anticipating the importance of age standards in assessing children's intelligence (though he did not develop the idea into a system of practical tests, as Binet and Simon did).

Sensory discrimination for this second sample was measured by a pitch discrimination task, and by rankings of the students' musical competence by their music teacher (Spearman argued that musical proficiency was more a matter of sensory than of intellectual ability). Spearman found that music or pitch correlated with the four intelligence scores at an average of .56, while music and pitch correlated with each other at .40, and the four separate intelligence scores intercorrelated among themselves at an average of .71. Plugging these into the formula for the true correlation between General Intelligence and General Discrimination, Spearman gave the following equation[6]:

$$\frac{.56}{\sqrt{.40 \times .71}} = 1.04.$$

Once again, Spearman dismissed the slight excess over 1.0 as the result of random error. Greatly impressed by this second example of a "perfect" relationship, Spearman wrote: "We reach the profoundly important conclusion that *there really exists a something that we may provisionally term 'General Sensory Discrimination' and similarly a 'General Intelligence'* [emphasis is Spearman's]."[7] In other words, from his perception that "General Intelligence" entered into these theoretically "perfect" relationships, Spearman inferred that it must be something *real*, and not merely an arbitrary mathematical abstraction.

In fact, Spearman's reasoning was not airtight here, and critics almost immediately noted that it involved an inappropriate use of the correction formula.* Nevertheless, these findings encouraged Spearman to proceed further with his consideration of "General Intelligence," and to turn up other evidence that was more persuasive.

The Two-Factor Theory of Intelligence

Convinced of the concrete reality of General Intelligence, Spearman investigated its apparent influence on the individual correlations among the six variables for his preparatory school subjects. He discovered yet another marvelous coincidence, in that the correlations were not only all positive, but also ranged themselves in a nearly perfect *hierarchy.* Intelligence scores based on Classics grades always achieved the highest cor-

---

*While the correction formula itself was recognized as valid, it was argued that the "reliabilities" ought to apply only to the intercorrelations between different administrations of the same test, not to the broad collections of variables such as Spearman's "intellectual" and "sensory discrimination" groups. Spearman himself eventually accepted this, and abandoned this particular line of argument for his General Intelligence concept.

relations with all the other variables, French intelligence the second highest, followed by English, Mathematics, Pitch, and Music, in nearly perfect order. The table below reproduces Spearman's reported correlations, whose hierarchical order is apparent from the regular decrease one observes reading across any row, or down any column[8]:

	Classics	French	English	Math	Pitch	Music
Classics	—	.83	.78	.70	.66	.63
French	.83	—	.67	.67	.65	.57
English	.78	.67	—	.64	.54	.51
Math	.70	.67	.64	—	.45	.51
Pitch	.66	.65	.54	.45	—	.40
Music	.63	.57	.51	.51	.40	—

From the universal *positiveness* of the correlations, Spearman inferred that there must be a single *factor* common to them all; this, he suggested, was General Intelligence, which he subsequently abbreviated by the symbol "*g*." From the fact that the separate variables differed systematically in their average *level* of intercorrelation, Spearman inferred that they must be differentially "saturated" with General Intelligence. That is, the Classics measure was the most highly saturated, and the "purest" index of General Intelligence among the tests used; Music was the least pure.

Spearman reasoned that any test with low saturation must strongly reflect something else besides *g*—something independent of the prerequisites for success on any of the other tests. This something, he suggested, was a *specific factor*, or "*s*" factor, which determines ability for that one field but not for the others. Tests highly saturated with General Intelligence, or *g*, require relatively little of an *s* factor.

Spearman generalized these views in his *two-factor theory of intelligence*. According to this theory, the performance of any intellectual act requires some combination of *g*, which is available to the same individual to the same degree for *all* intellectual acts, and of the *s* factor which is specific to that act and which varies in strength from one act to another. If one knows how a person performs on one task that is highly saturated with g—say in age-corrected Classics grades—one can safely predict a similar level of performance for another highly g-saturated task. Prediction of performance on tasks with high s factors, such as music or pitch discrimination, will be less accurate. Nevertheless, since g pervades *all* tasks to some extent or another, prediction in even those cases will be significantly better than chance. According to Spearman, the single most important bit of information to have about any person's intellectual ability is an estimate of his or her g level.

Spearman and Binet

In 1904, Spearman published all of these findings, and the first statement of his two-factor theory, in a paper in *The American Journal of Psychology,* entitled " 'General Intelligence,' Objectively Determined and Measured." The paper attracted much attention from the start, and in 1906 Spearman was rewarded with a junior academic appointment at University College London. Soon afterward he became that institution's first professor of psychology, and spent the rest of his career there developing and promoting the theory of General Intelligence.

Very early on, he realized that his own first ways of measuring "intelligence" through teachers' ratings and grades were cumbersome, and, like all other early techniques, superseded by the Binet-Simon tests of 1905 and 1908. Even though Spearman had correctly anticipated something of the importance of age standards in measuring children's intelligence, his methods were too closely tied to actual school performance to be of much use in assessing intelligence independently of the academic setting. And while his sensory measures were relatively independent of academic performance, these achieved relatively low g saturations and so had little practical value for predictive purposes. Binet and Simon, in contrast, had developed a technique which did have practical predictive value, and which did not depend too greatly on previous educational experience. Thus Spearman was greatly impressed by the practical utility of the Binet tests, when he learned of them.

He was less impressed by Binet's *theory*, however, which conceptualized intelligence as a congeries of diverse functions arranged in different and individualized patterns for different people. Spearman noted, not without a touch of resentment, that Binet had seemingly adopted his own general procedure of assessing intelligence by means of a "hotchpot" of several different tasks. Though the specific items in Binet's hotchpot were different from (and practically superior to) his own group of sensory and academic measures, Spearman found that when their scores were intercorrelated a familiar pattern emerged: all the correlations were positive, and fell into a roughly hierarchical pattern. The highest correlations were obtained by tests like the "similarities" questions, requiring a degree of abstract thinking.

For Spearman, this was evidence of a *g* factor underlying all of Binet's items, together with *s* factors of varying magnitudes for each. The Binet tests worked, he argued, not because they assessed uniquely patterned intelligences, but because their overall results offered reasonable estimates of the subjects' *g* levels. Spearman wrote:

> On the whole . . . it is difficult to avoid the conclusion that [Binet and Simon], though they believed themselves to maintain the theory that the tests measure some genuine "intelligence" consisting in one or more formal powers, nevertheless in their actual practice had totally abandoned this theory in favour of the opposite one of Two Factors.[9]

If intelligence was not a collection of diverse functions, but primarily the result of an all-important general factor subserved by numerous *s* factors, what was its underlying explanation? Spearman observed that it could potentially be accounted for "in an infinitude of different ways,"[10] but from this infinitude he strongly favored one interpretation in particular, based on brain physiology, and in complete accord with his long-standing anti-associationistic predispositions:

The [g] factor was taken, pending further information, to consist in something of the nature of an "energy" or "power" which serves in common the whole cortex (or possibly, even, the whole nervous system).

But if, thus, the totality of cognitive operations is served by some general factor in common, then each different operation must necessarily be further served by some *specific* factor peculiar to it. For this factor also, a physiological substrate has been suggested, namely, the particular group of neurons specially serving the particular kind of operation. These neural groups would thus function as alternative "engines" into which the common supply of "energy" could be alternatively distributed.[11]

Thus Spearman interpreted g, literally, as *brain power*, as the general level of mental energy which led people to perform well or poorly on all sorts of intellectual acts, but particularly those requiring abstract thinking. Here was the energy which enables people to overcome the power of previously acquired associations, and to perform those adaptive acts of learning and creative synthesis that had been emphasized in Wundt's voluntaristic psychology.

Consistent with his other mentor, Galton, Spearman also believed that each person's g level was probably acquired more by inheritance than through the environment. Though always more interested in the *theory* of intelligence than in its practical or political implications, Spearman nonetheless joined the Eugenics Society, and expressed the hope that tests of g might one day serve Galton's original purposes for mental tests. "One can . . . conceive the establishment of a minimum index [of g] to qualify for parliamentary vote, and above all, for the right to have offspring," he wrote in 1912.[12]

In general, then, Spearman chose to interpret g as a modern-day version of Galton's hereditary and physiologically based "natural ability," though adapted and fitted with new terminology to fit the findings of the newer and more practical Binet-type tests of intelligence.

Critical Reactions to Spearman's Theory

Spearman's case for General Intelligence was original and influential but hardly conclusive, and has been challenged from its inception on several scores. Unsurprisingly, Binet expressed doubts about Spearman's 1904 paper when he reviewed it the following year. Though he allowed it was "highly interesting," he also expressed considerable skepticism:

> [Spearman] judges [his] conclusion as *profoundly* important. It is possible. We ourselves are *profoundly* astonished at it, because of the defective character of the author's sensory experiments, and of the way in which he rated or secured ratings of total intelligence. Before pronouncing judgement it is necessary to wait for other investigators to obtain similar results.[13]

Had he lived, Binet would have found some justification for his doubts, because replications have generally produced findings less theoretically perfect than Spearman's. Low correlations between sensory and intellective measures—more on the order of Wissler's findings than Spearman's—have usually occurred; and while later studies usually revealed *rough* hierarchies in the intercorrelations among subtests, their structures were much less perfect than the one reported by Spearman in 1904. Indeed, when the statistics are recalculated from the raw data which Spearman appended to his own 1904 paper (and on which his reported correlations were supposedly based), the results turn out less perfectly than he reported. Corrected correlations between General Intelligence and General Discrimination deviate farther from 1.0 than Spearman indicated, and the hierarchy of intercorrelations is more irregular and headed by French rather than Classics. While we cannot explain the reason for these strange mistakes in Spearman's original calculations, they seem to suggest that he had a tendency to see what he wanted to in his data, sometimes at the expense of what was really there.[14]

Nevertheless, extensive research over many years has substantiated Spearman's most important *general* findings. All of the multitudinous subtests of intelligence that have been tried do tend to intercorrelate positively, with negative correlations being exceedingly rare. And the correlations also tend to range themselves into hierarchies, though almost never so perfectly as reported in Spearman's 1904 paper. A two-factor theory like Spearman's provides one plausible approach to explaining this repeatedly observed pattern.

It is not the *only* possible explanation, however, for the British statistician Godfrey Thomson (1881–1955) demonstrated in the 1920s that an identical hierarchical pattern of correlations would result if the measured "intelligence" really consisted of a large number of independent mental abilities, capable of being only "on" or "off." Thomson generated a large number of random "test scores" by throwing dice, as if they were produced by just such a multiplicity of independent factors, and showed that they too produced a hierarchical pattern of correlation coefficients. Thomson took pains to point out that this did not mean Spearman's theory was necessarily *wrong,* but only that an alternative and qualitatively very different theory could explain the observed patterns of correlations equally well. The existence of the hierarchies alone could not *prove* the validity of the two-factor theory.[15] The Thomson-Spearman exchanges ignited a controversy over the statistical structure of intelligence which continues unabated to the present day, and which we shall encounter again in the next chapter.

The biologist Stephen Jay Gould has recently taken Spearman to task in a different way, accusing him of the sin of *reification*—of treating an abstract pattern of mathematical correlations as if it were a real, concrete thing.[16] The most basic observation underlying g was the large number of positive intercorrelations among tests, from which Spearman inferred General Intelligence as the common *cause.* Gould points out that correlation alone cannot prove causality, however, and that variables may be strongly correlated in the complete absence of any meaningful common cause. For example, the world supply of underground petroleum, the distance between earth and Halley's comet, and the record time for running the mile have all been decreasing regularly in recent years, and so have been positively inter-correlated variables. Yet no one would suggest there is a single and common cause for these relationships, and so might the case be with the intelligence test correlations. Causal theories like Spearman's or Thomson's may not be required at all; they remain possibly true, but unproven.

Nevertheless, Spearman's conception of General Intelligence has had lasting appeal and influence. A unidimensional and inherited general ability was just what workers in the Galtonian tradition were hoping to find and measure, and Spearman's theory gave them a rationale for interpreting Binet test results as just that. All they lacked now was a means of *quantifying* their scores on a unidimensional scale. The basis for this was provided by a German psychologist named William Stern (1871–1938) in 1912, when he introduced the notion of the "intelligence quotient."

WILLIAM STERN AND THE INTELLIGENCE QUOTIENT

It is surprising that this second deviation from Binet's testing philosophy should have been initiated by Stern, who held general views markedly similar to Binet's. As a young man, Stern had been attracted to philosophy as well as to psychology, and had been strongly repelled by theories which interpreted human experience as little more than the mechanical, associationistic interaction of sensations and ideas. But unlike Spearman, who found his antidote to mechanistic association in the abstract energy of *g*, Stern found *his* solution in the notion of the *person*, the active and uniquely organized agent behind every behavior. At the turn of the century he decided that *individuality* was destined to be *the* psychological problem of the twentieth century, and he developed a scheme for what he called "personalistic psychology." As he recalled in his autobiography:

> Scientific psychology had so far been mainly a gener-
> alizing science, and had regarded individual differ-

William Stern (1871–1938) *(Archives of the History of American Psychology, University of Akron)*

ences, which occasionally occurred in the course of experiments, more as a hindrance to its own generalizing tendencies than as a unique problem. Thus the natural interest in individual variations was left entirely to unscientific treatments (e.g., phrenology, graphology, etc.). This condition I wanted to rectify through differential psychology; I undertook to give the psychological differences between one human being and another the status of an independent psychological problem.[17]

The primary methods of Stern's psychology involved classification of people according to *types, norms,* and *aberrations*—though he admitted that this procedure had some built-in limitations:

> Just like general psychology though to a lesser degree, [personalistic psychology] *generalizes.* For the concept of a "type" is itself a general functional rule for a group of human beings; the relegation of an individual to a type or to several types can never do justice to the ineffable particularity of his individuality.[18]

These views, of course, might almost be taken as a paraphrase of those expressed by Binet with Henri in their 1896 paper "Individual Psychology." There Binet identified the problem of individual assessment as paramount, and proposed the development of a small series of tests and dimensions for measuring the important characteristics of individuals, while still conceding that such techniques could never capture the real essence of individual personalities. To a remarkable degree, Stern shared both Binet's desire to investigate individuality, and his appreciation of the practical difficulties involved in doing so.

In yet another parallel to Binet, Stern became interested in child psychology through the observation of his own children. He and his wife, also a psychologist, published books in 1907 and 1908, describing their children's development of speech and the ability to give testimony about things. In the course of this Stern naturally encountered the work of Binet and other early investigators of the intelligence of children. He became briefly fascinated with this field, and reviewed its principal findings in a short 1912 book entitled *The Psychological Methods of Intelligence Testing.* Here, in the course of his review, Stern developed the idea of expressing intelligence test results in the form of a single number, the intelligence quotient.

The Intelligence Quotient

Stern's comprehensive review noted, and took a somewhat equivocal stance toward, Spearman's work. He agreed with Spearman that "intelligence does really signify a general capacity which colors in a definite way the mental behavior of an individual." Nevertheless, this endorsement was immediately tempered by a cautionary statement of a kind never found in Spearman, regarding the highly varied *qualitative* differences among individual manifestations of general intelligence:

> There are persons who have a pretty high grade of general intelligence, but who manifest it much better in critical than in synthetic work; again, there are persons in whom the receptive activities of the intelligence (apprehending and understanding) are superior to the more spontaneous activities, and so on.[19]

Along similar lines, Stern echoed Binet's sentiment that the same test scores can frequently mask significant differences between people's actual intelligences. He warned that a given test score "must not . . . be thought of as an absolutely unequivocal determination of a subject's intelligence, but only as a very rough quantitative determination of its value, without any implications as to its qualitative differences. . . . There never is a real phenomenological equivalence between the intelligence of two persons."[20]

Yet here again Stern equivocated somewhat, for he went on to argue that children who scored at the same level on Binet tests had intelligences which were "teleologically equivalent," if not "phenomenologically" so. The distinction between these technical terms is clarified by considering Stern's general definition of intelligence as, simply, "a general capacity of an individual consciously to adjust his thinking to new requirements, . . . a general mental adaptability to new problems and conditions of life."[21] Two people might differ in their *approaches* to adapting to new situations, illustrating the "phenomenological" dis-equivalence of their intelligences. But if they *succeeded* equally well, they would have shown the "teleological equivalence" of their two intelligences, in Stern's terms. On the assumption that Binet intelligence tests confronted subjects with a range of new tasks requiring mental adaptation, similar scores, however obtained, could be taken as signs of functional or teleological equivalence among the intelligences tested. Total test scores thus could be taken seriously.

A further aspect of Stern's attitude toward test scores was reflected in his use of the German term *Intelligenzalter*, meaning literally "intellectual *age*," as his translation of Binet's *niveau intellectuel* or "intellectual *level*." "Age" seems a more precise and absolutely measurable concept than does "level," and also carries more connotations of innate sequences of maturation and growth. Thus Stern became accustomed to thinking about each child's test score as a particular "mental age" (as his American translator G. M. Whipple rendered his *"Intelligenzalter"*), which could be directly compared with the actual or "chronological age" to determine the degree of retardation or advancement.

Moreover, Stern was struck by two studies which indicated that mental age and chronological age do not always increase at the same rate in the same individual. In the first study, children were re-tested on the Binet-Simon scale after a year's interval. Those who had tested nearly normally on the first try raised their mental ages by an average of one year on the second, exactly as expected. Children who had been clearly retarded on the first testing improved their mental ages by less than two-thirds of a year on the second, however, while those who had been clearly advanced the first time improved by considerably more than a year. Thus, retarded children fell ever farther behind as they got older, and "advanced" children moved increasingly ahead of their chronological ages. The absolute gaps between children's mental and chronological ages were not fixed, but were at least partly a function of their chronological ages.

The second study investigated the gaps between the mental and chronological ages of children who had been clearly diagnosed (by means other than the Binet tests) as imbeciles, morons, borderline retardates, or as individuals of low normal intelligence. The average gap for each group turned out to depend on the chronological ages of the children involved, as well as on the severity of their diagnoses. For example, eight-year-old imbeciles had an average mental age of 5.7, or 2.3 years behind their chronological age, while twelve-year-old imbeciles scored at 7.3, fully 4.7 years behind. The morons were retarded by 1.9 years at age eight, and by 3.3 years at twelve; thus the older morons were farther behind than the younger imbeciles. Twelve-year-olds in the low normal group were retarded 2.0 years, almost as much as the young imbeciles. In sum, this study showed that the absolute difference between mental and chronological age, considered by itself, was not an accurate index of the severity of retardation; its relationship to the chronological age had also to be taken into account.

As Stern summarized these findings, he made a simple but highly influential suggestion:

> Since feeble-mindedness consists essentially in a condition of development that is below the normal condition, the *rate* of development will also be a slower one, and thus every added year of age must magnify the difference in question, at least as long as there is anything present that could be called mental development at all. *With this in mind it is but a step to the idea of measuring backwardness by the relative difference; i.e., by the ratio between mental and chronological age, instead of by the absolute difference* [emphasis added].[22]

Stern named this ratio—the mental age divided by the chronological age—the *intelligence quotient;* in 1916 Lewis Terman, whom we shall meet in the next chapter, suggested multiplying the quotient by 100 to remove fractions, and abbreviated the term as "IQ." Thus was introduced one of the most popular terms in the modern psychological vocabulary.

The expressing of intelligence levels as quotients had theoretical implications beyond that of equalizing scores for children in the same diagnostic categories, but of different ages. Offering an apparently unitary and standard scale of measurement, intelligence quotients were readily interpretable as measures of something like Spearman's *g*. Further, Binet tests could now be employed in correlational studies, as the relationships between

IQ and other precisely measurable variables could be calculated. A whole new research industry was born with this quantification of Binet test results.

Of course, the merits of this development were, and remain, somewhat debatable. Despite its advantages, the quotient effectively removed from consideration the actual mental and chronological ages of the subject, and thus was farther removed from actual test behavior than the scores on which it was based. The number of different ways subjects could obtain the same final test score was multiplied manyfold, and one lost sight of even more of "those little facts that complete the physiognomy of the experiment," which had been emphasized by Binet. Binet was no longer alive in 1912 to criticize the quotient concept, but his collaborator Simon later called it a betrayal *("trahison")* of their scale's original objectives.[23]

It seems that Stern himself came to have second thoughts about his influential brainchild. He did little further work on intelligence testing per se after 1912, but continued to emphasize individuality and uniqueness in his personalistic psychology. He strongly transmitted this emphasis to Gordon W. Allport (1897–1967), his most famous American student, and the foremost advocate of individualized personality study in America. When Stern came to America shortly before his death, in 1936, he confided to Allport that a principal aim of his visit was to advocate his mature personalistic psychology as a counterbalance to the "pernicious influence" of his earlier invention, the intelligence quotient.[24]

Any such regrets came far too late, however, because by then, for better or for worse, the IQ was here to stay. Intelligence testing had firmly entered the public consciousness, and had become a big business. The first foundations for this public acceptance of intelligence testing had been laid by the popular writings of the American psychologist Henry H. Goddard (1866–1957), which moreover reunited the themes of intelligence testing and eugenics. We turn now to Goddard's story.

Henry Goddard and the Popularization of Binet Tests

Like Charles Spearman, Henry Herbert Goddard came late to the formal study of psychology, though following a first career in education instead of the army. Of New England Quaker background, he took both bachelor's and master's degrees from Haverford College, and then became a high school teacher and principal for six years. Only at age thirty did he enroll in the Ph.D. program in psychology at Clark University, in Worcester, Massachusetts.

Henry Herbert Goddard (1866–1957) *(Archives of the History of American Psychology, University of Akron)*

Clark was a particularly exciting place for people like Goddard, with interests in both education and psychology. Just recently founded in 1889, Clark was then exclusively a graduate school, offering only the Ph.D. degree. Modeled after the German Ph.D. programs, Clark imposed no formal requirements on its students beyond a thesis and final oral examination, to be taken whenever the students' advisors felt they were ready. The University's president and chief professor of psychology was G. Stanley Hall (1844–1924)—next to William James the most eminent American psychologist of the time. The first president of the American Psychological Association, Hall had founded the *American Journal of Psychology* as America's first regular psychology periodical in 1887. With broad interests dating from his own early career as a teacher, Hall had also been the leading American proponent of child and educational psychology. At Clark, he instituted a department of pedagogy under the direction of a psychologist, and in 1893—shortly before Goddard's arrival—founded *Pedagogical Seminary*, the first psychological journal to be devoted exclusively to issues of education and development.

Goddard throve at Clark, and completed his thesis under Hall in 1899 on the subject of psychological factors in "faith healing." He then accepted a teaching position at Pennsylvania's West Chester State Teacher's College. Though an energetic and capable enough professor, Goddard made little professional impact until 1906 when, at age forty, he was named director of research at the Training School for the Feebleminded, in Vineland, New Jersey. New to the field of mental retardation, he immediately set out to learn what other people were doing in the area, and by the end of 1908 developed the ideas and the program that would soon make him famous.

In the spring of 1908, Goddard traveled to Europe to learn firsthand about current developments there. In Paris, he tried but failed to meet Binet. This did not seem a great loss, however, for Goddard had not been much impressed by the 1905 Binet-Simon tests, and was not even aware that the greatly improved 1908 scale had just been published. Further, Binet's work enjoyed no great reputation at that time even among his Sorbonne colleagues; thus Goddard wrote in his travel diary: "Visited Sorbonne. Binet's lab is largely a myth. Not much being done. . . . There are no special classes in French schools, and only the worst cases are sent to . . . institutions."[25]

Only when he got to Brussels did Goddard learn secondhand that Binet's lab was in fact much more than a myth, and that his new revised scale had just been published. Though initially skeptical, Goddard translated this scale shortly after returning home and tried it out on the retarded children of Vineland. To his surprise it worked very well in classifying the children's degrees of retardation, and Goddard quickly metamorphosed from a skeptic into an enthusiast. By 1915 he had distributed more than twenty-two thousand copies of the translated test, and eighty-eight thousand answer blanks, to all parts of the United States.

In 1916 Goddard supervised the English translation of the complete Binet and Simon papers that had introduced their tests of 1905, 1908, and 1911. It was Goddard who suggested the now familiar word moron as the equivalent of Binet's *débile*, to denote the most common and highest grade of mentally deficient person. Through these efforts, Goddard became the world's leading proponent of Binet's testing methods, following the latter's death in 1911.

But while he was enthusiastic about Binet's methods, Goddard like Spearman was far from appreciating the Frenchman's rather loose and pragmatic theory of intelligence. Instead, he borrowed from the then-fashionable Mendelian theory of dominant and recessive genes, and conceptualized the vast majority of cases of "feeblemindedness" or moronity as inherited conditions caused by a single recessive gene. All individuals who received this gene from *both* their parents presumably developed as feebleminded, and, if allowed to reproduce, transmitted the deficiency to their offspring in turn according to the laws of Mendelian genetics.* Goddard summarized his outspokenly hereditarian view in 1920:

Modern proponents of the hereditary causation of intelligence differ from Goddard by hypothesizing that intelligence is determined by several different genes, not just a single one.

> Stated in its boldest form, our thesis is that the chief
> determiner of human conduct is a unitary mental pro-
> cess which we call intelligence: that this process is con-
> ditioned by a nervous mechanism which is inborn: that
> the degree of efficiency to be attained by that nervous
> mechanism and the consequent grade of intelligence or
> mental level for each individual is determined by the
> kind of chromosomes that come together with the union
> of the germ cells: that it is but little affected by any later
> influences except such serious accidents as may destroy
> part of the mechanism.[26]

Here was a conception of intelligence more unitary than
Spearman's, and more exclusively hereditarian than Galton's—
expressed by a man who was the world's leading advocate of
Binet's approach to tests! If ever there were a case of the disciple
transforming his master's message in the retelling, this was it.

Consistent with his hereditarian theory, Goddard was also a
super-enthusiast of the eugenics movement. His emphasis differed somewhat from Galton's, however, for whereas Galton had
originally been interested in *fostering* population growth at the
upper end of the intelligence distribution, Goddard became
obsessed with its *prevention* at the *lower* end. Convinced that most
feeblemindedness was caused by a single recessive gene, he
believed that this scourge could theoretically be eliminated if only
the genetically defective could be prevented from having children for a few generations; on the other hand, to allow continued uncontrolled breeding by these individuals seemed to invite
social disaster. To illustrate and dramatize his case, Goddard
published a book in 1912 entitled *The Kallikak Family: A Study in
the Heredity of Feeble-mindedness*. Addressed to the lay reader, this
book quickly became a psychological best-seller, and effectively
helped shape a new public appreciation for mental testing and
eugenics.

The Kallikaks

The Kallikak Family did not pretend to be a technically sophisticated book, for Goddard prefaced it with the frank

admission that "we have made rather dogmatic statements and drawn conclusions that do not seem scientifically warranted by the data. We have done this because it seems necessary to make these statements and conclusions for the benefit of the lay reader."[27] Because of his intensive association with the retarded, Goddard may have formed a low opinion of the intellect of the "lay reader" as well. In any event, *The Kallikak Family* hardly challenged the intelligence of its readers, but instead presented its case in simple language, and blunt, sensational, and sometimes sordid terms.

The book purports to be a survey of two branches of a single family, one containing the gene for feeblemindedness and producing an endless stream of human degeneracy and vice, while the other branch lacks the gene and produces only exemplary citizens. As when he coined "moron," Goddard looked to the Greek language while making up a fictitious name for this family, creating "Kallikak" from the combination of its words for "good" *(kalos)* and "bad" *(kakos)*.

The first member of this family to come to Goddard's attention was "Deborah," who, he tells us, came to the Training School "one bright October day, fourteen years ago, [as] a little eight-year-old girl." In the school's sheltered environment, Deborah grew up to be a very attractive and normal-looking young woman, with reasonable skills in sewing, carpentry, and housekeeping. Several photographs of Deborah and her work adorn the book, to support these points. Despite her accomplishments, however, she remained very backward in her *intelligence,* as assessed by the Binet tests. Repeated testing had confirmed her maximum mental age as nine. Goddard argued that such a person, however attractive and normal in appearance, presented a deceptive image—her attractiveness and "normality" made possible only by the sheltered environment of the institution. Outside, she would have no chance:

> Here is a child who has been most carefully guarded. She has been persistently trained since she was eight years old, and yet nothing has been accomplished in

> the direction of higher intelligence or general educa-
> tion. Today if this young woman were to leave the insti-
> tution, she would at once become prey to the designs
> of evil men or evil women and would lead a life that
> would be vicious, immoral, or criminal, though because
> of her mentality she herself would not be responsible.
> There is nothing she might not be led into. . . .
>   We may now repeat the ever insistent question, and
> this time we have good hope of answering it. The ques-
> tion is, "How do we account for this kind of individ-
> ual?" The answer is in a word "Heredity,"—bad stock.[28]

Goddard next set out to "prove" these points through an analysis
of Deborah's extended family. He learned that this family had
resided in the Vineland area for several generations, where it
had become notorious for producing "an appalling amount of
defectiveness." Elizabeth Kite, his assistant who had done most
of the Binet translations, was dispatched to interview as many
living members of the family as could be found, and to trace the
family's genealogy. She finally identified 480 relatives, living and
dead. On the basis of personal impressions and occasional Binet
tests on the living, and of historical accounts of the dead, definite
intellectual diagnoses were made for 189 of these people, while
the rest were categorized as "unknown or doubtful." Of the 189,
143 were "conclusively proved" to have been feebleminded, while
only 46 were diagnosed as normal. Tabulated according to other
categories, Deborah's immediate relatives included 36 illegiti-
mate children, 33 "sexually immoral persons, mostly prosti-
tutes," 24 confirmed alcoholics, 3 epileptics, 3 criminals, 8 bordello
keepers, and 82 children who died in infancy.

Kite brought back horrendous accounts of the depraved and
miserable conditions under which these people typically lived,
and photographed some of them for the book: dejected-
looking people in impoverished rural surroundings, who contrasted markedly with the attractive, demure, and well-dressed
Deborah at the Vineland Training School. Such was the *kakos*
side of the Kallikaks.

The *kalos* side of the family first became evident when, while
tracing Deborah's relatives, Kite occasionally found herself "in

the midst of a good family of the same name, which apparently was in no way related to the girl whose ancestry we were investigating." Soon, however, "these cases became so frequent that there gradually grew the conviction that ours must be a degenerate offshoot from an older family of better stock."[29] Further sleuthing revealed that this was indeed the case.

During the Revolutionary War a young man of good family, dubbed "Martin Kallikak Sr." by Goddard, had had a brief affair with a feebleminded tavern worker and fathered a son. Though abandoned by Martin, the woman named her child after him; he became "Martin Kallikak Jr." in the book's genealogy. Martin Jr. grew up mentally feeble but sexually potent, earning the nickname "Old Horror" and becoming the founding father of the debased Kallikak line. He was Deborah's great-great-grand-father.

After the war, Martin Sr. "straightened up and married a respectable girl of good family." From this union came 496 direct descendants, all of whom reportedly had normal or better intelligence. Three were "somewhat degenerate, but . . . not defective," and they were more than offset by a large number of true paragons of civilized virtue:

> All of the legitimate children of Martin Sr. married into the best families of their state, the descendants of colonial governors, signers of the Declaration of Independence, soldiers and even the founders of a great university. Indeed, in this family and its collatoral branches, we find nothing but good representative citizenship. There are doctors, lawyers, judges, educators, traders, landholders, in short, respectable citizens, men and women prominent in every phase of social life.[30]

Goddard argued that this proved the hereditary nature of feeblemindedness and its attendant social afflictions:

> We thus have two series from two different mothers but the same father. These extend for six generations. Both lines live out their lives in practically the same

> region and in the same environment, except in so far
> as they themselves, because of their different charac-
> ters, changed the environment. . . . We thus have a nat-
> ural experiment of remarkable value to the sociologist
> and the student of heredity, no one can doubt.[31]

One *can* doubt Goddard's conclusion, of course, but for the
moment we shall follow his argument further. He railed against
Martin Sr.'s youthful indiscretion, citing "the havoc that was
wrought by that one thoughtless act," and regretting that "society has had to pay the heavy price of all the evil he engen-
dered."[32] The only solution he could see to the problems posed
by people like the Kallikaks was to prevent their future breeding; feebleminded people must be prevented from having children, at all costs.

Goddard believed that compulsory sterilization of the feebleminded offered one possible solution to this problem, but thought
such a practice would offend too many people's sensibilities. Thus
he did not press for it as a realistic alternative. The best solution,
he argued, was to build many more institutions like Vineland,
where the feebleminded could be collected and kept as Deborah
had been: with kindness, but altogether like children corresponding to their mental ages. Most important, they could be
segregated by sex and closely supervised so as to conceive no
children. With enough institutions to house the bulk of the feebleminded population, the gene supposedly responsible for this
deficiency could be removed from the American population
almost completely within just a few generations. Goddard
acknowledged that this would be an expensive solution, but only
at first, for as the celibate feebleminded population declined, so
would the need for the institutions.

A related project occupied Goddard in the years immediately
following publication of *The Kallikak Family,* as he experimented
with Binet tests on samples of newly arriving immigrants to the
United States at Ellis Island. His primary purpose was simply to
demonstrate the usefulness of intelligence tests for identifying
feebleminded people—a practice which of course would have to

be perfected before any program of enforced institutionalization could be expected to work. A secondary effect occurred, however, when Goddard found large numbers of immigrants from eastern Europe with tested mental ages lower than twelve, and thus technically classifiable as morons. Goddard equivocated somewhat while explaining this finding, for while he believed that many of the people were unquestionably hereditarily feebleminded, he also allowed that poor early environments, and lack of familiarity with American culture, might have handicapped others of them.[33] Thus his work suggested the *possibility* that unrestricted immigration from eastern Europe would introduce unwanted degenerate stock into the American population, but he could not specify the exact extent of the threat. As we shall see in the next chapter, some other psychologists were soon to be more outspoken than Goddard on this issue, and with more explosive consequences.

Evaluation and Effect of Goddard's Work

In sum, Goddard successfully brought Binet-type intelligence tests to the attention of his fellow American psychologists, and alerted the American people to the presumed scourge of hereditary feeblemindedness. He did not really advance the *scientific* status of the nature-nurture controversy, however, because his data, like Galton's before him, were just as subject to environmentalist as to hereditarian explanations. Thus, among the Kallikaks, the bad side of the family had developed under environmental conditions immeasurably worse than those for the good side—a pattern that began when Martin Sr. abandoned the pregnant tavern girl to her unmarried lower-class fate, but went on to provide a privileged environment for his wife and legitimate offspring. Since Martin Sr. must be presumed by Goddard's own theory to have contributed primarily "good" intelligence genes to both sides of the family, it was essentially on the *environmental* level that his legacies to the two sides differed. Elizabeth Kite's reports clearly showed that environmental deprivation persisted for Deborah's side of the family, while the good side developed under uniformly middle- to upper-class conditions. Since the two branches had entirely contrasting environments *from the very beginning*, Goddard's assertion that they had been reared "in the same environment, except in so far as they themselves, because of their different characters, changed the environment" is patently unjustified.

Further, Goddard's basic data were not beyond question. He did not say exactly how all his diagnoses of feeblemindedness were made, but apparently only a few were based on actual Binet tests, while the majority came from possibly unreliable personal impressions. Even Goddard's photographic records were questionable, since several of his pictures of Deborah's rural Kallikak relatives were rather crudely retouched in facial features. Some have suggested that this represented a fraudulent attempt to exaggerate the unattractive and "retarded" qualities of these unfortunate people.[34] In fact, it is no longer possible to determine the exact motive for the retouching, and some more innocent possibilities exist: a desire to enhance low-contrast home snapshots for reproduction, for example, or to disguise the identities of the pictured individuals. But whatever the case may have been on this relatively incidental point, *The Kallikak Family* taken as a whole was much more a propaganda piece on behalf of eugenics and hereditarian theory than it was a dispassionate scientific study.

Nevertheless, it was *effective* propaganda, for it coincided with a rising national concern about incipient racial breakdown, which had several complex sources.[35] And while Goddard himself was relatively moderate in his prescriptions for how to deal with hereditary feeblemindedness, not everyone else was so reticent. Several states, on the basis of "evidence" like that in *The Kallikak Family*, passed laws mandating the involuntary sterilization of thousands of diagnosed retardates.* Sometimes these people were deliberately misled, as in the poignant case of a young woman who was told she was having her appendix removed when in fact

---

*Involuntary sterilization practices were adopted with particular enthusiasm by Nazi Germany. In the 1930s, even before the systematic genocide of the Jews, more than 200,000 "degenerates" of all kinds and races were sterilized there. Revulsion against the Nazi practices eventually helped reduce public support for sterilization laws in the U.S. and elsewhere.

she was being sterilized. Only much later, after she tried unsuc-
cessfully for years to have a child, were she and her husband
correctly informed about what had been done to her.[36]

Involuntary sterilization of retarded people is seldom practiced today, though some states still retain the laws in their books.
In the absence of an absolute faith in the hereditary causation
of retardation, and in the accuracy of the tests used to identify
it, such laws—however well intentioned—cannot avoid seeming
(and being) unjust. And even Goddard himself eventually came
to believe that his original theory of hereditary feeblemindedness had been overstated. In 1918 he left Vineland to direct studies
on juvenile delinquency for the state of Ohio, and in 1922 he
became professor of clinical psychology at Ohio State University
where his interests expanded to include gifted children. Perhaps
because of this expanded experience, he came to believe by 1928
that he had previously categorized "feeblemindedness" much too
rigidly. He now acknowledged that proper education could
markedly improve the performance of many children who originally tested as morons, and that strict institutionalization was
not required as often as he had previously thought. "I think I
have gone over to the enemy," he now conceded.[37] In fact, of
course, by agreeing that hereditary limits on intelligence were
more flexible than he had previously thought, he was really
moving toward a view of intelligence more in accord with that
of his original hero, Binet.

Nevertheless, Goddard had helped set the stage for the next
major developments in American intelligence testing. The first
really large-scale user of the Binet testing methods, he had demonstrated their potential relevance to major social issues. In his
wake, other psychologists would come along and apply the tests
to increasing numbers of the *non*retarded population, for an ever
increasing number of important social purposes. The next chapter will tell how this came about.

Suggested Readings

Autobiographies by Spearman and Stern appear in
Volume 1 of *The History of Psychology in Autobiography*, edited by Carl

Murchison (Worcester, MA: Clark University Press, 1930). For interesting additional information about these men see Bernard Norton's "Charles Spearman and the General Factor in Intelligence," in *Journal of the History of the Behavioral Sciences* (*15:*142–154, 1979), and Gordon W. Allport's "The Personalistic Psychology of William Stern," in Allport's *The Person in Psychology: Selected Essays* (Boston: Beacon, 1968).

The three major primary sources discussed in this chapter are Charles Spearman's " 'General Intelligence,' Objectively Determined and Measured," in *American Journal of Psychology* (*15:*201–293, 1905); William Stern's *The Psychological Methods of Intelligence Testing* (Baltimore: Warwick and York, 1914); and Henry H. Goddard's *The Kallikak Family: A Study in the Heredity of Feeble-mindedness* (New York: Macmillan, 1912). Stern's book is also to be recommended because it gives an interesting survey of the general state of intelligence testing at the time of Binet's death.

For a good brief overview of Spearman's and Goddard's roles in the development of modern intelligence testing, see Read Tuddenham's "The Nature and Measurement of Intelligence," in Leo Postman, ed., *Psychology in the Making* (New York: Knopf, 1962). Stephen Jay Gould's *The Mismeasure of Man* (New York: Norton, 1981) presents a highly critical account of Spearman's and Goddard's work from a current-day perspective; for a much more appreciative recent account of Spearman's *g* see the first two chapters of Arthur Jensen's *Straight Talk about Mental Tests* (New York: Free Press, 1981).

4 The Rise of Intelligence Testing

When the United States entered World War I in April of 1917, the psychologist Robert Yerkes (1876–1956) stood among the millions of patriotic Americans suddenly eager to serve their country. As president of the American Psychological Association, Yerkes was also eager to demonstrate the usefulness of his young science, which at that time did not loom very large in public consciousness. Accordingly, he induced the APA Council to establish twelve committees for exploring various possible military applications of psychology. Yerkes himself was primarily an animal psychologist, but he had also worked on intelligence tests as a sidelight; thus he named himself chairman of the committee charged with developing proposals for the psychological testing of army recruits.

To form his committee, Yerkes called on all of the leading American intelligence testers, including Henry Goddard and Lewis Terman (1877–1956), the Stanford University psychologist who had just introduced an outstanding new American version of the Binet tests. From the outset, Yerkes had big plans for his committee, believing they should aim to achieve more than just the obvious goal of helping screen out mentally defective recruits. "We should not work primarily for the exclusion of intellectual defectives," he declared, "but rather for the classifi-

Robert Mearns Yerkes (1876–1956) *(Archives of the History of American Psychology, University of Akron)*

cation of men in order that they may be properly placed in the military service."[1]

This ambitious goal required an extraordinary broadening of available intelligence testing technology in two ways. First, the sheer numbers of recruits who would have to be assessed ruled out the *individual* test procedure required by the Binet-type scales, with a single examiner for each single subject; instead, a *group test* would have to be developed, capable of being given to large numbers of subjects at the same time. Second, these new tests would have to be used for positive as well as negative selection purposes—not only screening out the mentally retarded as Binet tests had been designed to do, but also identifying candidates with *superior* ability for officer training and higher military responsibilities.

An energetic salesman, Yerkes interested the Surgeon General of the army in his audacious proposal, though the navy turned a deaf ear. Yerkes's committee quickly put together two prototype tests, one for recruits literate in English, and another which did not require reading, for the large numbers of illiterate recruits and recent immigrants who could not read English. A trial of these tests on eighty thousand men impressed army administrators sufficiently to authorize the testing of *all* new recruits by the beginning of 1918, with the results to be made available to commanders as a supplement to the traditional military criteria for making personnel decisions. An exultant Yerkes proclaimed to the newspapers: "Psychology has achieved a position which will enable it to substantially help to win the war and shorten the necessary period of conflict."[2]

The two tests, revised and named the *Army Alpha* for literate subjects and the *Beta* for illiterates, were soon being administered at the rate of 200,000 per month. By war's end in November of 1918, some 1,750,000 men had been given one or the other of the tests—a truly impressive organizational and logistical feat. The trial had been too brief for a conclusive demonstration of military usefulness, however, and army commanders had been somewhat divided regarding the tests' potential value. Even so, the monumental exercise had clearly succeeded in placing psychology and intelligence testing on the map of public consciousness. The American people were now quite familiar with the *idea* of intelligence tests, so when Yerkes, Terman, and others introduced group tests for the general population after the war, they found ready and lucrative markets. Moreover, the huge mass of data produced by the army testing was intensively analyzed after the war, leading to a widely publicized and sometimes acrimonious discussion of America's level of "national intelligence." Both effects—the near ubiquity of intelligence testing and the dispute about the intellectual makeup of the American population—continue today.

In this chapter we shall examine the lives and careers of three men who were intimately involved with these developments: Yerkes and Terman, who helped direct the original army testing, and David Wechsler (1896–1981), who served as a young tester in the army program and went on to develop the most successful of the individual intelligence tests in use today.

ROBERT YERKES AND THE MASS TESTING OF THE ARMY

Robert Mearns Yerkes, the firstborn child in a rural Pennsylvania farming family, grew up uninspired by farm life, and early aspired to something better. "The physician's life appealed to me as less harshly laborious, more interesting, exciting, heroic, useful, and altogether profitable than that of the farmer," he recalled in his autobiography.[3] A supportive uncle in Collegeville, Pennsylvania, put him on the road toward his medical goal by financing his tuition at the local Ursinis College, in return for which Robert lived at his house and did chores. After four "happy, toilsome years [which] would have been perfect if I could have afforded and arranged to have Saturday as a holiday,"[4] Yerkes was graduated, and confronted with a choice. He could go to Philadelphia for medical training, as originally planned, or he could accept an unexpected offer of a loan for a year's tuition at Harvard, to do graduate work in biology before commencing his medical training. He finally decided to broaden his horizons, and went to Harvard.

Once there, Yerkes became especially interested in animal behavior, a subject with psychological as well as biological implications. Indeed, he found this so interesting that he postponed medicine again, to study comparative psychology—the study of the differences and similarities in the behavior of different animal species—in Harvard's Psychology Department. He wound up abandoning medical plans altogether, taking his Ph.D. there, in 1902 and then being appointed to its Psychology faculty.

All of these moves entailed substantial financial sacrifice, for Yerkes had had to borrow extensively to finance his Harvard education, and his new academic post was not highly paid. But Yerkes was very good at his work, and together with his friend John B. Watson (1878–1958)—the Johns Hopkins psychologist who founded the famous "Behaviorist Movement"—he helped establish comparative psychology as a major specialty in America. It was mainly for this work that his colleagues recognized him in 1917, by electing him president of the American Psychological Association.

But while Yerkes's primary work and reputation were in animal psychology, financial and other pressures had gradually conspired to draw some of his attention to intelligence testing. He had to supplement his salary for many years by teaching general psychology at the Radcliffe College summer school; this involved him in issues of human as well as of animal psychology. Another necessary part-time job expanded his interests further, when in 1912 he became director of psychological research at the Boston State Psychopathic Hospital. Here he first encountered intelligence tests, which were being investigated as possible aids for making psychiatric diagnoses.

Two of Yerkes's Harvard professors, who later became colleagues and friends, had also provided vital influences. The psychologist Hugo Münsterberg (1863–1916) had brought from his native Germany a keen elitism and regard for the work of experts. As one of the first proponents of applied psychology in America, he strongly supported applied research on the newly developed mental tests. Yerkes's biology professor Charles B. Davenport (1866–1944) was the leader of the eugenics movement in America. Davenport corresponded regularly with Galton during the latter's old age, and taught in his courses that "characteristics" inherited along Mendelian lines were the "atoms" of the new biology. Just as new or different chemical substances could be created by varying the combinations of atoms, so could new or different varieties or species be created through different combinations of inherited characteristics.* Yerkes was early "converted" by Davenport, and became an outspoken supporter of the eugenics movement—which of course had strong historical ties to intelligence testing.

Still another nudge came from the Harvard administration.

---

*Goddard's "feeblemindedness," as described in Chapter 3, was considered by Davenport and him to be one important example of a "characteristic" inherited along Mendelian lines.

Always ambitious, the young Yerkes wanted to establish a formal research institute for comparative psychology at Harvard, but was dissuaded by President A. L. Lowell. Yerkes recalled, "Instead of receiving encouragement in such seemingly impractical planning as I had been indulging in, I was tactfully advised by the . . . administration that educational psychology offered a broader and more direct path to a professorship and to increased academic usefulness than did my special field of comparative psychology."[5] Though Yerkes claimed in his autobiography to have disregarded this advice, he nevertheless became increasingly involved in the work on intelligence tests at Boston Psychopathic Hospital. Here was an ideal secondary field for research, combining its implications for the recommended educational psychology with potential psychiatric applications, and having historical connections to eugenics. For a few years, this secondary interest came to occupy more of Yerkes's time and energy than did comparative psychology.

Yerkes's earliest work on intelligence tests involved the conversion of Binet's tests into a "point-scale test," giving results as the simple number of points scored on a large array of items, rather than as a "mental age" or as a quotient. The major advantage of this approach, he believed, was a reduction in the heterogeneity of items measuring intelligence at the different age levels. In a standard Binet test, for example, items from the five-year-old's scale required the comparison of weights, the naming of colors, the making of aesthetic judgments, and the defining of objects; the eight-year-old's items, by contrast, required counting backward, comprehension of questions, giving similarities between pairs of things, and vocabulary. Thus, Yerkes observed,

> the measurements made on different individuals of different ages are not strictly comparable, for the obvious reason that different forms or aspects of behavior have been measured in the two cases. . . . Even the most enthusiastic believer in the Binet scale and method cannot hope to maintain the thesis that at each or even at

two ages precisely the same forms or aspects of human
behavior are measured.[6]

Such, of course, was completely acceptable according to Binet's
flexible theory of intelligence. In *Yerkes's* ideal test, however, *all*
subjects—not just those of a certain age—would be asked to take
all of the different types of tests: remembering digits, defining
words, giving similarities, and so on. He believed that all subjects' results, combined into single scores, would then be directly
comparable to one another. Norms could be established for each
different age, but age itself would not be a criterion for selecting
the items.

Yerkes believed that the difference between the Binet and the
point-scale approaches was "the difference between a relatively
unscientific procedure and one which is striving to fulfill the
essential requirements of scientific method."[7] Those "essential
requirements," in his view, were that the data produced must be
quantitative and subject to statistical analysis. The purposes of
"science" could best be served, he thought, by combining all types
of intelligence test items into a single, unilinear scale—contrary
to Binet's conception of intelligence, but generally consistent with
Spearman's or Goddard's—and comparing the average results
of different groups of subjects. In early 1917, Yerkes gave his
conception of an ideal research program, using the point-scale
measure:

> With the application of the Point Scale to increasing
> numbers of individuals, the norms, whether for age,
> sex, race, educational or social status, become increas-
> ingly numerous and reliable, and the value of the
> method correspondingly increases. In order to use the
> Point Scale profitably for a new race, or social group, it
> is necessary only to make a sufficient number of exam-
> inations to yield reliable norms. They immediately
> become standards of judgement.[8]

Shortly after expressing this idea, Yerkes got the chance to
put it into practice, and on a larger statistical scale than he had

ever dreamed possible. America entered the World War, and he initiated proceedings for the testing of the army.

The Army Tests

Both the Alpha and the Beta forms of the army tests had to be administered to large groups of men, often under highly cramped conditions. This testing situation, of course, made it impossible to tailor specific questions to the different mental ages or levels of the subjects, so all recruits had to try all parts of their tests. Scoring was essentially on the point-scale basis that Yerkes had recommended before the war, though for army use the point scores were further converted into letter grades from A to E. A grade of A was said to denote "a high officer type when backed by other necessary qualities"; B indicated "splendid sergeant material"; while C was "good private type, with some fair to good N.C.O. material." D scorers were characterized as "usually fair soldiers, but often slow in learning," while men a half-grade lower at D— were judged just barely fit for regular service. Recruits graded at E were declared intellectually unqualified for regular army service.[9]

The Alpha tests included arithmetic problems, word pairs to be rated as synonyms or opposites; number sequences to be completed; multiple-choice questions of general information and "common sense"; and scrambled word lists which had to be unscrambled to make sentences, which then had to be designated as true or false (for example: *sides every has four triangle*). Yerkes claimed that the items had been designed to minimize cultural or educational biases, yet some of the questions clearly required familiarity with American culture and history. Subjects had to know that the Overland car was manufactured in Toledo (not Buffalo, Detroit, or Flint), for example, and that Crisco was a food product and not a disinfectant, toothpaste, or medicine. One sentence-completion item read "Washington is to Adams as first is to __?__."

The Beta tests supposedly provided roughly equivalent tasks, but did not require the subjects to read: for example, tracing the correct paths through mazes, finding the missing element in pictures, imagining how pictured geometrical forms could be fitted together, or substituting symbols for numbers according to a given code. Though these items were unquestionably fairer than the Alpha's for illiterate or immigrant subjects, they were not entirely culture-free by any means. Several picture-completion items required familiarity with middle-class culture, for example, such as a tennis court without a net, or an Edison phonograph lacking the sound-horn. Moreover, while Beta did not require subjects to read, it did demand the circling, drawing, or filling in of correct answers with a pencil. For totally uneducated people who had seldom or never held pencils in hand before, this presented a marked disadvantage quite independent of innate intelligence.

A further disadvantage for many of the Beta subjects was that their instructions were given in extremely brief and arbitrary commands, in contrast to the rather full and reassuring written instructions that were printed on the Alpha test forms. In a recent dramatization of this problem, Professor Stephen Jay Gould gave the army Beta, under exactly the conditions specified in its original manual, to his class of students at Harvard. While more than half the class earned the expected A grade, 30 percent of this highly select group got B's and more than 10 percent C's—little more than private material according to the World War I testers.[10]

Yerkes and his colleagues were aware of at least some of these problems, and tried to alleviate them partially be re-testing very low Alpha scorers on the Beta, and low Beta scorers on an individually administered intelligence test. When this policy was followed, the average re-test scores rose significantly at each step. Unfortunately, however, the pressures of rapid and mass mobilization precluded re-testing in the vast majority of cases when it was warranted. Most soldiers were rushed through a single testing session, the results of which remained with them for their military careers, no matter how low or unfairly reduced they may have been.

Given these practical problems, it is hardly surprising to learn that the tests met mixed success in their prediction of soldiers' military careers. One validation study revealed correlations in the low .60's between Alpha test scorers and officers' independent ratings of their men's intelligence; for Beta, the correlations ranged in the high .50's. Correlations of test scores with ratings of actual military performance were lower, though still moderately positive for men who had been commissioned as officers. As might have been suspected, the tests worked best for the literate and native American recruits from whom the officers were primarily drawn.[11]

Official army reactions to the tests were also mixed. Some commanders were more than happy to have a quick and roughly accurate guide for personnel decisions that they would only have had to make on the basis of *other* imperfect data in any case. The use of tests received a boost in July 1918, when General Pershing, the commander-in-chief of the expeditionary force, complained that too many mental incompetents were getting sent to Europe following the traditional selection procedures. But there still remained many commanders who resented the time and space testing took up at their camps, and who regarded the testers as pests and "mental meddlers" who interfered with military efficiency.[12] The issue was never resolved, because the war and mass mobilization both ended in November 1918, too soon for any consensus to be reached. Yerkes could and did argue that the tests had helped to win the war, but the army—to Yerkes's immense disappointment—was less convinced, and discontinued the testing program from its peacetime force.

Though Yerkes may have been disappointed, and though the actual military value of his program may have been ambiguous, he and psychology had nevertheless scored a public relations triumph. Intelligence testing had been practiced on the widest scale ever, and its *potential* usefulness had been demonstrated to more people than ever before. Afterward, civilian organizations such as schools and businesses began to seek intelligence tests for their own purposes. And even the army was permanently influenced, for while testing was deemphasized during peacetime, the return of hostilities in World War II found the entire United States military ready to make extensive use of intelligence and aptitude testing, on a much more organized scale than in 1917 and 1918. Thus, the army testing program firmly established the place of psychological testing in American society.

Postwar Analyses of the Army Data

The army testing program also provided an enormous mass of data, which Yerkes and his colleagues could analyze after the war according to those statistical procedures which he regarded as the hallmarks of pure science. These yielded a statistical profile, supposedly representative of the intellectual makeup of the nation as a whole. When these basic results were published in Yerkes's massive, eight-hundred-page *Psychological Examining in the United States Army* (1921), and extensively commented upon in his junior colleague Carl Brigham's *A Study of American Intelligence* (1923), a heated controversy over America's "national intelligence" arose. These books emphasized three statistical findings which aroused particular debate.

The first pertained to the average intelligence of the army recruits, considered as a whole. Point scores on Alpha and Beta were converted into mental age equivalents, on the basis of norms from a sample of subjects who had taken both the army and the Binet tests. The average inferred mental age for all recruits came out to be just over thirteen years. At this time the "average adult" mental age was considered to be sixteen, and the upper borderline for moronity in adults was taken to be twelve. Rather than interpreting his results to mean that there was something wrong with the standard, or that the army scores had been artificially depressed by the factors noted earlier—for example, the failure to re-test most low Alpha scorers on Beta, as was supposed to have been the case—Yerkes asserted that the *native intelligence* of the average recruit was shockingly low. The tests, he said, were "originally intended, and now definitely known, to measure native intellectual ability. They are to some extent influenced by educational acquirement, but in the main the soldier's inborn intelligence and not the accidents of environment determined his mental rating or grade."[13] Accordingly, a very substantial proportion of the soldiers in the U.S. Army were actually morons. To Yerkes the eugenicist, these data indicated that Goddard's fear was coming true, and the native American stock was deteriorating intellectually; the young adult generation was barely able to meet the normal standards of American society. Strong and immediate eugenic measures seemed required.

The second and related controversial finding to emerge from the army data pertained to the average test scores obtained by recruits of different national origins. Compared to native-born American whites, immigrants from northern Europe scored slightly lower, and those from southern and eastern Europe considerably so. Indeed, a clear majority of this last group fell below Yerkes's standard for moronity, with mental age equivalents below twelve. Yerkes's colleague Carl Brigham made much of these findings in his book, and explained them on a genetic-racial basis. Borrowing from a then-fashionable (but scientifically unfounded) anthropological theory, Brigham asserted that the higher intelligence of native Americans and northern Europeans was due to their superior "Nordic" blood, as opposed to that of the inferior "Alpine" and "Mediterranean" racial types who presumably preponderated among southern and eastern Europeans. Brigham further observed that immigration by these presumably inferior races had been greatly increasing in recent years, and argued that restrictions ought to be imposed soon before the American population became swamped with inferior blood.

Brigham's voice was not alone here, for there already existed a strong national mood against immigration, and in 1924 the Congress passed a bill setting strict quotas for each national group. Moreover, these quotas were based on the population makeup of the United States from *1890,* which was *before* there had been very substantial immigration from southern and eastern Europe. Thus the new quotas for those countries were very low, and further immigration from them was severely restricted. Given the national mood, these restrictions would have been passed even without the encouragement of the army testers. Nevertheless, the pronouncements of eminent psychologists like Yerkes and Brigham regarding deteriorating national intelligence and supposed racial differences did not hurt the cause.

In fact, the army data contained substantial evidence which could have been used to support an *environmentalist* explanation of the tested differences between immigrant groups. Immigrants' test scores were shown to correlate positively with the length of time they had been resident in America, regardless of their particular origins. Thus those who had been present in the country for twenty or more years achieved an average mental age of 13.74, higher than the overall average for recruits in general; those who had been present six to ten years averaged 11.70; and the most recent immigrants, with up to five years of residence, scored only 11.29.[14] As it happened, the greatest proportion of the older residents came from northern Europe, while the more recent ones came predominantly from the south and east. Thus the "Nordic" immigrants had had a substantially longer average time than their "Alpine" and "Mediterranean" peers to familiarize themselves with the American culture and history they were asked about in the tests. Here was surely an explanation for at least part of the national differences in average test scores, yet it was minimized or overlooked by Yerkes, Brigham, and others who feared the tainting of the American stock through unrestricted immigration.

The third controversial finding in the army statistical summary was a very low average score for native American blacks, lower even than for any immigrant group. Once again data were at hand to support environmental explanations for the differences, since blacks had had much less schooling, and came from much more poverty-stricken backgrounds than did their white counterparts. Further, blacks from many northern states outperformed whites from several in the south. Brigham's explanation of these findings, however, was that the blacks had received less schooling because they were innately less intelligent, and had thus dropped out more quickly or never even bothered to attend. The higher scores of northern blacks he attributed to a selective northward migration by the more intelligent segment of the black population, and to a greater admixture of white blood in northern blacks. Like Goddard with the Kallikaks, he observed a *cor-*

relation between low intelligence test scores and poor environment, and assumed that the low intelligence *caused* the environment. Of course, the reverse was equally plausible.

The Environmentalists' Response

Both well-respected psychologists, Yerkes and Brigham received many positive reviews for their books. Their interpretations did not pass unchallenged, however, either in the popular or in the professional press. Thus the columnist Walter Lippman wrote a series of articles for *New Republic* magazine ridiculing Yerkes's claim that the "average" intelligence of adult recruits was that of a "normal" thirteen-year-old, and arguing that the age standards applied to the army point scores must have been ludicrously inappropriate.[15] Brigham's neglect or dismissal of environmentalistic explanations, and several statistical peculiarities in the test-score distributions which tended to undermine his nativist interpretations, were noted by several critical professional reviewers in psychological journals.[16]

The most significant environmentalist response, however, came a few years later from psychologists who adopted the "culture concept" of Columbia University anthropologist Franz Boas (1858–1942). Boas argued that many important "racial" characteristics get transmitted from generation to generation not because of heredity, but because members of the same race tend to be reared in a distinctive and similar *culture* from birth onward, with its own formative language, childrearing patterns, and institutionalized values. In a real sense, Boasian anthropology represented a fulfillment of the sketchy "ethology" program which John Mill had proposed in the nineteenth century.

Among the first to apply the culture concept to group differences in intelligence test scores was Otto Klineberg (b. 1899), a graduate student in psychology who happened to study anthropology with Boas in the mid-1920s. On a field trip to Washington State, Klineberg gave some intelligence test items to a group of Yakima Indian children, and observed the following unexpected result:

> The Indian children appeared almost completely indifferent to the amount of time required to complete the tasks. No matter how often I repeated or emphasized the words "as quickly as possible" they paid no attention. On the other hand they made fewer mistakes.[17]

In Yakima culture, quickness was not considered a sign of "intelligence," but to the contrary was believed to reflect impetuosity and lack of control. So here was a culture in which the most intelligent people, by their own standards, would be actually *penalized* on all intelligence test items requiring speedy responses. Here was a clear demonstration of how nongenetic, cultural factors could produce group differences in intelligence test scores.

This experience attuned Klineberg to the general importance of cultural factors in tested intelligence. He expanded his study of cultural attitudes toward speed for his Ph.D. thesis,[18] and then spent several years studying black migration patterns in the United States. His book, *Negro Intelligence and Selective Migration,*[19] argued that it was superior environmental and cultural advantages, and *not* selective migration, which had resulted in northern blacks scoring higher on intelligence tests than did their counterparts who remained in the south.

As a result of these related developments, all but the most diehard of hereditarians came to concede significant effects to culture and environment in producing "racial differences." Genetic factors perhaps were not ruled out completely, but even Carl Brigham admitted by 1930 that he had seriously overstated their case in his book five years earlier.[20] Thus began an era of relative consensus in the nature-nurture debate, when even those who believed there was a strong innate component to differences in intelligence also acknowledged a very important role for culture and nurture.

A brief episode punctuated this calm in 1940, when psychologists from the University of Iowa reported a series of studies showing large IQ gains for children who had been adopted into good foster homes. The Iowa psychologists interpreted their results as demonstrating the great malleability of intelligence to environmental influence. A group of Stanford University psychologists, led by Lewis Terman, severely criticized the studies on methodological grounds, and argued that the environmental effect had been grossly exaggerated.[21] This flare-up was short-lived, however, and since neither side could prove its case conclusively, it was followed by another period of relative calm. This lasted until the explosive events of the late 1960s, which shall be taken up in Chapter 5.

Meanwhile, developments had proceeded apace since World War I in intelligence testing technology, as increasingly sophisticated tests were developed and applied in a widening variety of situations. Lewis Terman played a leading role in these events too. In the next section we shall see how Terman came to be the leading test constructor of his time, and pioneered the use of intelligence tests for the identification of "giftedness" in children.

LEWIS TERMAN AND THE STANFORD-BINET IQ TEST

Lewis Madison Terman was born on January 15, 1877, the twelfth of fourteen children in a moderately prosperous Indiana farm family. Like most farm children, young Lewis spent much of his time doing chores. His family was also relatively well supplied with books, however, and an older brother and sister had already left the farm to become schoolteachers, so he was encouraged in academic pursuits as well. When he entered the local one-room school at age six, he so outshone his fellows that he was promoted directly to the third grade after a single term. By twelve he had completed the eighth grade and exhausted the formal educational opportunities available near his home. Too young to go away to school, he did independent "postgraduate work" for a year or two under the supervision of his brother.

In the meantime Lewis, like young Robert Yerkes, was finding

Lewis Madison Terman (1877–1956) *(Archives of the History of American Psychology, University of Akron)*

farm work increasingly uninspiring, as he was "forever plough-ing the same fields, doing the same chores, and getting nowhere."[22] His youthful ambitions for better things were stim-ulated by the visit to his home of an intinerant book peddler, selling a work on phrenology. After feeling young Lewis's head, the peddler predicted a great future for him on the basis of the science presented in the book—which the Terman family bought and Lewis avidly read. The experience not only fired his ambi-tion and self-confidence, but also introduced him to the "sci-ence" of personality assessment. Like his future intellectual hero

Galton, Terman was influenced toward a belief in innate individual differences through a youthful brush with phrenology.

In order to leave the farm and fulfill his ambitions, Lewis needed more education, and for that there was only one route available: "For the farmer boy of 1890 in Indiana, to get an education meant, first of all, that one must prepare to teach school. That step accomplished, it was possible to earn one's way through college and to enter a profession."[23] Thus as a fifteen-year-old Terman entered Central Normal College, an unaccredited but efficient producer of rural schoolteachers some twenty-five miles from his home. After attending classes half-time for two years—returning home to help on the farm during warm seasons—Terman qualified for his first teaching post at seventeen, in a one-room schoolhouse much like the one he had attended. He managed to take two of the next four years off for further study at Central Normal, and finally left at age twenty-one with three different bachelor's degrees—in arts, sciences, and pedagogy. Though this college's degrees were not recognized as equivalent to those awarded by "standard," accredited universities, it did provide excellent practical training for an aspiring educator. Terman was immediately appointed principal of a township high school, with responsibility for the entire curriculum of its forty students. Never having attended high school himself, Terman was challenged, and developed an interest in the art and science of pedagogy that would remain throughout his life.

This job was but a stepping-stone for the ambitious Terman, for within three years he not only married and had a son, but also accumulated sufficient capital to matriculate at last at a "standard university," Indiana University at Bloomington. There he majored in pedagogy and, largely because of interests aroused by his developing young son, psychology. With characteristic diligence, he earned three and a half years of credit in two years, and a master's as well as a bachelor's degree. He also began to show entrepreneurial ability, helping to finance himself by renting a large house and letting rooms to fellow students at a reasonable profit.

Terman wrote long papers at Indiana on "degeneracy" and

une great man theory," as well as a master's thesis on leadership in children. Though these were not major scholarly contributions in themselves, their preparation exposed Terman "to almost everything I could find in the library, in English, German, or French, on the psychology of mental deficiency, criminality, and genius."[24] Figuring prominently in this reading were the works of two men who became his intellectual ideals:

> Of the founders of modern psychology, my greatest admiration is for Galton. My favorite of all psychologists is Binet, not because of his intelligence test, which was only a by-product of his life-work [and which had not yet been developed when Terman first read him in 1901 and 1902], but because of his originality, insight, and open-mindedness, and because of the rare charm of personality that shines through all his writings.[25]

Inspired by Galton and Binet as well as his Indiana teachers, Terman "became fired with the ambition to become a professor of psychology and to contribute something myself to the science."[26] This ambition seemed thwarted when funds ran short, however, and Terman prepared to return to high school teaching. Then in the midst of his job search he received an unexpected offer of a graduate fellowship for Ph.D. study at Clark University. With a substantial loan from his family, Terman was able to accept, and to study under the eminent G. Stanley Hall as Henry Goddard had just finished doing.

Terman was at first awed by Hall, from whose seminars "I always went home dazed and intoxicated, took a hot bath to quiet my nerves, then lay awake for hours rehearsing the clever things I should have said and did not."[27] Under Hall's "hypnotic sway," Terman wrote a literature survey on precocity, and a follow-up questionnaire study to his master's research on leadership in children. Hall found these good enough to publish in his journals, and they became Terman's first professional publications.[28]

Terman's interest in precocious and exceptional children deepened, and his reading soon led in the direction of mental tests. Hall did not really approve of this subject, in part because he distrusted the "quasi-exactness" of the mathematical methods employed by most testers, and also probably in part because he did not get along well with American testing pioneer James McKeen Cattell. Terman, however, sensed that the future lay in this undeveloped field, despite Hall's reservations. With some reluctance but the courage of his convictions, Terman finally decided to abandon Hall's supervision, and do his Ph.D. research on mental testing under the nominal supervision of E. B. Sanford, a less renowned psychologist who allowed him to work out his own ideas independently.

Terman chose a research problem much in keeping with his own previous experience. As a teacher and principal, he had always had a few students capable of sailing through the entire curriculum with great ease, picking up almost everything at a single try. He himself had been such a student. But also since childhood he had been mystified and intrigued by those "backwards" students whose experiences were obviously so opposite to his own. As an educator, he had been further baffled by those students, who seemed unable to keep up no matter what educational tricks he tried. For his Ph.D. thesis, Terman decided to see what mental tests could do in distinguishing unusually backward students from very bright ones. He entitled his completed study "Genius and Stupidity: A Study of the Intellectual Processes of Seven 'Bright' and Seven 'Stupid' Boys."

Terman did not then know of Binet and Simon's work, which was proceeding simultaneously with his own, but he adopted a working strategy remarkably similar to theirs, though on a smaller scale. He gave a diverse series of tests to fourteen schoolboys between ten and thirteen years old, seven of whom had been picked as exceptionally bright by their teachers, and seven as exceptionally dull. His tests were much more like Binet's than like Galton's, Cattell's, or Spearman's in their emphasis on "higher" and complex cognitive functioning, and fell into eight categories:

1. Tests of *invention and creative imagination* required subjects to manipulate objects and numbers imaginatively: for example,

by determining how five chains of three links each could be made into a single long chain with only three weldings.*

2. A typical test of *logical processes* was the "ball-in-field" situation: "A ball is lost in a round field. The grass is so tall you can only see ten feet on each side of you. Show [with a pencil on a circular diagram] what path you would take in looking for the ball."[29]

3. Several tests of *mathematical ability* involved basic arithmetic, fractions, money changing, probability and chance, and elementary algebra.

4. To demonstrate *language mastery*, subjects were asked to solve anagrams, fill in the blanks in stories with appropriate words, and read a text aloud.

5. In the *interpretation of fables*, subjects were asked to derive the morals from twelve proverbs or short fables.

6. All subjects were told the rules of *the game of chess* (a new game to all), and then rated for the numbers of errors in their games, and their ability to improvise appropriate strategies of play.

7. To test *memory*, Terman asked his subjects to observe and then reproduce chess moves and geometric figures, and to repeat short stories from memory.

8. Tests of *motor skill* required such activities as balancing a book on the head while walking, or catching a ball in a small cup.

Much as Terman had anticipated, the bright boys' average performance surpassed the dull boys' on all of these tests except for motor skill. Nevertheless, only in mathematics and chess learning were there nonoverlapping distributions; in all others, the best of the "dull" boys surpassed the worst of the "bright." Given the stringency with which the groups had been selected—presumably from the very top and very bottom of a large school population—these results surprised and disappointed Terman. The tests were far from infallible indicators of "brightness" or "stupidity," even with such extreme groups.

Terman noted in passing, but did not emphasize, one fact which

---

*The solution is to disconnect all three links from one short chain, and use them to join the remaining four short chains together.

could have helped explain his imperfect results: namely, that the dull boys were on average almost a full year older than the bright boys. Had his two samples been matched for age, his results would have worked out better, for his tests were in fact much like those used by Binet and Simon. But of course in early 1905 Binet and Simon had not yet publicized the importance of age standards, and Terman, like so many others, failed to appreciate it. Thus Terman's thesis *seemed* like a relative failure when he published it in 1906; only later would he find the experience invaluable as he revised and perfected the Binet-Simon scales for American populations.

As he concluded his Ph.D. thesis, Terman inserted an almost offhand remark on the nature-nurture question. "While offering little positive data on the subject," he wrote, "the study has strengthened my impression of the relatively greater importance of *endowment* over *training,* as a determinant of an individual's intellectual rank among his fellows."[30] He did not provide the factual basis for this judgment or elaborate further in any way. It shows, however, that Terman began his investigations of intelligence with an inclination toward the hereditarian explanation of individual differences—an inclination which persisted through his clash with the Iowa psychologists in 1940.

All such issues became temporarily academic, however, as Terman sought a job. He had suffered a severe attack of pulmonary tuberculosis at Clark, and knew he would have to live somewhere with a year-round salubrious climate. This severely restricted the job choices open to him, and forced him to accept a high school principalship in San Bernardino, California, rather than a university position as he would have much preferred. After a year there he was appointed to teach pedagogy and child study at Los Angeles State Normal School—an improvement over the principalship, but still leaving him outside of psychology per se, and without much opportunity to do research. Thus for four years Terman concentrated on regaining his health and paying off his debts: "I read only moderately, tried to forget that I was ever interested in research, and spent as much time as possible out of doors."[31]

This fallow period ended in 1910, when E. B. Huey, a friend and classmate from Clark, declined an assistant professorship in educational psychology at Stanford University, but recommended his old friend instead. Terman was only too delighted to accept when he was asked. At last he had a position fully within psychology, and with excellent research opportunities.

Huey performed a second vital service when he visited Terman just before his first term at Stanford. Terman recalled: "I was 'boning' on the courses I was to give and was naturally in a receptive state of mind. At this time [Huey] told me . . . about the work of Binet and Goddard. He urged me to start at once with the Binet 1908 scale for measuring intelligence."[32] Terman never received better advice in his life, for his subsequent work on the Binet tests soon catapulted him both to academic recognition and financial fortune.

The Stanford-Binet Tests

Terman was highly impressed with Binet and Simon's techniques for intelligence testing, which accorded well with his own predilections from his Ph.D. research. He saw that with the advantage of age standards both his and their test items could predict school success reasonably well. He also saw that the Binet-Simon tests needed revision and refinement, however, primarily through validation on larger and more representative samples of American subjects than had been used previously. In attacking this problem, Terman demonstrated his capacity not only for experimental work per se, but also for the administration and supervision of large projects carried out by teams of graduate students. If the subject sample for his Ph.D. research had been almost laughably small, he now built an efficient research empire for the testing of thousands of subjects.

First, with his graduate student H. G. Childs, Terman showed that the available versions of Binet tests seriously overestimated mental age for young American children, but underestimated it for older ones. For example, five-year-old children earned average mental age scores of almost seven, while thirteen-year-olds averaged about eleven. Only in the mid-ranges between eight and ten was the correspondence between chronological and average mental age reasonably close. Clearly, many items and scoring criteria from the Binet-Simon scale needed to be altered to make the tests more accurate for American populations.

Terman and Childs, assisted by two other graduate students, prescribed some of these alterations in their 1912 article "A Tentative Revision and Extension of the Binet-Simon Measuring Scale of Intelligence."[33] Here several original Binet-Simon items were removed altogether, and several new ones were added—including the "ball-in-field" test, fable interpretation, and fill-in-the-word items from Terman's Ph.D. study. Some few hundred children of varying ages constituted the standaridization sample for this revision.

In 1916, with the aid of several more graduate students, Terman produced an even better test, standardized on more than twenty-three hundred individuals. This "Stanford Revision of the Binet-Simon Scale," soon called simply the "Stanford-Binet," was by far the best of all available individual intelligence tests, in terms of its reliable norms for all ages from early childhood through mid-adolescence. The Stanford-Binet quickly dominated the field, and became the standard against which all subsequent American intelligence tests—whether group or individual—would be measured.

The 1916 Stanford-Binet also brought with it a popular new term. Terman adopted William Stern's suggestion that the ratio between mental and chronological age be taken as a unitary measure of intelligence, but then multiplied that result by 100 to get rid of decimals. This resulting "intelligence quotient," which Terman dubbed the "IQ" for short, has ever since been given in countless psychology textbooks by the now-classic formula

$$IQ = \frac{\text{Mental Age}}{\text{Chronological Age}} \times 100.$$

The Stanford-Binet established Terman's high reputation among mental testers, and made him one of the first to be tapped by Yerkes in 1917 for service on the army testing program. Terman put that experience to good use by learning the techniques of group intelligence testing. Shortly after the war, Terman collaborated with Yerkes and some others to introduce the *National Intelligence Tests,* constructed on the army Alpha model, to measure the intelligence of groups of schoolchildren. This was the first of many group tests to come onto the educational market, all of which were validated primarily by showing good correlations with the Stanford-Binet. The market had been primed by the army project's publicity, and intelligence testing soon became a big business. With royalties from the sale of his tests, Terman became a wealthy as well as a prominent psychologist. In 1923, he was elected president of the American Psychological Association, in recognition of his professional achievements.

Studies of Gifted Children

Test development per se was only one aspect of Terman's signal contribution to the intelligence testing movement. Equally important was his successful advocacy of *high* IQ as an index of giftedness or even "genius" in children, and his promotion of research on the gifted.

Terman had long been interested in the subject of intellectual precocity, beginning with his own academically accelerated childhood and continuing through his studies with Hall. Many people at the turn of the century associated childhood precocity with adult abnormality, as expressed in the popular catchphrase "Early ripe, early rot." This popular belief was supported mainly by anecdotes about child prodigies who later went to ruin and school dullards who grew up to be great men, but definitive research had not been done. Terman privately suspected (perhaps thinking of himself as an example) that the folk wisdom was the reverse of the truth.

Binet testing methods offered a convenient approach to studying this issue, because they apparently provided quantitative measures of intellectual "advancement" as well as of retardation. Binet himself had done a few preliminary studies of children with intellectual levels in advance of their ages, but had died before reaching any firm conclusions about the meaning of such advancement. Terman resolved to carry this sort of research much farther, as an approach to the study of precocity.

The primary question for Terman was whether or not high IQs in childhood are systematically related to intellectual success or failure in adulthood. He addressed the question in two ways: first, by estimating what the childhood IQs *might have been* for highly eminent individuals from history; and second, by identifying a large group of present-day children with very high IQs and following their progress longitudinally over many years.

The first kind of study was inspired by the publication of Karl Pearson's major biography of Francis Galton in 1914, documenting for the first time Galton's precocious childhood development which we reviewed in Chapter 1. Much involved with his new IQ concept when he read this biography, Terman estimated that young Galton's more spectacular exploits occurred at about half the age at which normal children can do them; this suggested a childhood IQ of close to 200. In a 1917 paper, Terman reported that this figure exceeded by far any single IQ yet obtained from the thousands of California schoolchildren who had taken the Stanford-Binet, and concluded that Galton had been an extraordinary child genius.[34]

One may question the literal accuracy of Terman's astronomical assessment, which was based on selected documents from a family with a strong wish to emphasize their child's precocity, and which ignored other evidence indicating more ordinary childhood abilities. This was no real substitute for test data obtained under standardized conditions, by an examiner with no vested interest in the outcome. Even so, however, one must grant Terman his *basic* point that Francis Galton had been precocious, if not so extraordinarily so as Terman wished to believe. Here was at least one case to counter the early ripen–early rot dogma, for Galton showed high intelligence throughout his entire life span.

To see if a similar pattern occurred in the lives of great men in general, Terman set his graduate student Catherine Cox to investigating the childhood biographies of some three hundred people rated among history's greatest geniuses. For her Ph.D.

thesis, Cox compared the ages at which these individuals were reported to have done things in childhood with the ages at which average children would be expected to do so, and used the ratios to estimate their IQs. The average value came out to 155, and not a single score fell below the "normal" figure of 100. Coincidentally, Galton's environmentalist counterpart John Stuart Mill received the highest single estimate (190) in this group. The lowest estimates were received by individuals such as Copernicus and Cervantes, about whom very little childhod information was available; Terman and Cox believed that if more were known, estimates of their IQs would surely rise.[35] Thus the point of this study was *not* to compare the exact IQs of famous historical figures, for any fair comparisons were admittedly impossible. But the findings did seem to support Terman's *general* point, namely, "that the genius who achieves highest eminence is one whom intelligence tests *would have* identified as gifted in childhood [emphasis added]."[36] Those of the three hundred individuals about whom satisfactory childhood data existed had both ripened early *and* resisted subsequent rot.

Of course, the finding that adult geniuses had tended to be intellectually precocious children did not prove that most precocious children grow up to be eminent, or even necessarily above average in achievement. It was still possibly true that many or most precocious children go to subsequent ruin. To investigate this question directly, Terman initiated one of psychology's largest and longest-running research programs. In the early 1920s, his assistants tested more than 250,000 California schoolchildren in order to find a sample of 1500 boys and girls, all with IQs above 140. Extensive background data were collected on all these children, and then their academic, social, professional, and familial careers were investigated at regular intervals thereafter. Following the initial selection in 1922, surveys were conducted by Terman himself in 1929, 1950, and 1955, and after his death by his scientific executors in 1960 and 1972. A new follow-up is imminent. To date, more than three hundred of the original subjects have died, and the rest are now of retirement age. Nevertheless, more than nine hundred of these "Terman's Termites" (as they jokingly call themselves) are still in active and enthusiastic contact with the researchers. The project is yet another monument to Terman's administrative and organizational skill.

And just how have these highly selected, high IQ individuals fared in their lives? The answer is not uncomplicated, though *on the average* they have led from the beginning of the study much healthier, happier, and generally more successful lives than a randomly selected group would have. A very high proportion entered the professions, with many achieving national or international reputations as scientists, lawyers, bankers, and businessmen. So far, more than thirty have been listed in *Who's Who*, exceeding the chance figure several times over. Notable successes in the creative arts were rarer, though the sample does contain a noted science-fiction writer, an Oscar-winning motion picture director, and some university heads of music or art departments.* No subject has won a Nobel Prize or become a celebrated "genius," though this is not too surprising given the size of the sample, and the odds against anyone's doing so.

In 1960, when the male subjects were in the prime of their occupational lives, the one hundred "most successful" and the one hundred "least successful" (according to a series of objective and subjective ratings) were singled out for separate study. The most successful men—the "A group"—had average incomes almost five times the national average; the least successful "C group" still exceeded the national average, but only by about 1.4 times. The A group had a very high proportion of professionals, containing twenty-four university professors, eleven lawyers, eight research scientists, and five physicians; the C group had only five men working in professions, in relatively low-level positions. The A men also came out much better on measures approximating "quality of life," with alcoholism rates five times lower and divorce rates three times lower than the C's. Thus there was considerable variation in the life outcomes of the Terman gifted men.

---

*Names of the individual subjects in this project have been kept confidential, except for those of a few (who mainly became psychologists) who have voluntarily identified themselves.

Some fared exceptionally well, and the great majority were considerably above average. But the C group was not much better off than a random sample drawn from the general population. With average IQs near 150, these men demonstrated that high IQs by themselves offer no guarantee of unusual success or happiness in life.

The women in the study showed a somewhat similar pattern, winning professional honors and citations in biographical dictionaries much more frequently than chance would predict. Reflecting the dominant pattern of their times, however, the majority of the women became housewives, and reported no career at all when contacted in mid-life. Their subjective reports indicated that many suffered particularly acutely from the lack of intellectual fulfillment in their lives—the sort of frustration which has more recently given rise to the women's movement.[37]

Terman's Legacy

In general, Terman's studies firmly laid to rest the early ripe–early rot myth, and went a good way toward establishing the opposite: unusually precocious children were more likely to turn out well than poorly in their later lives. Indeed, so successful was Terman in establishing this point that a person with a high IQ is often popularly regarded in our society as synonymous with a "genius." This view, however, is really something of an exaggeration, as can be shown by a brief consideration of the research since Terman's, investigating the ability of IQ scores to predict success in various ventures.

Many studies have investigated the correlations between IQ scores and grades in school. Typically, these correlations average in the .60's for elementary school students, but fall to the .50's for high school students, the .40's for college students, and the .30's for graduate students. California psychologist Arthur Jensen, a leading modern proponent of IQ testing, argues that the reason for the decline is not that IQ becomes less important at higher educational levels, but that its range becomes progressively much more restricted. People with low IQs tend to fail in the lower levels, and so never enter the higher ones. If they did, they would presumably continue to fail, and hence to maintain the higher correlations. Thus, for Jensen, the best estimate of the "true" relationship between IQ and academic accomplishment is the elementary school figure, based as it is on the most representative range of subjects.[38]

A somewhat different explanation has been proposed by Richard Herrnstein, another leading advocate of testing. Herrnstein believes that the relationship between IQ and scholastic success really *is* stronger at the lower levels:

> Children with low I.Q.s almost always do poorly in school, while children with high I.Q.s cover the range from excellent down to poor. For school work, as for many other correlates of I.Q., intelligence is necessary but not sufficient. Another way to put this is to say that a low I.Q. predicts poor performance more reliably than a high one predicts good performance.[39]

The idealized graph below illustrates Herrnstein's conception. At the lowest levels of IQ, school grades too are low, and do not show much variability. With increasing levels of IQ the variability increases along with the average level of success. The bulge at the bottom of the graph indicates a generally greater tendency for high IQ people to *under*perform in school than for low IQ people to *over*perform. From a historical perspective, of course, it is unsurprising that the tests should work somewhat better at the low end of the distribution, since they were originally developed to diagnose retardation rather than to identify giftedness.

For success variables other than school grades, somewhat lower but still solidly positive correlations with IQ are routinely observed. Income levels, or ratings of the social prestige of people's occupations, typically correlate with IQ in the .40's, for example. The exact meaning of these correlations remains debatable, however, since the success variables also correlate strongly with education. Some investigators argue that the correlation between IQ and

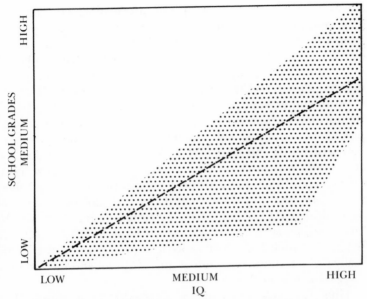

The relationship between IQ and school grades. Adapted from Richard J. Herrnstein, *I.Q. in the Meritocracy* (London: Allen Lane, 1973), p. 50.

success is primarily an indirect reflection of the education-success relationship; that is, IQ adds little to a person's prospects for success beyond its contributions to his or her educational career, which is the main determiner of success.[40] Other theorists believe that IQ has a continuing and independent positive effect on success in life, citing cases of high IQ individuals who did poorly in school but went on to achieve professional or financial success anyhow, presumably because of their intelligence.[41] We see here once again the inability of mere correlations to permit conclusions regarding causality.

In summary, it is fair to say that IQ scores are *moderately* good predictors of conventional success in our society, in an absolute sense. In a relative sense, they are *very* good predictors, since it is hard to think of any other single measure that can do better.

IQ scores can potentially be useful information, not only for diagnosing retardation, but also for identifying gifted children from unlikely backgrounds. Several of "Terman's Termites," for example, believe that the very fact they were selected as subjects in the study opened up new vistas for them, helping them and their families to realize previously unsuspected possibilities.*

On the other hand, even the most enthusiastic supporters of IQ tests must acknowledge that the scores are far from perfect predictors. Assuming with Jensen that the true general correlation between IQ and school grades is about .60, children scoring at the 90th percentile on IQ tests will perform academically at an average of only the 77th percentile, with half falling below that figure. As was also shown by Terman's study of gifted children, a high IQ by itself offers no firm guarantee of success. Organizations such as "Mensa," which admit members solely on the basis of their high intelligence test scores, inevitably contain many people whose actual intellectual achievements fall substantially short of their IQ levels.†

Thus Terman's legacy of the IQ test has been a useful but imperfect gift. IQ scores can be important bits of information, but they must be interpreted and used with great caution. First, of course, it must be certain that the test was appropriate for the subject—that his or her cultural and environmental background is similar to those for which the test was developed and standardized. Granting this, it must be further recognized that the test's predictive value is only approximate, so that important decisions about an individual's life should always be supported

---

*Of course, this suggests that some part of the unusual success achieved by Terman's gifted children may not have been due to their high IQs per se, but simply to their having been *labeled* as gifted. Such are typical of the ambiguities of research on the nature-nurture question.

†In a spoof of Mensa pretentiousness, an organization called "Densa" has recently been established in Toronto, with membership open to anyone of self-professed low intelligence willing to pay the $10 membership fee. Members receive lapel buttons with a turkey insignia, and promote the philosophy that since intelligent people have made such a mess of the world already, it is time to give stupid people a chance.

by other sorts of information besides IQ. Finally, it must be recognized that a single IQ score can never be more than a global assessment of an "intelligence" that may well have many individually varying facets and complexities—particularly if one accepts Binet's as opposed to Spearman's basic conception of intelligence.

Indeed, it was appreciation of this last factor which led our next protagonist, David Wechsler, to develop a new set of tests which retained the basic IQ concept but also permitted the making of more individualized diagnoses in line with Binet's theory of testing.

DAVID WECHSLER AND THE ASSESSMENT OF ADULT INTELLIGENCE

David Wechsler was born in Romania in 1896, but emigrated with his family to America at age six (ironically, as part of the tide of eastern European immigrants who aroused such concern for Yerkes and Brigham).[42] He grew up in New York City, taking a B.A. from its City College in 1916, and then enrolling as a graduate student in psychology at Columbia. When America entered World War I in April of 1917, Wechsler was in the midst of a Master's thesis studying memory loss in patients with Korsakoff's psychosis, an organic brain condition associated with long-term alcoholism.

As an aspiring psychologist, Wechsler was naturally attracted to Yerkes's testing program. While awaiting his own induction into the army he served as a volunteer scorer of the army Alpha tests. Then, as a junior officer in the army himself, he was appointed to the testing program and assigned the duty of administering *individual* intelligence tests (usually the Stanford-Binet) to recruits who had been specially referred—usually because of their poor performance on the Alpha and/or Beta. All of this experience gave Wechsler an excellent working knowledge of the major intelligence tests of the time, and an

David Wechsler (1896–1981) *(Archives of the History of American Psychology, University of Akron)*

appreciation of their practical weaknesses as well as their strengths. In particular, he began to sense that the Stanford-Binet did not always pose questions that were suitable for the assessment of adults.

At the end of hostilities, Wechsler was briefly posted in England, where he was able to study with Spearman. He was impressed by Spearman's notion of General Intelligence, but felt that it was too narrow and overlooked the importance of "nonintellective" factors in intelligence, such as motivation and personality.

By the time Wechsler returned to Columbia after the war, he had acquired a great deal of both practical and theoretical expertise with intelligence tests. He gained further testing experience as he completed his Ph.D., working part-time as a psychologist for the New York Bureau of Child Guidance. Many of his emotionally disturbed clients here, as in the army, came from immigrant families. With his own personal experience of being an immigrant, this made him responsive to the work of his Columbia compatriots Boas and Klineberg, who were just then beginning to stress the importance of cultural influences on intelligence test scores.

For the first few years after he completed his Ph.D. in 1925, Wechsler continued to practice psychological testing, both for the Psychological Corporation and privately. During this time his major research interest lay not in intelligence testing per se, but he nevertheless published two short articles which reflected his developing attitudes toward that field. First, he showed in 1926 that the relative variability of mental age scores tends to decrease with increasing chronological age throughout childhood.[43] Though not absolutely conclusive, Wechsler thought this reflected a homogenizing influence of *education* on IQ scores— that is, as children got more and more education, their scores became relatively more similar. This interpretation, of course, reflected Wechsler's conviction of the partial plasticity of intelligence, and its susceptibility to environmental factors.

Six years later, Wechsler published another brief paper reporting that, for diagnostic purposes with disturbed patients, he had found the army Alpha test to be more useful than the Stanford-Binet.[44] The reason was that the Alpha used the same types of items at all intelligence levels, and thus made possible the diagnosis of *special* abilities and disabilities in addition to global intelligence. For example, one might learn that a subject with average overall intelligence was particularly good on items requiring abstract reasoning, like similarities questions, but deficient in questions requiring general practical knowledge. This was, of course, one of the advantages Yerkes had cited for a point scale, as opposed to a mental age form of test, many years earlier.

Wechsler soon had an opportunity to put his convictions about testing into widespread practice, for in 1932 he was appointed chief psychologist at New York's enormous Bellevue Hospital, where he was charged with supervising the testing of thousands of mental patients, from highly diverse national, linguistic, and socioeconomic backgrounds. He now became more than ever convinced of the limitations of existing intelligence tests for populations like this, and set out to develop his own. As he did so, he felt there were two major problems to be solved. First, he wanted to develop an individual intelligence test tailored specifically to *adults* rather than to children, and second, he wanted to exploit the point scale's potential for assessing intelligence as a multifaceted entity, representable by more than just a single IQ score.

Assessing Adult Intelligence

The Stern-Terman IQ formula had suffered from one major limitation ever since its inception: it was fully appropriate only for children and adolescents whose mental ages could be assumed to be developing in pace with their chronological ages. With the kinds of items that worked best for estimating mental age, improvement typically slowed down dramatically by the late teens and leveled off in the twenties; performance actually *declined* slowly but progressively thereafter. Whether recalling digits, solving analogies, or arranging blocks into designs, people were as good as they would ever be by twenty, and over the hill by thirty.

The meaning of this general finding is ambiguous. Some take it to mean that "intelligence" truly peaks in the early twenties, and that young adults are on average the smartest segment of the population. Others—especially older people, perhaps—may argue that this finding exactly reflects a major shortcoming of the "intelligence" measured by IQ tests, namely, that the tests fail to assess those qualities of "wisdom" or "creativity" which are the most important determinants of genuine, mature intellectual contributions to society. One fact is clear, however: the failure of mental age scores to increase after adolescence rules out the application of the traditional IQ formula to adult subjects.

One early approach to this problem was to assign an arbitrary chronological age of fourteen to all adult subjects. Another was made by Terman with his 1937 revision of the Stanford-Binet, when he added three levels of "Superior Adult" items to the mental age scale. But while these techniques made it possible to assign various above-average intelligence levels to adult subjects, they still lacked the precision and conceptual neatness of the IQ calculations for children.

An alternative technique, of course, was the point-scale method, and it was this which Wechsler refined when he introduced the Wechsler Bellevue Scale in 1939, and its revision, the Wechsler Adult Intelligence Scale, or "WAIS," in 1955. These tests, generally accepted today as the best available measures of adult intelligence, give final scores which are referred to as *deviation quotients* or *deviation IQs*.

To obtain these scores, subtests are selected not because of any specific relation to age (though they are of the same general type as those used in the Binet and army tests), but because their results, when scored on a point scale, tend to fall in bell-shaped, normal distributions for all age groups of adults. The *mean* raw scores, however, can and do vary among different age groups. Thus on the WAIS items, for example, sixteen-year-olds earn an average of 103 points, twenty-five-year-olds average 114, forty-year-olds return to 103, and sixty-year-olds average only 93. These figures reflect the general finding that absolute point scores tend to peak for people in their twenties, decline to about the same level as that of the mid-teens in middle age, and then fall progressively as old age approaches. Graphs representing the overall point-score distributions for these four age groups are shown on page 154.

Wechsler used basic statistics such as these for converting each person's raw score into a "deviation IQ" which expressed his or her performance *relative to the appropriate age group*. To make these values maximally comparable to traditional IQs, Wechsler arbitrarily assigned a score of 100 to any result exactly at its age group average; thus 100 was the WAIS IQ assigned to sixteen- or forty-year-olds with total point scores of 103, to twenty-five-year-olds with 114, or to sixty-year-olds with 93. Wechsler converted raw scores above and below the mean in such a way that

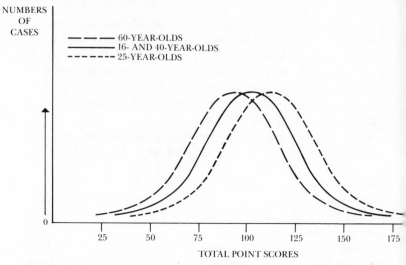

NUMBERS OF CASES

—— —— —— 60-YEAR-OLDS
———————— 16- AND 40-YEAR-OLDS
— — — — — 25-YEAR-OLDS

TOTAL POINT SCORES

Overall point-score distributions for 16-, 25-, 40-, and 60-year-olds. The graph is based on data presented in David Wechsler, *The Measurement and Appraisal of Adult Intelligence,* 4th ed. (Baltimore: Williams & Wilkins, 1958), p. 95.

IQ distributions for all age groups had standard deviations of 15. Simply put, this meant that more than two-thirds of all IQs fell between 85 and 115 (one standard deviation below and above the mean, respectively), and percentile equivalents were assignable to them according to the following scheme:

IQs AND THEIR CORRESPONDING
PERCENTILE RANKS

IQ	Percentile	IQ	Percentile
145	99.9	100	50.0
140	99.6	95	36.3
135	98.9	90	24.2
130	97.7	85	15.9
125	95.0	80	8.8
120	90.3	75	4.5
115	84.1	70	2.3
110	74.2	65	0.9
105	63.7	60	0.4

Thus a person with a deviation IQ of 85 always stands at about the 16th percentile of his or her age group, a person with 105 stands near the 64th, a 135 approaches the 99th, and so on.

So successful was this technique in removing the inconsistencies of IQ calculation for varying ages that it has by now been adopted by almost all IQ test constructors, working with children as well as adults. Even the Stanford-Binet's later revisions dispensed with the traditional formula, and now provide deviation IQs.

Individual Patterns of Intelligence

Though Wechsler designed his tests to give global IQ scores, his experience with the army Alpha also led him to seek a more individualized assessment of each subject's particular strengths and weaknesses, and of factors that might have artifically depressed the final IQ score. He achieved this by establishing norms not just for the total point scores, but also for each of the eleven separate subtests included in his scales. Thus a *profile* of comparative strengths and weaknesses can be drawn for each subject, reflecting relative performance levels on the following eleven individual WAIS subtests:

1. *Information* items inquire about specific aspects of our society and culture, such as the number of weeks in a year, the distances between certain major cities, or the nature of famous literary works.
2. *Comprehension* questions assess practical judgment or "social intelligence" by asking, for example, what to do when a fire breaks out in a theater.
3. *Arithmetic* questions vary in difficulty, and are scored partly for speed as well as accuracy of response.
4. *Digit Span* requires subjects to remember and repeat back varying series of random digits, both forward and backward.
5. *Similarities* questions require subjects to state the essential common elements for various pairs of things, such as an orange and a banana.
6. *Vocabulary* items vary from simple words such as "donkey" to relatively uncommon ones such as "travesty."

7. *Picture Arrangement* requires subjects to arrange separated and scrambled comic-strip-style pictures so they tell a meaningful story. Bonus points are awarded for speedy correct solutions.
8. *Picture Completion* items are drawings of scenes and objects lacking essential features which must be identified: for example, a pig without a tail.
9. *Block Design* tests require subjects to arrange red and white painted blocks, as quickly as possible, so they duplicate various pictured designs.
10. *Object Assembly* tasks involve putting scrambled, jigsaw-puzzle-like pieces together as quickly as possible, to make the shapes of familiar objects whose natures are not divulged to the subjects beforehand.
11. *Digit Symbol Substitution* entails the writing of symbols under different digits, according to a specified code, while being timed.

A sharp-eyed reader may have noticed that the first six subtests from this list, which Wechsler designated as *Verbal tests*, assume a degree of education and bear a close resemblance to the items in the army Alpha; the final five *Performance tests* are closely akin to the army Beta. This is no accident, for Wechsler purposely included both kinds of subtests so a subject's levels can be compared. A person scoring substantially lower on the culturally loaded Verbal tests than on the Performance items might be suspected of being culturally disadvantaged, for example. If independently obtained information supports this hypothesis, then the Performance tests alone might be considered to give a truer estimate of the subject's overall intelligence than the full-scale IQ. If the Performance scores lag substantially behind the Verbal ones, an examiner might well recommend a follow-up neurological examination, since some of the Performance subtests are particularly affected by certain kinds of brain damage or other organic pathology. These are merely hints and suggestions, not hard and fast rules, for Wechsler recognized that Verbal-Performance differences may be created by many different kinds of factors:

> Occupation is frequently an important factor, so that carpenters, mechanics, and engineers will do better on Performance, and clerical workers, school teachers, and lawyers better on Verbal items. There also appear to be cultural and possibly racial differences which in individual cases may have to be taken into consideration, but owing to the large overlap between such groups, this fact alone cannot be used as an unfailing criterion. All this means, of course, that the significance between a subject's Verbal and Performance score cannot be interpreted *carte blanche*, but only after weight is given to the various factors which may have contributed to it.[45]

A clinician can also find important clues in individual subtest scores. Arithmetic and Digit Span, for example, are especially susceptible to interference from anxiety; if subjects score lower on these than on the other subtests, one might suspect the presence of some emotional or neurotic difficulty hindering attention and concentration. Depressed people often fail to muster the energy to complete the *timed* tests at a level equal to their other scores. A large body of research and experience has by now demonstrated the usefulness of all WAIS subtests for suggesting these and other kinds of clinical hypotheses. In the hands of skillful interpreters, the Wechsler test patterns provide multi-perspectived views of the intellectual workings of many different kinds of people.

Wechsler's approach to measuring adult intelligence proved so effective and popular among clinicians that he extended it to the testing of children as well. The Wechsler Intelligence Scale for Children ("WISC"), originally introduced in 1949, provides deviation IQs and subtest profiles for children between the ages of five and fifteen; the 1963 Wechsler Preschool and Primary Scale of Intelligence ("WPPSI") does the same for those between four and six and a half. Allowing as they do for individualized profile analyses as well as for global IQ scores, all of these tests mark a genuine return to the attitudes and philosophy of Binet. Their one major drawback is that they are *individual* tests which take time to administer and score, and a substantial degree of clinical sensitivity to interpret with maximum effectiveness.

The Structure of Intelligence

The Wechsler tests provide a handy illustration of the way the debate about the *structure* of intelligence has evolved following Spearman's original introduction of the two-factor theory. Recall that Spearman believed all variability among intelligence test scores could be accounted for in terms of just a single general factor (*g*) pervading everything, combined with individual *s* factors unique to all specific subtests. Subsequent research with tests like the WAIS, however, and the development of the statistical techniques of *factor analysis,* have indicated that this two-factor conception is oversimplified at best.

The typical pattern of intercorrelations among WAIS subtests illustrates the major issue. As Spearman would have predicted, all of the correlations are positive, and range from about .30 to the mid .80's. The subtests' correlations also arrange themselves in a generally hierarchical manner, with Similarities, Information, Block Design, and Picture Completion achieving relatively high average correlations, while Digit Span and Object Assembly get relatively low ones. Here is Spearman's classical evidence in favor of the *g* factor.

The matrix of WAIS subtest correlations shows a further degree of organization, however, because on the average the Verbal subtests all intercorrelate more highly with each other than they do with the Performance tests. Performance tests, in turn, are more highly intercorrelated among themselves than they are with the Verbal measures. Thus the correlation matrix contains two statistically distinct *clusters* of subtests—one measuring generally verbal functions, the other nonverbal performance.

When groups of subtests different from the WAIS's are intercorrelated, a similar result generally occurs: positive correlations overall, but also clustering into distinct groups of especially highly correlated subtests. The specific nature of these clusters of course varies with the particular pattern of subtests thrown into the matrix, but some typical results have been clusters of tests which particularly involve memory, numerical ability, spatial visualization ability, or reasoning—as well as verbal and performance groups similar to those on the WAIS.

The central theoretical question raised by this clustering tendency concerns how much emphasis to place on it, as opposed to the general tendency toward positive correlations overall. On the one hand, some psychologists retain Spearman's basic position and argue that the general positiveness of all correlations indicates a preeminently important g factor. For these investigators the separate clusters represent *group factors* which have more generality than s factors, and are moderately interesting to know about, but which are still definitely subsidiary to g. Arthur Jensen has recently expressed this view:

> Although psychologists can devise tests that measure only one group factor, they cannot devise a test that excludes g. . . . The ubiquitous common factor to all tests is g, which has been aptly referred to as the primary mental ability. . . . And the same g permeates scholastic achievement and many types of job performance, especially so-called higher-level jobs. Therefore, g is most worthy of our scientific curiosity.[46]

From this point of view, global IQ scores—particularly if derived from instruments like the WAIS with many highly g-saturated subtests—express the most important fact about different people's intelligence. Individual profiles and group-factor scores are of secondary interest.

An opposed conception of the structure of intelligence was proposed by the University of Chicago psychologist L. L. Thurstone (1887–1955) and his followers. Thurstone was much more impressed with the importance of clustering among subtests. With the aid of statistical factor analytic techniques of his own devising, and with wide samplings of subtests, Thurstone discerned seven distinct clusters of "Primary Mental Abilities," which he labeled Verbal Comprehension, Word Fluency, Number Facility, Spatial Visualization, Associative Memory, Perceptual Speed, and Reasoning. He believed each of these represented a largely independent element of the intellect, and interpreted the *g* factor as nothing more than a general average, of decidedly secondary interest to an individual's particular pattern of Primary Mental Abilities.[47]

California psychologist J. P. Guilford has carried Thurstone's approach even further, positing a three-dimensional "Structure of Intellect" which classifies intellectual acts into 120 separate categories. The *materials or contents dimension* classifies the subject matter of all intellectual acts as verbal, figural, symbolic, or behavioral. On the *operations dimension*, acts are classified as involving cognition, memory, divergent thinking, convergent thinking, or evaluation. And on the *products dimension*, the outcome of any act is said to involve units, classes, relations, systems, transformations, or implications. Among the four content, five operation, and six product categories, there are 120 possible combinations, constituting the most basic kinds of intellectual processes. According to Guilford, "intelligence" is thus much too complex to be subsumed by a few primary mental abilities, much less by a single *g*-factor value or IQ score.[48]

Unfortunately, there is no unequivocal way to choose among these contrasting interpretations of the structure of intelligence. Mathematical factor analytic techniques have been devised to describe subtest matrices *either* as permeated by a large *g* factor with small and subsidiary group factors, *or* as collections of sharply defined and largely independent factors, where *g* emerges only as a secondary finding. Neither of these complex statistical approaches is necessarily more "correct" than the other, for they merely describe the same complicated patterns of correlations from different mathematical perspectives. The whole controversy reflects once again some of the uncertainties which inevitably arise when dealing with relations that are merely correlational, and have not been demonstrated to be causal.[49]

In general, then, the debate about the structure of intelligence retains many of its features from 1910. It is still possible to follow Binet and regard intelligence as an individually patterned collection of diverse functions, as Wechsler, Thurstone, and Guilford have all done in their own distinctive ways. On the other hand, it is also still possible to follow Spearman by emphasizing the overall positiveness of intertest correlations, and positing a supremely important *g* factor, as Jensen has done. All views have a degree of plausibility, but none is proven.

This basic uncertainty about the basic nature and structure of intelligence naturally complicates any interpretation of research on the *genetics* of intelligence, for one must always address the prior question of just what it is that is supposedly being inherited. If "intelligence" is taken to be a relatively unitary characteristic such as *g*, represented fairly by a global IQ score, the research may be regarded as simpler and more straightforward than if intelligence is believed to be a grouping of largely independent elements, each with its own separate set of causes. Here is just one more source of continuing discord on the highly charged issue of the genetics of intelligence, which is the general subject of the next chapter.

SUGGESTED READINGS

Autobiographies of Yerkes and Terman appear in Volume 2 of *The History of Psychology in Autobiography*, edited by Carl Murchison (Worcester, MA: Clark University Press, 1930). On David Wechsler, see his obituary by Joseph Matarazzo in *American Psychologist* (*36*:1542–1543, 1981). For a highly appreciative account of Terman by a former student of his see May V. Seagoe, *Terman and the Gifted* (Los Altos, CA: Kaufmann, 1975); for a much more critical view of both Terman and Yerkes, see Stephen Jay Gould's *The Mismeasure of Man* (New York: Norton, 1981).

Good accounts of the army testing program of World War I are given in Daniel J. Kevles's "Testing the Army's Intelligence: Psychologists and the Military in World War I," *Journal of American History* (*55*:565–581, 1968); and in Franz Samelson's "World War I Intelligence Testing and the Development of Psychology," *Journal of the History of the Behavioral Sciences* (*13*:274–282, 1977).

5 | Twins and the Genetics of IQ

Once in the early 1930s, a young telephone repairman named Edwin was accosted by a new co-worker with the greeting, "Hello Fred, how's tricks?" Upon learning that Ed was not the Fred he had once met elsewhere, the new acquaintance was astonished. Later, *another* man greeted Ed as Fred, and explained his mistake by saying that Ed looked exactly like a Fred he had known in another city. With a name to go on now, and a dim memory of a lost brother from his distant past, Ed set out to find his look-alike. When he located Fred, a sort of fantasy or "family romance" that many people secretly hold, but that exceedingly few actually realize, turned out to be true.

Ed and Fred had been born identical twins in a New England town, but had been adopted by different families when six months old. The two adopting families were of the same middle-class status, but did not know each other and each boy was raised as an only child. They attended the same school for a while, where their remarkable similarity of appearance was sometimes noted, but they did not become friends. While they were still very young, one family moved to Iowa and the other to Michigan, so they completely lost contact until Ed tracked down Fred.

Once reunited, they discovered that they had led very similar lives. Both had been mediocre students and had dropped out of high school; both had become electricians and worked for the telephone company; both had married and had a son at about the same time; and both even had a pet fox terrier named Trixie.

Shortly after their reunion, the twins learned that three scientists at the University of Chicago were widely advertising for early-separated pairs of identical twins to visit Chicago and be studied, all expenses paid and at the time of the extremely popular 1933 World's Fair. Since their funds were scarce, the scientists required some advance assurance that applicants actually were identical twins. Only too happy to volunteer, Ed and Fred sent photographs proving their similarity of appearance, and were accepted for the study.

Edwin (left) and Fred at the time of their first meeting, shortly before arriving in Chicago.

In Chicago they had a marvelous time and gained much publicity. They attended the fair with a pair of female twins from the study, stealing attention from some Siamese twins on formal exhibit there. Their picture and unusual story appeared in popular journals, and helped give rise to the sort of popular mythology about separated twins that is caricatured in Charles Addams's cartoon. Of greater importance to the scientists, the twins were given several psychological tests, including the Stanford-Binet intelligence scale. Ed's IQ came out to 91, Fred's to 90.[1]

Separated at birth, the Malifert twins meet accidentally. (*Drawing by Charles Addams; © 1981 The New Yorker Magazine, Inc.*)

The study of groups of separated identical twins like Ed and Fred *potentially* represents the most effective use of Galton's twin-study method to distinguish the effects of nature from those of nurture. As *monozygotic* (MZ) twins who have developed from a single fertilized ovum which subsequently split in half—opposed to fraternal or *dizygotic* (DZ) twins who have developed from two separate ova fertilized by two separate sperm—such individuals have completely identical genes. In the language of geneticists, their *genotypes* are identical. Accordingly, any differences which develop in their body structure or character—their so-called *phenotypes*—must be caused by differences in their experience and environment. This means further that, under ideal scientific conditions, the correlation coefficient expressing the similarity of traits such as IQ for a sample of separated MZ twins can be a precise indicator of the *heritability* of those traits—a mathematical statement of the proportion of the trait's variance which is attributable to hereditary factors. If the IQ correlation were 1.0, all of the IQ variability would be genetic; if .5, half the variance would be genetic and the other half due to environment and measurement error; if 0, then none of the variability could be attributed to heredity. No other group of kinship pairs offers so theoretically clear-cut an analysis of the respective contributions of nature and nurture, so it is no wonder that behavior geneticists have been extremely interested in these imagination-catching cases.

Thus it is unfortunate for scientific reasons, if not so for humanitarian ones, that it has proven impossible in practice to conduct a completely ideal and definitive separated-twin study. Several crucial conditions have always been lacking, to one degree or another. For example, a definitive study would have to employ twins who represent a genuinely random sample of the general population, and who have been *randomly* placed for adoption in a range of homes representative of the entire population. A definitive study would also have to demonstrate that its sample genuinely represents the full population of separated twins, and is not biased toward including only certain kinds of cases. Finally, in an ideal study all twins should have been *completely* separated from each other soon after birth, with no opportunity to communicate with each other or influence each other prior to their testing. As it happens, none of these conditions has ever been fully met.

A first practical difficulty arises because cases of separated twins are quite rare. When twins are put up for adoption, there is a natural tendency to try to keep them together in the same adoptive family. Failing that, they are often placed in similar and nearby homes, frequently maintained by separate branches of the same family. If they do go to separate and independent families, these families tend to be similar in background, and matched to the adoption agency's information about the backgrounds of the twins' biological parents. In all cases of adoption, of course, obviously deprived or pathological homes are screened out to begin with, so the range of adoptive homes cannot be truly representative of the entire population. In sum, the entirely justifiable practice of *selective placement* makes it inevitable that separated twins get sent to adoptive homes of greater than chance similarity. Thus any similarity the twins show in characteristics such as IQ is potentially explainable on environmental as well as hereditary grounds.

Ed and Fred were among the more completely separated twins who have been studied so far, according to a recent survey of the entire separated-twin literature.[2] And even they were adopted by childless couples of similar socioeconomic status, had some contact with each other as children, and were reared under generally similar conditions. In more typical cases of "separated" twins who have been available for study, the correspondences and contacts have been even greater.

Separated-twin studies also inevitably tend to be biased in their selection of twins. If twins have been truly separated without knowledge of each other, any discovery of their twinship is likely to follow an experience like Ed's, where their great similarity is remarked upon by a third party. This means, of course, that only similar-seeming twins can be so identified; separated twins who grow up to look and / or act very differently from each other will not be noticed and thus will be excluded from study. The Chicago scientists introduced a further explicit bias in this direction by investigating only twins who seemed very likely to be monozygotic on the basis of photographs. *Di*ssimilar-looking twins—who might have been dizygotic but who also might just have been the most unlike of monozygotic pairs—were systematically disqualified from participation.

When one adds to these factors an understandable tendency of twins who have communicated with each other before the study to perhaps overemphasize the similarities and coincidences of their lives which make them such an extraordinary story, it is clear that any observed findings may represent an exaggeration of their genetically determined similarity. Any observed IQ correlation for such imperfectly separated twins, preselected partly because of their overt similarity, is almost certainly an overestimation, to some degree, of the true heritability of IQ.

These considerations were recognized by Ed and Fred's Chicago examiners—Horatio Newman, Frank Freeman, and Karl Holzinger—who in 1937 reported a correlation of .67 for the Stanford-Binet IQs of the nineteen pairs of separated identical twins they had been able to study. They also reported a tendency for the largest IQ differences among their pairs to occur in those twins who had been reared in the most strikingly different environments. Here was positive evidence for an environmental factor of some kind, though the three authors did not completely agree about how much weight to give it. Newman, a biologist, was inclined to emphasize it less than the psychologist Freeman or the statistician Holzinger. Nevertheless, all three agreed that the issue was uncertain, and that *both* nature and nurture played significant roles in producing the correlation. They concluded the book describing their research by saying:

> If, at the inception of this research project over ten years ago, the authors entertained any hope of reaching a definitive solution of the general nature-nurture problem . . . in terms of a simple formula, they were destined to be rather disillusioned. The farther one penetrates into the intricacies of the complex of genetic and environmental factors that together determine the development of individuals, the more one is compelled to admit that there is not one problem but a multiplicity of minor problems—that there is no general solution of the major problem nor even of any one of the minor

problems. . . . We feel in sympathy [with the] dictum
that what heredity can do environment can also do.[3]

The Newman-Freeman-Holzinger study, supported by other
findings, contributed powerfully to the consensus view which held
until well into the 1960s, that both heredity and environment
are major and interacting determinants of individual differences in human intelligence. While there was some room for
disagreement—as among Newman, Freeman, and Holzinger
themselves—exponents of nature and nurture were substantially at peace with each other. Each was willing to grant a substantial if not a predominant importance to the other side.

This relative tranquillity changed in the 1960s, however, after
the eminent British psychologist Sir Cyril Burt (1883–1971)
published a spectacular separated-twin study, with a larger sample than in any previous investigation, and apparently minimally
tainted by selective placement and the other major problems of
separated-twin studies. Burt's results suggested an IQ heritability of more than 80 percent, *greatly* outweighing all combined
environmental effects. Then in 1969 the University of California psychologist Arthur Jensen (b. 1923) cited Burt's studies in
support of an argument that compensatory education programs
for culturally deprived children had failed in the past, and were
likely to continue to do so in the future, because of the great
preponderance of hereditary over environmental factors in
determining intelligence. Jensen further hypothesized that genetic
factors may have been partially involved in creating the observed
IQ difference between black and white Americans.

This suggestion of a radical alteration in the presumed heredity-
environment balance, and the reintroduction of the highly
charged racial issue, aroused a firestorm of controversy. In the
ensuing years, violent and even scandalous acts came to light on
both sides of the question, and many psychologists despaired of
ever arriving at an evenhanded assessment. Indeed, the situation has yet to be completely resolved today, though the outline
of a solution seems to be discernible.

Many different individuals have participated in this latest

eruption of the nature-nurture controversy, but the main lines of the argument are all present in the activities of Burt, Jensen, and Leon Kamin (b. 1927), the Princeton psychologist who became the most effective critic of Burt, and a vigorous proponent of a completely environmentalist explanation of IQ differences. By focusing on the stories of these three men, we shall see once again how personal and biographical factors have continued to predispose different investigators toward widely different positions on this most contentious of psychological issues.

CYRIL BURT AND THE NEW CASE FOR HEREDITY

Cyril Lodowic Burt was born on March 3, 1883, in a working-class section of London, England. Though his larger environment, including his first schools and playfellows, was lower class, his home situation was not. His well-educated father was completing medical training, and supporting his wife and young son by running the local pharmacy.

As a child Cyril got on reasonably well with his lower-class playfellows, acquiring a cockney accent which he would enjoy turning on or off at will throughout his life, and developing sympathy for the lot of underprivileged city children. These early experiences helped make Burt an effective worker with delinquent children after he became a psychologist; they may also have led him to adopt a certain street wisdom, and a win-by-your-wits-at-any-cost attitude that carried over into some of his later controversies with *intellectual* adversaries.[4]

In contrast, young Cyril's immediate family stressed strictly middle-class and intellectual values. His autobiography relates that his earliest and most treasured possessions were not ordinary toys, but books, paints, and musical instruments. Constantly encouraged intellectually by his parents, he was given Latin lessons by his father even before he was out of his baby's bed.

A crucial change occurred when Cyril was nine, as his father moved from London to take up a rural medical practice where his patients included a brother and sister of Francis Galton. Burt

Cyril Lodowic Burt (1883–1971) *(British Journal of Educational Psychology, Methuen London Limited)*

recalled that his father always liked to inspire him with stories about his famous patients or their relatives, so "I heard more about Francis Galton than about anyone else. Next to Milton and Darwin he was, I think, my father's supreme example of the ideal man; and as a model he had the further merit of being really alive." Further inspired by a personal meeting with Galton when he accompanied his father on his rounds, Burt obtained Galton's *Inquiries into Human Faculty* from his school library and observed "with a superstitious thrill" that it had been published in 1883, the year of his own birth. From that moment a strong identification with Galton and his values was established.[5]

Like young Francis Galton many years before, Cyril Burt was led by parental pressure to crave competitive academic success. He recalled,

> As ... examinations drew near, my mother regularly related how my father had once won so many prizes at ... school that a cab was necessary to cart them home, and I felt I should be disgraced if I did not bring back at least one prize. To make quite sure, I generally aimed at the Scripture prize, which nobody else seemed to covet.[6]

Burt particularly channeled his energies into acquiring a stunning array of miscellaneous and often recondite information. This enabled him to win several scholarships, and prizes in "out-of-the-way subjects, like Scripture or Music."[7] His penchant for miscellaneous information and "out-of-the-way subjects" continued throughout Burt's life, as his later scientific papers were regularly studded with footnotes and incidental information, lending them an air of great scholarly authority. Sometimes, his opponents occasionally complained, the notes also served to swamp his papers with obscure information, while evading the major points at issue.

After completing preparatory school with a commendable record, Burt studied "the Greats" (classical languages and philosophy) at Oxford, and was graduated respectably if not spectacularly with second-class honors in 1907, at the age of twenty-four. His training had included absolutely no science or mathematics, and only during his final year did he study psychology, or "mental philosophy" as it was then called at Oxford. His teacher for this crucial experience, William McDougall (1871–1938), knew and admired the aging Francis Galton, and was a strong supporter of the eugenics movement. Learning of Burt's long-standing interest in Galton, McDougall put him to work on the standardization of some of Galton's anthropometric tests. While doing so, Burt met another McDougall protégé, the fast-rising Charles Spearman who had just recently introduced the concept of General Intelligence.

Burt felt he had now found his calling, but since Oxford offered no higher degrees in psychology he had to enroll in a year's teacher training course to continue with McDougall. He now immersed himself not only in psychology but also mathematics and statistics, and won a scholarship which enabled him to study psychology in Germany for the following year. Then a new job as lecturer in experimental psychology opened up at the University of Liverpool. With little formal psychological training, but abundant energy, ambition, and the recommendation of McDougall, Burt won the job.

Burt's First Research

His career now launched, Burt quickly became a popular teacher and began conducting his own research. His first published article, the 1909 "Experimental Tests of General Intelligence,"[8] clearly set the direction for much of his later work. As its title suggests, this study drew heavily on Spearman's theory, and Burt publicly acknowledged Spearman's personal assistance.

As in Spearman's original study,* Burt secured teacher ratings of "intelligence" for thirty boys from an ordinary elementary school and thirteen from an exclusive preparatory school, and then intercorrelated these ratings with a series of other tests. These other tests were more numerous than Spearman's, however, and were subclassified as (1) tests of *sensory discrimination;* (2) *motor* tests (for example, dealing cards or sorting letters); or (3) *association* tests (for example, drawing while watching the hand in a mirror, or touching a series of patterned moving dots with a pencil).

As in Spearman's study, all of the tests and ratings intercorrelated positively and arranged themselves in a hierarchy, though a much less perfect one than Spearman's. Thus Burt interpreted his findings as *generally* though not perfectly supportive of Spearman's theory of general intelligence.

*See Chapter 3, page 87 ff., for a description of Spearman's original study.

In one important way, Burt went far beyond Spearman in interpreting his data. Although he had no *direct* way of comparing the "general intelligence" of his two groups of subjects (since both had been ranked on intelligence only within themselves), he noted that the exclusive prep school boys scored higher than their ordinary counterparts on those tests which had achieved the highest average correlations, and were therefore presumably most highly saturated with general intelligence. From this, Burt concluded that the prep school boys *had* more general intelligence, and the question now arose as to why.

Burt's answer might have been lifted directly from Galton's *Hereditary Genius* of forty years before. He did not believe tests such as mirror drawing or dot marking relied much on previous training, and in any event the ordinary schoolboys had come from reasonably adequate environments. Thus Burt argued that environment or training could not have been very important, and the differences must have been innate. This was not surprising to him, considering that the *fathers* of the ordinary schoolboys were typically "local tradesmen," while those of the prep school boys were "in nearly every case . . . men of eminence in the intellectual world, . . . Fellows of the Royal Society, University Professors, College Tutors, and Bishops."[9] The boys had obviously inherited their general intelligence from their parents, Burt believed, and he added that such inheritance occurs "to a degree which few psychologists have hitherto legitimately ventured to maintain."[10]

The hard evidence for this position was slight, of course, since Burt had studied only forty-three individuals, and had never had a direct comparative measure of the general intelligence of his two groups. His faith in the major role of heredity here was in some ways surprising, because in *other* contexts the Burt of this period was quite sensitive to environmental factors. In 1912, for example, he surveyed the literature on sex and race differences in mental capacity. He concluded that sex differences in innate mental constitution were "astonishingly small—far smaller than common belief and common practice would lead us to expect."[11] On race, he observed, "the differences . . . in innate mental capacities between civilised and uncivilised races, though characteristic, appear astonishingly slight. . . . In the case of the individual, we found the influence of heredity large and indisputable; in the case of race, small and controverted."[12] This peculiar predisposition to insist upon the hereditary determination of intellectual differences among *individuals*, while accepting environmentalistic explanations for other important questions, persisted throughout Burt's life.

Clinical Work with the London County Council

Burt was able to put both his hereditarian and his environmentalist inclinations into practice after 1913, when he was hired as Britain's first professional educational psychologist by the London County Council, the agency which ran all of London's publicly funded schools. Here he had responsibility for advising one of the world's largest school systems on practical issues regarding hundreds of thousands of pupils.

Burt's first task was to diagnose and place retarded children, for Britain too had passed universal education laws like those in France which had stimulated Binet and Simon's work. Burt now learned firsthand about Binet testing methods, which he adapted to his own English-speaking population. In the absence of well-standardized tests in English, he took a flexible, "clinical" approach, adapting tests or modifying scores as he thought the particularities of individual cases demanded. In his first year alone, he oversaw the testing of more than two thousand suspected retarded children, more than two-thirds of whom he ultimately diagnosed as normal. Generally, he impressed his employers and co-workers as a sensitive clinician whose recommendations made sense.

After developing a system for diagnosing retardation, Burt became increasingly concerned with two further issues. First was the excessive degree to which he believed the school system was geared to the needs and abilities of the "ordinary" child, a condition which ill-served the very bright as well as the retarded. Burt strongly advocated the testing of children for high as well as for low ability, and the "streaming" of classes according to test results. It was particularly important, he believed, to identify bright children from the working class and educate them commensurately with their abilities. Owing to the hereditary nature of intelligence, these children might be a very small proportion of the total working-class population, but they were many in absolute numbers, and a potentially invaluable social resource to be tapped.

Second, Burt became increasingly interested in juvenile delinquency, which he attributed primarily to environmental causes. From his own childhood background in the London slums, he was sympathetic to the plight of delinquent children. His 1925 book, *The Young Delinquent,* vigorously attacked the then-popular argument that most delinquents were "moral imbeciles," suffering from an innate lack of moral sense in the same way that genuine imbeciles lack innate intelligence: "As in physical disorders, so in moral," he wrote, "contagion is all too often mistaken for heredity."[13] Clearly, Burt was no raving hereditarian as he worked for the London County Council. In general, he served his employer well, and set a reasonable precedent of sensible clinical practice for the generations of professional psychologists who would follow in his footsteps.

During the late 1920s, however, this clinical and practical phase of Burt's career gradually came to an end. He began to teach educational psychology at the London Day Training College for teachers, where he proved an effective lecturer and came to the notice of the British Broadcasting Corporation, which began employing him as a psychological commentator in its radio broadcasts. He also attracted a substantial number of research students, one of whom he married in 1932. That same year brought another important change, as Burt's old mentor Charles Spearman retired from his professorship at University College London, and Burt was appointed his successor in this prestigious post.

University College London

When Burt accepted his new position, he realized that he would have to shift gears somewhat in his work. "I was reminded that the Department of Psychology had always been regarded as a research department," he recalled, so "I had now to deal with general rather than applied psychology."[14] In charting a new course for himself and his new department, Burt remembered that University College London had a long association with the Galtonian approach to psychology. Galton himself had conducted research there, and upon his death endowed the chair which had long been held by his biographer and disciple, Karl Pearson. Spearman's work on General Intelligence had of course been inspired by Galton's writings. Burt, with his own almost reverential attitude toward Galton, and his predilection for at least parts of the hereditarian case, had little hesitation in deciding to maintain the tradition.

Burt now shifted the major focus of his own work to *factor analysis*—the statistical analysis of interrelations among tests which had originated in Spearman's attempts to demonstrate the nature and importance of the g factor. With remarkable ease for a person totally lacking in formal mathematical training, Burt mastered the basic factor analytic techniques and soon began making original contributions of his own. He became particularly influential in showing the importance of *group factors,* midway in generality between the g and s factors which had been primarily emphasized by Spearman, and which were also being highlighted by the work of Wechsler and Thurstone in America.

Burt also used his prominent position to promote some important national social programs. He testified to British government committees that children's intelligence levels were largely fixed by the age of eleven or so, and were accurately measurable by standard tests given at that age. Thus Burt's was one of several influential voices which helped produce the so-called "eleven-plus" examination system in Britain, under which all eleven-year-olds were given a series of academic and intelligence tests, the results of which streamed the top-scoring minority into intellectually demanding "grammar schools," and the majority into the less challenging "modern schools." It was virtually impossible for a child to move from a modern to a grammar school, and grammar school training was required for eventual acceptance into a university. Thus the eleven-plus system steered some poor but high-scoring children toward an academic career that might otherwise have been unavailable to them, but also effectively precluded the very possibility of higher education for *most* children, at a very early age. Burt felt this was proper, given their innately fixed and accurately measured low intelligence levels.

Even as Burt's national reputation and influence were distinctly on the rise, some not-so-happy traits began to emerge in his personality. After working essentially on his own for many years, he now daily had to confront highly ambitious colleagues and graduate students who could be regarded his intellectual equals and "competitors." He did not always behave well in these confrontations, as younger colleagues and brighter students sometimes found him overbearingly insistent on "winning" intellectual arguments with them, even if he had to resort to unscrupulous debating tricks. In a half-humorous reference to his earlier book, some students began calling Burt "The Old Delinquent."

By the late 1930s, subtle indications of more serious misbehavior began to appear. Burt claimed in a footnote to a 1937 article, for example, that he had been the first person to suggest the use of a certain equation for factor analysis, in his first 1909 paper on general intelligence. Spearman, retired but still alert, promptly wrote to Burt reminding him that *he* had originated the equation, and supplied it to Burt in a personal letter dated several months before Burt's paper was published. Burt apologized to Spearman, but this marked the first of an increasingly insistent campaign to "rewrite the history" of factor analysis, exaggerating his own importance in its development and minimizing Spearman's.

Somewhat later Burt asked H. J. Eysenck, one of his best graduate students, to help with an article on factor analysis by calculating the statistics, while Burt wrote the text. Eysenck has reported:

> Burt ... showed me the paper he had written under our joint names, and I thought it was very good. I was rather surprised when it finally appeared in the *British*

Journal of Educational Psychology in 1939 with only my name at the top, and with many changes in the text praising Cyril Burt.[15]

Following Spearman's death in 1945, Burt's campaign of self-aggrandizement intensified. He took great advantage of the fact that he was editor of the *British Journal of Statistical Psychology*, publishing many of his own unrefereed papers there, which inflated his own role in the history of factor analysis and minimized Spearman's. He also filled that journal with articles actually written by himself, but signed with fictitious names—such as a 1954 paean of praise to Cyril Burt by one "Jaques Lafitte," purportedly a French psychologist minutely familiar with the details of Burt's previous work.

A few psychologists apparently had begun by then to suspect Burt's historical fabrications and exaggerations, but no one publicly called him to account. It probably seemed a small matter, as Burt in any case was making positive and legitimate contributions to mathematical psychology and the theory of factor analysis. Besides, Burt's public reputation had continued to grow. In 1946, primarily for his contributions to educational and practical psychology with the London County Council, he had become the first British psychologist ever to be knighted. Thereafter, to attack the work of *Sir* Cyril Burt was to question the integrity of an acclaimed public figure.

Even so, storm clouds began to appear on the horizon. Burt had been understandably upset when much of his accumulated data, stored at University College London during World War II, was destroyed by bombing. His marriage ended acrimoniously, and he became increasingly afflicted with Ménière's disease, a condition of the inner ear which impaired his hearing and sense of balance. When he reached mandatory retirement age in 1950, he quarreled with his colleagues over the choice of his successor, and then made himself so disagreeable to the person chosen that he was completely barred from the Psychology Department. At about the same time, there began to appear some sharp attacks on the eleven-plus examination system, and on intelligence testing in general, which challenged some of Burt's most firmly held beliefs and threatened to undermine his practical achievements. Against this troubled background, Burt embarked on the culminating events of his career—his spectacular separated-twin studies.

Burt's Twin Studies

The stage for these studies had been set by a paper Burt published in 1943, entitled "Ability and Income." In a brief passage there he mentioned that he had previously tested large numbers of London schoolchildren during his tenure with the County Council, including many pairs of twins. He reported an IQ correlation of .86 for sixty-two pairs of *un*separated MZ twins, and added: "in the few cases (15 in number) where the 'identical' twins had been reared separately the correlation was .77."[16] Burt provided no details about the circumstances of the twins' separations, or indeed even about their ages, sex, or the specific tests he had used. In fact, this short passage has been characterized by one of Burt's former students as a "throw-away line," not directly related to the main subject of Burt's paper, but simply inserted to help make the general point that intelligence is highly heritable.

One heard no more about these twins until 1955, when the retired Burt felt compelled to respond to some recent attacks on the eleven-plus examination system, and the intelligence tests which it used. Particularly galling to him were works by Brian Simon, a Marxist lecturer on education at the University of Leicester, and Alice Heim, a psychologist at Cambridge University.[17] Simon, a former schoolteacher, deplored the academic demoralization which occurred because so many British children were effectively excluded from meaningful higher education so young, on the basis of intelligence tests which he felt were of doubtful validity as long-term predictors of academic ability. He advocated a new system of "comprehensive schools," which all children would attend together regardless of their early academic records. Heim criticized Spearman's theory of General Intelligence, was skeptical about the genetic implications of twin studies, and championed Binet's pragmatic and non–theory-laden approach to measuring intelligence.

To answer these and some other critics, Burt wrote a paper entitled "The Evidence for the Concept of Intelligence." Complaining that "few of the critics show a clear or correct understanding of what the term [intelligence] really designates or of the reasons that have led to its introduction,"[18] Burt attempted to set them right by showing that "intelligence" is highly heritable and follows ordinary genetic laws. This being the case, he assured his readers that intelligence must be something real and accurately measurable.

In making this case, Burt referred to his 1943 paper, and added that a "Miss Conway" had collected some of the twin data reported there and had computed the correlations. Since then, she had continued to be busy:

> Thanks to numerous correspondents, she has been able to increase the number of cases, particularly for the small but crucial groups of monozygotic twins reared together or apart. The total numbers now amount to . . . 83 monozygotic or one-egg twins reared together, and 21 reared apart.[19]

Burt reported that the crucial twenty-one pairs showed a correlation of .771 for a "Group Test" of intelligence, .843 for "Individual Tests," and a rousing .876 for "Final Assessments." None of these tests was described further, though "Final Assessments" evidently referred to the sorts of clinical judgments Burt had commonly made with the London County Council, when raw test scores had been adjusted upward or downward according to his knowledge of the special circumstances of each case.

Two years later, Burt was honored by an invitation to deliver the Walter Van Dyke Bingham Memorial Lecture, and elected to speak on "The Inheritance of Mental Ability." Here he discussed the alleged scarcity of separated twins, and argued that such cases are really much commoner than most investigators think. Single mothers of twins quite often feel unable to rear two infants at once, he argued, and so keep one twin themselves while putting the other up for adoption:

> Owing to the strong popular prejudice against separating twins, [the mother] not unnaturally tries, as a rule, to keep these arrangements secret. But patient and tactful inquiries show that cases of twins brought up in different environments almost from birth are much commoner than is usually believed. We have now collected over 30 such cases.[20]

Burt reported IQ correlations for this recently enlarged sample of separated twins of .771, .843, and .876 for Group Tests, Individual Tests, and Final Assessments, respectively.

In 1958, "J. Conway" herself published a paper in Burt's *British Journal of Statistical Psychology*, reporting that "our collection [of separated twins] has been still further enlarged," and now included forty-two pairs. Conway added that many of these twins had been unusually well separated:

> Among our later cases most were discovered through personal contacts; and, as a result, many of them came of educated parents, usually school teachers or members of a university staff: when the pair was separated, one twin generally remained with the mother and shared her cultural environment, while the other was boarded out, usually with persons of much lower intellectual status.[21]

As an example, Conway cited "George" and "Llewellen," sons of an Oxford don who died just before their birth. George, reared by the mother, had a spectacular academic career and won high honors in modern languages. Llewellen, adopted by an elderly farming couple in North Wales and given little formal education, grew up to be a successful farmer. Llewellen's IQ was tested at 137, George's at 136. For the whole sample of separated twins, Group Tests reportedly correlated .778, Individual Tests .846, and Final Assessments .881.

In the early 1960s, Burt once again found his cherished beliefs under attack, most notably by the explicitly left-wing psychologist John McLeish in his book *The Science of Behaviour*. Here McLeish attacked the whole Spearman tradition of regarding intelligence as a general, unitary, and quantifiable entity, and also emphasized the *environmentalist* implications of the Newman-Freeman-Holzinger twin study. McLeish also criticized Burt himself, describing Burt's admission that he sometimes "adjusted" tests scores by clinical intuition while assessing innate intelligence as scientifically "shocking."[22] Burt privately complained that this book was "libellous," and wrote McLeish a long and haranguing letter of complaint.[23] More deviously, he published a long, pickily critical review in his statistical journal, but under the pseudonym "M. Howard" rather than his own name.[24]

Burt's most important response to McLeish and other environmentalist critics, however, was his 1966 paper, "The Genetic Determination of Differences in Intelligence: A Study of Monozygotic Twins Reared Together and Apart." Here he reported that his separated-twin sample had now increased to fifty-three pairs, becoming the largest in the literature. Of greater scientific importance, he now claimed to have evidence proving that his twins had been truly separated and randomly placed in adoptive homes. While acknowledging the sad fact that *other* investigators had had difficulty finding truly "separated" cases, Burt claimed that he and his colleagues, with privileged access to an unusually large number of twins, had been able to be more discriminating: "We included in our group . . . no cases in which both had been brought up by a relative, except for five in which one relative lived in a town and the other in the country."[25] Burt went on to present a table rating the "Occupational Categories" of the 106 twins' adoptive parents on a scale from 1 ("Higher Professional, etc.") through 6 ("Unskilled"). The correlation between the adoptive parents' occupations for the twin pairs, worked out from this table, is an astoundingly low $-.03$. Thus the reported Burt-Conway sample was not only the largest in the literature, but it also almost perfectly met the most important requirement for the heritability tests—the randomness of the adoptive placements. The IQ correlations Burt gave for this nearly ideal sample were .771 (Group Tests), .863 (Individual Tests), and .874 (Final Assessments).

Other Kinship Correlations

Throughout the period when Burt's twin studies were appearing, he also reported important IQ correlations for other kinship relations (parent-child, grandparent-grandchild, uncle-nephew, etc.), derived from his supposedly unparalleled data base in the London school system. In papers that were models of mathematical and statistical sophistication, and that legitimately advanced the *theory* of behavior genetics, Burt showed how these correlations could be used to estimate IQ heritability after allowing for such genetic complications as dominance, assortative mating, and the like. In the 1966 paper he gave correlations for many different kinship pairings, including some such as uncle-nephew which had never been reported by any other investigator. With uncanny accuracy, all of these correlations led to IQ heritability estimates of almost exactly .80 when fitted into Burt's elegant theoretical model. In short, the separated-twin data were perfectly corroborated.

Up until 1966, Burt's separated-twin data had not aroused inordinate attention. Even though his correlations were the highest on record, they were not *that much* higher than those from other studies. And like those from other studies, they could be interpreted as having been inflated by selective placement and the other inherent problems of twin research. When Burt reported nonselective placement for his twins in 1966, however, the situation changed entirely. No one else had been able to do that, so his figures took on a new significance. Moreover, they suggested a rather radical revision of the consensus which had developed regarding the relative importance of nature and nurture, with nature now seeming *many times* more powerful than nurture.

By now, a few other workers in the field began to entertain some *private* doubts about certain aspects of Burt's studies. He had never presented detailed case studies of his subjects, as other investigators such as Newman, Freeman, and Holzinger had.

184 THE INTELLIGENCE MEN

"George and Llewellen" were the only twin pair Burt or Conway ever described specifically; for all others, basic information regarding age, sex, or specific IQ scores was completely lacking. When other psychologists wrote to Burt asking for his raw data, they were usually politely but effectively put off with references to obscure documents from the 1910s and 1920s, or excuses regarding the unavailability or uncodability of data. Finally, when the American sociologist Christopher Jencks requested simply a list of the fifty-three pairs of IQ scores, and the occupational ratings for the adoptive parents, Burt provided this bare-bones information—but only after a delay of several weeks. This represented the maximum detail with which he ever described his basic data.

At this point, a few British psychologists evidently realized that Burt had sometimes used fictitious authors' names for his own papers; "Jaques Lafitte" had seemed an improbable personage to some, and "J. Conway" was totally unknown to psychologists at University College London, the institutional affiliation given for her in her article. This did not seem a *major* sin, however, and since those investigators who had had difficulty obtaining raw data had not communicated among themselves to spread suspicion, no one during Burt's lifetime publicly voiced serious question about the legitimacy of his work. Thus when he died in 1971, a few private questions were being asked, but Sir Cyril Burt was still one of the most highly respected psychologists in the world.

Among the most eloquent of eulogists following Burt's death was the prominent American educational psychologist Arthur Jensen. Jensen had been justifiably impressed by Burt's theoretical and statistical erudition, and had also taken Burt's empirical estimate of 80 percent IQ heritability at face value. Considering that to be the best available estimate, Jensen had recently brought a storm of controversy about himself, by drawing some of its apparent logical implications for social and racial policy. Confident of Burt's integrity as a man and as a scientist, and of the great if unpopular importance of his work, Jensen wrote an obituary which described Burt as "a born nobleman" whose "larger, more representative samples than any other investigator in the field has ever assembled" assured him a place in the history of science.[26]

Soon enough, Jensen would find reason to change his opinion about Burt, though not necessarily about the larger issue of IQ heritability. Before returning to the spectacular conclusion and aftermath of the Burt case, however, we shall turn to Jensen's own story, and the factors which made *him* such a central figure in the IQ controversy.

ARTHUR JENSEN AND THE "JENSENISM" CONTROVERSY

The son of a lumber and building supplies dealer, Arthur Jensen was born in 1923 in San Diego, California. As a youth he enjoyed practicing magic and "mind-reading" tricks on his friends, though his major interests were musical rather than

Arthur Jensen (b. 1923) *(Institute of Human Learning, University of California)*

psychological. An excellent clarinetist, he played with the San Diego Symphony at seventeen and nurtured early ambitions of becoming a symphony orchestra conductor. Also while a teenager he developed "an overwhelming fascination with Mahatma Gandhi," and a firm conviction that "one should use his life in ways relevant to serving his fellow man."[27]

At the University of California in Berkeley, psychology supplanted music as Jensen's major passion, though he still enjoys reading musicians' biographies, and conducting recorded symphonies at his home with a chopstick as baton. His altruistic inclinations pointed him toward a career in applied psychology, so Jensen did some social welfare casework for a few years after earning his B.A., and then entered the clinical psychology program at Columbia University Teachers College in 1952. There he was trained in the psychoanalytic tradition, under the able supervision of the noted personality researcher Percival Symonds (1893–1960). Jensen's Ph.D. thesis and earliest few publications dealt with psychoanalytic topics such as projective tests and the expression of aggression in fantasy and real life behavior. More practical psychodynamic training was provided during a year's clinical internship at Baltimore's Psychiatric Institute, before Jensen received his Ph.D. in 1956.

But while Jensen became adept at the psychodynamic techniques he was exposed to, and while he always retained respect and affection for Symonds, he gradually began to have doubts about what he was doing. As he wrote in his autobiography:

> The usual diagnostic procedures and techniques, as well as the psychological theories which were the basis for the "dynamic" interpretations in our clinical reports, seemed to me much too pat, speculative, and inadequate for understanding the problems of the patients we were trying to help. . . . It all came more and more to seem to me to be a kind of literary, rather than scientific, activity.[28]

A turning point came during Jensen's final student year when he read *The Scientific Study of Personality* by H. J. Eysenck, Burt's former student and by then a well-known British psychologist in his own right. Already on his way to becoming one of psychology's most prolific, iconoclastic, and controversial figures, Eysenck had written papers documenting the apparent ineffectiveness of psychoanalytically oriented psychotherapies, and had attacked psychoanalysis in his popular book *Uses and Abuses of Psychology*. Now advocating a quantitative and experimental approach to personality measurement which relied heavily on the factor analysis of test scores, Eysenck was generally contemptuous of "unscientific" psychoanalytic approaches, and had some critical comments to make about Symonds's work in *The Scientific Study of Personality*. Indeed, Jensen originally read the book because Symonds had asked him how he might respond to these criticisms. Ironically, Jensen found himself won over as "the quantitative and experimental approach to personality research espoused by Eysenck had much greater appeal to me, and seemed a much sounder basis for investigating human behavior than the more literary and speculative psychoanalytic variety."[29] Jensen went on to read Eysenck's other works, and was so impressed that he applied to work in the Englishman's laboratory. He was accepted, and immediately after receiving his Ph.D. went to London on a two-year postdoctoral fellowship.

Once there, Jensen became increasingly convinced that real progress in personality research would have to await the solution of certain "basic" problems in human learning theory. Accordingly, he began an extensive program to study the so-called *serial position effect*, which occurs when subjects try to memorize lists of random stimuli such as words, letters, numbers, or nonsense syllables. Almost always, subjects learn the items from the middle parts of the lists last. Though apparently simple, this situation posed a fundamental learning problem and provided several interesting variables for experimental manipulation, such as the length and nature of the lists to be learned, and individual differences among the subjects. Jensen became a recognized expert on this topic, publishing more than a dozen articles on it within a few years.

This early work was satisfying but distinctly noncontroversial, and Jensen has since observed that "it is hard to think of any conceivable practical importance of most of the research problems arising from serial rote learning."[30] Nevertheless, it is worth noting that the work was begun under the auspices of Eysenck, an outspoken individual who never shunned controversy or the opportunity to apply his psychological theories to large social issues. Over the years Eysenck has been very much a newsmaker in Britain, expressing controversial views about not only psychoanalysis, but also such diverse topics as astrology or the link between cigarette smoking and cancer. Further, he has been an outspoken hereditarian in the IQ controversy. As a psychologist willing and even eager to brave public notoriety, Eysenck may have served as something of a role model for Jensen. In any case, Jensen's studies of serial learning began to shade into increasingly "relevant" and controversial areas following his return to the United States in 1958.

Jensen encountered one other important influence during his stay in London, though he did not immediately appreciate its significance when it occurred. In May of 1957 he went to hear Cyril Burt deliver his Bingham Memorial Lecture on the inheritance of mental ability. This was not because of any prior interest in the subject, but because "Burt . . . was England's greatest and foremost psychologist, and I merely wanted to see him in person." At this lecture, of course, Jensen learned not only about Burt-Conway's growing sample of separated twins, but also about some of Burt's important theoretical innovations in the field of behavior genetics. Like most of the audience Jensen was impressed, and concluded, "It was probably the best lecture I have ever heard. . . . But at the time, the message of Burt's lecture met no immediate need in my thinking or research and was merely stored away in my memory for future reference."[31]

The "future reference" occurred well after Jensen had assumed a teaching position at his alma mater, the University of California at Berkeley, in 1958. There, his work on serial position learning gradually came to concentrate on *individual differences:* that is, on questions such as "If John and Bill can both regularly recall 8 digits after presentation, why is it that after a 10 seconds delay John can recall 7 and Bill only 6 digits?" or "Do some persons have a better memory in the auditory than in the visual modality, and vice versa?"[32]

Jensen's expertise in testing for individual differences of this type led to his being consulted in the early 1960s by a graduate student who had been working part-time as a school psychologist. The student posed a research problem concerning retarded children, which marked a turning point in Jensen's career.

"Direct Learning" in the Retarded

While working with retarded children, Jensen's student had observed that many of the children who came from minority groups seemed much more alert and less "retarded" in general demeanor than their white, middle-class counterparts, when outside the classroom situation. He wondered if Jensen knew of a good "culture-free" test which might be used to check this impression. Jensen went to see for himself, and agreed that the minority-group children "appeared much brighter socially and on the playground, often being quite indistinguishable in every way from children of normal intelligence, except in their scholastic performance and in their performance on a variety of standard IQ tests."[33] In contrast, the white middle-class retarded children seemed to be more generally retarded in *all* of their behavior.

The short-term memory tests that Jensen had already developed required a minimum of previous experience, and seemed reasonable candidates for the culture-fair measures his student had sought. And, in fact, retarded children of black or Chicano background turned out to perform significantly better on these tests than did their white, middle-class schoolmates. At first, Jensen thought that these rather simple tests of what he called "Direct Learning" might just prove to be the long-sought, culture-fair tests of intelligence.

He changed his mind, however, after obtaining Direct Learning scores for minority and white children from the *normal* as well as the retarded school population. With this full range of subjects, Jensen found that the correlation between Direct

Learning and standard IQ measures varied with the socioeconomic status (SES) of his subjects. For middle and high SES children, the correlations were in the fairly hefty .50 to .70 range, indicating that a high score on Direct Learning was a reasonably good predictor of IQ, and vice versa. For low SES (and predominantly minority group) children, however, the correlations were only between .10 and .40. This helped account for Jensen's earlier findings with the retarded minority children: their low IQ scores, which had been largely responsible for their diagnosis as retarded, were not highly correlated with their Direct Learning skills; hence most of them showed Direct Learning scores considerably higher than their IQs. In the higher ranges of IQ, the reverse was true: high IQ but low SES children scored relatively much *worse* on the Direct Learning tasks. Thus the higher Direct Learning scores for retarded minority-group members were counterbalanced by lower scores for the academically proficient. At the low end of the IQ scale, Direct Learning tests favored low SES subjects, but at the high end they penalized them.

Trying to make theoretical sense out of these puzzling findings, Jensen hypothesized that there are two basically distinct "levels" of intelligence. "Level I," measured by the likes of his Direct Learning tasks, he presumed to involve the simple input, storage, and output of untransformed information, as in rote memorization and recall. "Level II," on the other hand, he supposed to involve some sort of internal transformation or active processing of the stimulus input, before a response is provided. The best tests of Level II, Jensen believed, were those subtests from intelligence scales requiring reasoning, abstraction, or the like—precisely those tests which factor analytic studies had shown to be most heavily loaded with Spearman's *g*.

Furthermore, Jensen came to believe that Level II intelligence primarily determines one's success in school, particularly in the later stages. Level I might be useful in the early stages, and perhaps be necessary in some degree before Level II can develop, but by itself it is insufficient for academic success. Thus Jensen no longer believed that the minority children with whom he had begun his investigations had really been "unfairly" diagnosed;

he now believed that most of them had genuinely lacked the Level II ability necessary for success in the standard school curriculum. But these children also often possessed some Level I strengths which gave their nonacademic demeanor a "brighter" quality than that of the middle-class retarded children, who were deficient in both levels.

Thus Jensen came away from his research convinced that standard IQ tests, particularly those most heavily loaded with g, are in fact reasonably good indicators of intelligence and scholastic aptitude, even for minority-group members so long as they are not handicapped by obvious language problems, or the like. He now became interested in the question of *why* minority-group members tended to achieve lower average IQ scores than white children, since their deficit apparently could not be accounted for just by the "culture unfairness" of the tests. As he investigated the literature on the psychology of the culturally disadvantaged, Jensen became increasingly impressed by the potential importance of genetic factors.

The Genetics of Racial Differences

The mid-1960s, when Jensen began this next phase of his work, were years of great social ferment in the United States. Ever since racial segregation in schools had been declared unconstitutional by the U.S. Supreme Court in 1954, American blacks had been pressing increasingly for an end to the legal and social discrimination they all too regularly faced. Under dynamic leaders such as Martin Luther King Jr. (1929–1968), they campaigned for integration of public lunch counters and buses as well as schools, and for the repeal of unfair voting registration laws which made it impossible for them to vote in many states. These civil rights campaigns met much and violent opposition, particularly in the South, but also piqued the conscience of much of the country. The federal government, particularly under President Lyndon B. Johnson in the mid-1960s, responded with a spate of programs and legislation intended to produce a greater measure of social justice.

Part of this response was the so-called "War on Poverty," in which large grants were allocated to programs intended to relieve the causes of poverty, which was particularly rampant in the black population. Inadequate education was naturally assumed to be one major cause of poverty, a problem which was compounded because many black children apparently lacked sufficient aptitude (reflected by low IQ scores, among other things) to succeed in school even if decent education were made available to them. Many psychologists, led by J. McVicker Hunt of the University of Illinois, believed that the intellectual deficit was caused by the impoverished and stultifying early environments in which so many black children were reared. Accordingly, many of the War on Poverty funds were devoted to projects like "Operation Head Start," whose purpose was to provide cultural enrichment experiences for very young children of the poor—who were also largely black.

When Jensen began to survey the literature on the psychology of the culturally disadvantaged, early reports on projects like Operation Head Start were just becoming available. As he read these, Jensen thought he detected a strong *dis*inclination by their authors to consider the accumulated evidence pointing to a possible *genetic* role in the problem:

> In the few instances where genetics was mentioned, it was usually to dismiss the issue as outmoded, irrelevant, or unimportant, or to denigrate the genetic study of human differences and to proclaim the all-importance of the social and cultural environment. . . . So strongly expressed was this bias in some cases, and so inadequately buttressed by evidence, that I began to surmise that the topic of genetics was ignored more often because of the author's social philosophy than because the importance of genetic factors in human differences had been scientifically disproved.[34]

In retrospect, Burt's Bingham Lecture seemed highly relevant, so Jensen read its published version and then Burt's other articles, until "soon I found myself reviewing the total world literature on the genetics of abilities."[35] He was particularly impressed by Burt's mathematical theorizing, as well as by his findings suggesting 80 percent heritability for intelligence within the English population. Already knowledgeable in basic statistics, Jensen now mastered the mathematical techniques for estimating IQ heritability from different kinds of kinship correlations, and published some original contributions of his own to this field in 1967 and 1968.

In those same years he began giving talks expressing his growing conviction that genetic factors were too often shoved beneath the rug by educational theorists:

> I voiced the opinion that failure to give due weight to the biological basis of individual and group differences in educationally relevant traits . . . may hinder efforts to discover optimal instructional procedures suited to a wide range and diversity of abilities. Inappropriate educational procedures, often based on the notion that all children learn in essentially the same way except for easily changed environmental influences, can alienate many children from ever entering *any* path of educational fulfillment.[36]

Citing his own work on Levels I and II of intelligence, Jensen suggested that one possible educational improvement might be the structuring of remedial programs to emphasize minority children's rote learning and memory capacities, presumably less innately impaired than their Level II abilities.

Jensen's talks interested the editors of the *Harvard Educational Review (HER)*, a well-regarded education journal which, like a law review, was put out by graduate students at Harvard. The student editors invited Jensen to write a long article on the question "How much can we boost IQ and scholastic achievement?" Their letter of invitation to him proposed that his article would be "a lead piece in a discussion," to be followed by commentaries from other experts "with diverse perspectives on the nature of intelligence." Jensen was specifically requested to review the concept of intelligence and the controversies surrounding it, and to include "arguments against the extreme environmentalist position [and] a clear statement of your position on social class and racial differences in intelligence."[37]

Jensen gladly accepted this opportunity to set right what he perceived as an imbalance in the literature, and submitted a two-hundred-page typescript in November of 1968. This was hurried to press as the only article in the Winter 1969 issue of *HER*, the longest single piece it had ever published. Because of deadline pressures the solicited commentaries, and a final rejoinder by Jensen, had to be postponed until the next issue. Almost immediately, the article set off a furor that apparently had the young editors wishing they had handled the matter differently, and led to some controversial reactions on their part. Before returning to these more emotional aspects of the "Jensenism" issue, however, we must summarize the contents of the incendiary article itself.

Jensen's 1969 Article

"How Much Can We Boost IQ and Scholastic Achievement?" lost little time in proffering an answer to its title's question, for its first sentence read: "Compensatory education has been tried and apparently it has failed."[38] The following literature review indicated that the large programs designed to increase the IQs and scholastic aptitudes of culturally deprived children had produced marginal gains at best, and no improvement at all at worst. To suggest reasons for these apparent failures, Jensen next discussed the nature of "intelligence" itself.

Here he revealed himself as a strong defender of Spearman's *g*, which he called "the nuclear operational definition of intelligence, . . . [which] has stood like a Rock of Gibraltar in psychometrics, defying any attempt to construct a test of complex problem solving which excludes it."[39] Thus Jensen interpreted "intelligence" as a distinct unitary entity, presumably determined by some specific set of neurological functions, and most clearly measured by tests heavily loaded with *g*.

Jensen went on to chide writers who have argued that human intelligence is extremely plastic. Though the tone of most of his article was scholarly and restrained, here his language took on a certain edge:

> The notion of "fixed intelligence" has assumed the status of a popular cliché among many speakers and writers on intelligence, . . . who state, often with an evident sense of virtue and relief, that modern psychology has overthrown the "belief in fixed intelligence." . . . When we look behind the rather misleading term "fixed intelligence," what we find are principally [issues] calling for empirical study rather than moral philosophizing. . . . The first issue concerns the genetic basis of individual differences in intelligence.[40]

Turning to this crucial genetic issue, Jensen quoted with disapproval writers who assert that "there is no evidence that nature is more important than nurture," or that "we can attribute no particular portion of intelligence to heredity and no particular portion to environment." In Jensen's view, such statements represented an "ostrich-like denial of biological factors in individual differences, and [a] slighting of the role of genetics in the study of intelligence [which] can only hinder investigation and understanding."[41] In fact, Jensen argued, there exists substantial evidence pointing to the very much greater importance of nature than of nurture.

Jensen cited many different investigators in support of his case, but his greatest approbation was reserved for Cyril Burt as "probably the most distinguished exponent of the application of [quantitative genetic] methods to the study of intelligence." Jensen added that Burt's writings "are a 'must' for students of individual differences," providing "the most satisfactory attempt to estimate the separate [hereditary and environmental] variance components [of IQ]."[42] Taking several studies into consideration, but weighing Burt's more heavily than the others, Jensen concluded that IQ heritability ranged from .70 to .90, and centered around .80 for the various populations which had been studied. Thus the best evidence pointed to a hereditary factor far more important than the environment. Here was the primary hard fact which the environmentalist "moral philosophers" constantly ignored or belittled, in their "ostrich-like" way.

Had Jensen concluded his argument here, even its jibes would have aroused little controversy outside the academic circles. He went on, however, to consider the implications of high IQ heritability for the interpretation of the observed *racial* differences in IQ levels. Ever since the army studies of World War I, American blacks had been observed to get lower average scores than whites on intelligence tests—approximately 15 points lower on newer tests such as the Wechsler scales. Most investigators, including Jensen, noted the substantial overlap between the white and black populations, and emphasized that the *statistical* difference does not justify any predictions about *individuals*, based on race alone. Jensen also agreed that the long history of social and economic discrimination against American blacks played an important role in producing their lower average IQ scores. But Jensen also asked whether the accumulated findings "raise any question as to the plausibility of theories that postulate *exclusively* environmental factors as sufficient causes for the observed differences [emphasis added]."[43] And here, whether he intended to or not, he opened Pandora's box.

Jensen admitted that the evidence bearing on this difficult question was incomplete, and that all extant IQ heritability studies had been conducted on non-black populations. Nevertheless, the apparently high heritability found for white groups, and a few studies which suggested that some part of the IQ deficit remained even in middle- and upper-class black populations, led Jensen to make the following tentative statement:

> We are left with various lines of evidence, no one of which is definitive alone, but which, viewed all together, make it a not unreasonable hypothesis that genetic factors are strongly implicated in the average Negro-white intelligence difference. The preponderance of the evidence is, in my opinion, less consistent with a strictly

environmental hypothesis than with a genetic hypothesis, which, of course, does not exclude the influence
of environment or its interaction with genetic factors.[44]

In essence, Jensen's article argued that compensatory education programs had failed largely because they could not offset
the enormously important genetic causes of low intelligence
among poor people. Further, one could not and ought not rule
out the possibility that part of the genetic handicap which prevented success for many of the targeted black children was part
of their racial heritage.

In general, Jensen's tone was tentative and scholarly, and he
did not espouse policies that were overtly racist or contrary to
the rights of individual blacks. He argued, with evident sincerity,
that many blacks would be helped more in the long run by accurate and objective appraisals of their true mental potential than
by optimistic wishes.

Nevertheless, Jensen had touched on an explosive issue, and
his occasional jibing references to the environmentalistic "moral
philosophers" echoed Francis Galton's contemptuous dismissal
of *his* supposedly tenderminded opposition exactly a century
before. And just as environmentalists like Mill had been ready
to take vigorous moral exception to statements like Galton's, so
were their latter-day counterparts quick to do battle with Jensen.
Not all of their initial reactions were as reasoned as Mill's, however, and the early furor they aroused about "Jensenism" did
not entirely cast credit on their case.

The "Jensenism" Controversy

Jensen's article aroused immediate, emotional
reactions in both lay and professional groups. Student activism
was near its apex in the United States in 1969, and Harvard's
black and liberal student groups lost no time in attacking the
Harvard Educational Review's editors for publishing a "racist" article.
The student editors apparently panicked, and issued a statement to the press denying that they had ever asked Jensen to
discuss the racial issue, and blaming Jensen for releasing his arti-

cle to the public prematurely. Only after Jensen sent the Harvard newspaper a copy of his original invitation from the editors, which had explicitly requested "a clear statement of your position on social class and racial differences in intelligence," did he receive a private apology from an *HER* editor. Even so, Jensen complained that the *HER* did nothing publicly to counteract the false impression created by their original statement to the press.[45]

The *HER* editors also withdrew their Winter issue from public sale altogether, and made the extraordinary decision to distribute Jensen's article further *only* in the spring when it could be bound together with their collection of solicited rebuttals and counterarguments. Even Jensen's personal order for reprints of his own article went unfilled until the rebuttals were published, and Jensen himself was required to purchase the rebuttals along with his article.

When the long-awaited rebuttals finally appeared, they were generally temperate in tone, and not overly damaging to Jensen's case. They noted some minor inconsistencies in his presentation, and offered some differing interpretations of the literature. The geneticist James Crow, for example, praised Jensen's understanding of research methods and his diligence in tracking down sources, but concluded: "I have somewhat less confidence than [Jensen] in the quantitative validity of his methods. . . . I don't mean by this that I would reach opposite conclusions; I am simply more agnostic."[46] Even J. McV. Hunt, the most eminent of the advocates of compensatory education who had been chided by Jensen, admitted that "on the whole, Jensen's criticism comes in a constructive spirit." Hunt found "many points in his paper with which I agree heartily," though he complained that Jensen held a too limited conception of the learning process, overlooked cultural factors, and had too hastily accepted the failure of compensatory education on the basis of a few imperfect experiments.[47] No critic questioned the basic legitimacy of the studies on which Jensen had based his genetic case, and he could say in his final rejoinder, with only slight exaggeration, "Seldom in my experience of reading the psychological literature have I seen the discussants of a supposedly 'controversial' article . . . so much in agreement with all the main points of the article they were asked especially to criticize."[48]

Not all critics, however, responded with the restraint of Jensen's *HER* commentators. The leadership of the Society for the Psychological Study of Social Issues (spssi), a division of the American Psychological Association, declared Jensen's views "unwarranted by the present state of scientific knowledge," and urged members to write their local newspapers in opposition. Jensen complained that they did not recommend that their members actually *read* his article, however, and that they directed some of their fire against points which he had never even tried to make. Another group calling itself "Psychologists for Social Action" circulated a petition demanding Jensen's summary expulsion from, or at least censure by, the American Psychological Association. The American Anthropological Association conducted a "panel discussion" which unanimously and vigorously condemned Jensen and his views, without inviting him or anyone else sympathetic to the hereditarian argument to offer a defense.[49]

In general, many of these supposedly "expert" and "professional" reactions showed signs of panic, generated more heat than light, and helped fuel an even more irrational and violent response among lay groups. The term "Jensenism" rapidly became a popular new term of opprobrium synonymous with "racism." Angry student groups began disrupting Jensen's speeches and classes, and for a time his seminars had to be held in secret locations. Signs saying "Jensen Must Perish" and "Kill Jensen" appeared on campus walls, and Jensen received enough written and telephoned threats of violence that the University of California had to hire personal bodyguards for him.

In this superheated atmosphere, those who spoke out in favor of Jensen's argument were also harassed and threatened. In the case of William Shockley, the Stanford University physicist who had won the Nobel Prize for his work on inventing the transistor, this was perhaps unsurprising. Though Shockley's professional background lay outside genetics, he had long and loudly proclaimed the genetic inferiority of black Americans, and endorsed eugenic measures to curtail their breeding. When he gladly seized upon Jensen's article as helping to prove his case—a contention that went well beyond anything Jensen himself said or believed—he was often confronted with hostile demonstrations.

A similar fate awaited psychologists who tried to support all or parts of Jensen's case more moderately. When Jensen's old mentor Eysenck spoke out on his behalf in England, he was physically assaulted by his lecture audience. Harvard's Richard Herrnstein endorsed Jensen's genetic though not his racial hypotheses in his *Atlantic Monthly* article on IQ, and suffered the mistreatment described in the Preface to this book.

Throughout these difficult times, Jensen conducted himself remarkably calmly, and tried patiently to correct the patent errors and misperceptions that marked so much of the reaction against him and his supporters. The more reasoned objections to his view, such as those solicited by the *HER,* had perhaps dented but certainly not demolished his hypotheses; and the violent excesses of his more febrile opponents undoubtedly gained him sympathy in the long run. Indeed, as the initial hysteria faded, Jensen seemed to have revived Francis Galton's case, lending it not only a new visibility but scientific respectability as well. There did in fact seem to be plausible evidence for regarding heredity as much more important than environment in producing intellectual differences, and the hypothesis of genetic causes for racial differences thus seemed at least an open question.

In 1972, however, the nature-nurture argument took another surprising and dramatic turn, as a completely new and unexpected figure entered the fray. The Princeton psychologist Leon Kamin had made his professional reputation by studying learning in animals, but had been drawn into a reading of the major IQ literature almost by chance. With a fresh eye, he found things that had previously gone unnoticed or unmentioned by experts in the field, whether of environmentalist or hereditarian orientation. When he revealed them, Kamin stood the IQ testing world on its head.

Though new to IQ testing per se in 1972, Kamin had been in

a way prepared to play his new role by his earlier life and experience, to which we turn now.

LEON KAMIN AND THE NEW CASE FOR ENVIRONMENT

Leon Kamin was born on December 29, 1927, the son of a Polish rabbi who had immigrated to the small Massachusetts city of Taunton some time before the restrictive immigration laws of 1924. Today, Kamin believes that the experience of growing up Jewish in a small and predominantly Christian town strongly sensitized him to the power of the social environment in shaping personality.[50]

Kamin's family highly valued reading and scholarship, and he grew up always "knowing" somehow that he would go to college and become a professor some day. As a boy, he particularly loved arithmetic and "playing with numbers." He became a "lightning calculator," able to solve complicated problems in his head—not as quickly as those professional calculating prodigies whom Binet had studied, perhaps, but very impressively nonetheless.

The family moved to Boston for Kamin's high school years, a period greatly saddened by the death of his father. Considerably upset and wanting a change from high school, he began applying to Boston area colleges at the age of 15, as was possible during World War II because many schools were then accepting more classes, at earlier ages than usual. An excellent student, Kamin was accepted by Harvard as a sixteen-year-old freshman in June of 1944.

Shortly before entering Harvard, Kamin had read a novel about a confused young man who ultimately "found himself" and settled his life by becoming a diplomat. Identifying with this fictional hero, and hoping a similar solution might work for himself, Kamin decided to major in government. "Insane as it sounds," this vigorous controversialist now relates with amusement, "when I went to college at age sixteen I wanted to be a diplomat."

During his freshman year, however, Kamin found himself being bored by long Victorian treatises on government, while a room-

Leon Kamin (b. 1927) *(Stephen Cassell)*

mate kept bringing home fascinating case histories from his psychology course. One case in particular described a young college student with problems and concerns similar to Kamin's own, and he felt increasingly impelled to change his major. Thus he was led to psychology at Harvard by "a fascination with problems in clinical psychology, and of course speculation about my own normality or abnormality, as the case may be."

Kamin's undergraduate academic record was uneven. After eighteen months in the army following his sophomore year, he returned to earn an A+ average as a junior. The senior year was altogether different, however, as Kamin found himself bored and repelled by academic psychology. Lectures on topics such as the learning of nonsense syllables seemed as far removed from real life as anything could be, and Kamin's marks reflected his lack of interest.

By now, Kamin was in fact already embarked on a course that would make him a figure in national controversy for the first time. Coincident with his disdain for academic psychology, he had developed "a deep commitment to reforming the world" through political activism. Impressed by some older and seemingly more politically sophisticated Harvard students he knew, Kamin had joined the Communist party. Following his graduation from Harvard he became the New England editor of the party's weekly newspaper. In the rising anti-Communist atmosphere of the times in America, this was a dangerous course to follow.

To complicate matters further, Kamin's enthusiasm for the party soon diminished. As he developed progressive doubts about many of the party's positions, his earlier goals of reforming the world seemed futile, and the academic life began to seem attractive once again. He resigned from both his job and the Communist party in 1950, and applied to Harvard's Ph.D. program in Psychology and Social Relations. He was relieved when the admissions interviewer seemed more concerned with his spotty undergraduate record than with his recent occupational past, but Kamin accurately sensed that his political record would eventually rise to haunt him.

Because of his undergraduate academic inconsistency, Kamin was not admitted directly into the Ph.D. program, but was invited to serve as a volunteer research assistant for the summer of 1950. If all went well, he would be officially admitted in the fall. Fortunately, he was made a statistical assistant, a position which gave him a chance to show off his spectacular calculating talent. Kamin recalls the effect this had on his summer supervisor:

> He would sit there over an old adding machine, one of the great big clanking things, and be putting in a whole pile of numbers, and I would look at the pile of num-

bers and say, for example, "The answer is going to be 3,412,610." And he would puff on his pipe for a while and keep cranking in the numbers, and then he'd say, "My God, you're right!" So I impressed him with my calculational speed, and it was probably on that basis that he recommended I be admitted.

Once admitted, Kamin hoped to concentrate in social psychology and study politically relevant subjects such as voting behavior. He also needed a job, however, and so accepted an available assistantship to study avoidance learning in dogs. At first just a source of income, this work in behavioristic animal psychology soon came to seem very interesting in its own right. The studies required much statistical analysis, which Kamin both loved and excelled at doing. Further, the area was ideologically uncontentious, and as anti-Communist fever began sweeping the United States under the leadership of Wisconsin's senator Joseph McCarthy, Kamin thought it wise to keep a low profile.

As Kamin had foreseen, however, his past soon caught up with him anyway. Harvard, as a bastion of eastern liberalism, became a choice target of McCarthy's nationwide hunt for Communist "subversives." Kamin's previous role as an employee of the party naturally came to light, and he was among the handful of Harvard people subpoenaed to testify before a Senate subcommittee in March of 1953. Under oath, he was asked the names of other people he had dealt with while a party member, a procedure he and his fellow witnesses found odious because any named individuals—however innocent or nonpolitical their contacts might have been—would automatically fall under a cloud of suspicion, and perhaps be blacklisted or subjected to other forms of persecution. To avoid naming names, Kamin and his fellow witnesses refused to answer all substantive questions on the only sure legal grounds available, the Fifth Amendment; that is, on grounds that answers might possibly lead to self-incrimination. This *legally* safe course had a major disadvantage, however, because it had to be applied consistently to *all* questions, including those whose answers might be favorable to Kamin's personal case. Thus he was unable to get it on the court record that he had resigned from the party, for example, or that he had never engaged in treason against the United States. An implied cloud of "self-incrimination" hung over him just as he was winding up his graduate study, and made him effectively unemployable in any U.S. university.

Accordingly, when McCarthy came to Boston to hold new hearings in 1954, Kamin adopted a new and legally risky strategy. He now specifically waived the Fifth Amendment and testified fully under oath about his own involvement in the party. He declined to name the other people he had associated with, however, asserting, "I do not think that my duty to my country requires me to become a political informer." He added that he would be willing to name names only if convinced that espionage, sabotage, or treason had been involved. Predictably, McCarthy loudly doubted at the publicly broadcast hearing whether Kamin had ever really left the party, and demagogically blamed him and his "co-conspirators" for "the deaths of thousands of American boys" in the Korean War.[51] Even more important, he filed charges of criminal contempt of Congress against Kamin for his refusal to answer all questions. The subsequent trial extended sporadically over many months, and concluded with the judge's decision that McCarthy's questions had exceeded his subcommittee's mandate from the Senate. Acquitted on these rather narrow technical grounds, Kamin was by now something of a national figure whose picture had appeared in the *New York Times* and other leading newspapers.[52]

But even though his legal gamble had succeeded, Kamin still found himself unemployable in the United States because of his politically suspect past. Fortunately, Canadian universities were somewhat more tolerant, and he got temporary jobs at McGill University and Queen's University before finally gaining a regular assistant professorship at Ontario's McMaster University in 1957. There he rose impressively through the ranks, being named full professor by 1963 and chairman of the Psychology Department in 1964. During this time he published some thirty well-regarded papers on animal learning, a field whose continuing appeal for Kamin lay in the opportunities it provided to "play with numbers" in complex statistical analyses. He became something of a legend among his students for his ability to glance at a sheet of complicated raw data and accurately predict the general statistical trends that subsequent calculations would reveal. He also earned a reputation as a dynamic and popular lecturer.

By 1968 political conditions had changed in the United States, and Kamin's professional reputation was such that he could assume one of the top academic positions in American psychology, as professor and chairman of the Psychology Department at Princeton University. Fully exonerated and with an outstanding reputation in an uncontroversial area of psychology, Kamin was now primed—though he perhaps did not realize it himself at first—to re-enter the arena of socially charged debate. The opportunity to do so came in early 1972, from an unexpected quarter.

Kamin had invited Richard Herrnstein, an old acquaintance from Harvard, to visit Princeton and lecture on one of his specialties, the visual world of the pigeon. Herrnstein, of course, had recently become the target of the Boston student left's "Fall Offensive," for his *Atlantic Monthly* article on IQ which had given a favorable account of part of Jensen's genetic argument. Radical students at Princeton learned of Herrnstein's projected visit, and began planning tactics to "force" him to confront questions on IQ, even though his talk was supposed to be on something else. In the wake of his bad experiences elsewhere, Herrnstein felt unsatisfied by Princeton's security guarantees, and finally cancelled his talk.

In the midst of this, some of the radical students at Princeton approached Kamin to ask if he had read Herrnstein's IQ article, or had any opinion on the subject. Kamin said no to both; he had never been much interested in the subject before, and when teaching about IQ in introductory psychology he had always simply presented the standard textbook material. Sometimes he had cited Burt's studies, of which he had only read brief secondary accounts, as evidence pointing to some sort of hereditary influence. He had taken no strong stand on the nature-nurture issue, however, and had given it no deep thought. Now confronted by the radical students, Kamin defended Herrnstein's right to free speech but also felt obliged to read the article and offer them an honest opinion. Thus began his serious involvement with the IQ issue.

The Exposure of Burt

Kamin saw at once upon reading Herrnstein's article that Burt's studies represented the crown jewels of the hereditarian case, and decided that any knowledgeable opinion would have to be based on a reading of Burt's original papers. He started with Burt's last and largest study of 1966, which reported the perfectly uncorrelated environments for fifty-three separated-twin pairs. Kamin was highly skeptical of this study at once, as he animatedly recalled some ten years after the event:

> I think it is true to say that within ten minutes of starting to read Burt, I knew in my gut that something was so fishy here that it just *had* to be fake. He anticipates every possible objection to the hereditarian case, and comes out with a definitive empirical rebuttal to the objection. The work was so incredibly patly perfect and beyond cavil, and beyond challenge, that I just couldn't believe it. My experience of the messy nature of the real world was such that I just could not believe that what this guy was writing was true.
>
> At the same time there was a kind of vagueness and ambiguity, and *under*description and *under*presentation of method and detail. He didn't even name the IQ test used, no case histories, no information about the sex composition of the samples, or the times they were tested. So I was profoundly suspicious at once, and then started reading other Burt articles.

With his fresh eye and keen sense of number, Kamin quickly discovered many gaps and flaws in Burt's work that had apparently gone unnoticed before even by the experts who had taken it seriously. Kamin found that the actual tests were *never* described satisfactorily, even in the early and obscure papers to which Burt had customarily referred his later readers for technical details. He found that Burt's highest IQ correlations were always reported for "Adjusted Assessments," which an objective observer might reasonably expect had been consciously or unconsciously biased by Burt's hereditarian attitudes to begin with. And most damaging of all, Kamin noted that Burt's reported correlations for the separated twins often remained perfectly constant—to the third decimal place—even as the reported sample size was increasing from twenty-one to fifty-three; for example, the "Group Test" correlation for twenty-one twin pairs in 1955, "over thirty" in 1958, and fifty-three in 1966 was always reported as exactly .771. Kamin knew that it was statistically reasonable to expect only *approximate* similarity among the correlations; the changing makeup of the samples made it almost infinitely improbable that they would come out exactly the same. Finding several other examples of these invariant correlations over varying sample sizes, Kamin became privately convinced that Burt's twin studies were not simply flawed, but fraudulent.

After concluding that the Burt studies were worse than worthless for estimating IQ heritability, Kamin turned to the other major literature bearing on the issue. Here he found much more complete and obviously honest reporting of data, but also much more evidence of that "messy nature of the real world," which rendered any observed correlations doubtful as exact measures of heritability. Most of the messiness, he thought, was such as would artificially inflate the heritability estimates. Once Burt's studies were removed from consideration, the evidence of high IQ heritability did not seem particularly compelling to Kamin.

Now aroused, he looked into the history of American IQ testing, and was appalled to come across the racial theories propounded in the 1920s by respected psychologists such as Yerkes and Brigham. No doubt reflecting that his own middle-European family could have been excluded by the restrictive immigration laws these men supported, Kamin concluded that an arrogant and unfounded assumption of IQ heritability had helped produce an unjust social policy in the 1920s. He saw dangerous parallels in the 1970s, with questionable hereditarian arguments being used by Jensen and others to suggest the curtailment of programs for black youngsters.

Activist tendencies now reawakened, Kamin began to publicize his findings in a lecture entitled "Heredity, Intelligence, Politics, and Psychology," which he gave at several places throughout 1973, including the annual meeting of the Eastern Psychological Association. In 1974 he expanded his case further in a book, *The Science and Politics of I.Q.* Both the lectures and the book opened with an account of the more deplorable racist sentiments expressed by leading intelligence testers in the 1920s, and then asked "whether the policy recommendations of today's mental testers are any more surely grounded in scientific knowledge. . . . What kind of evidence in fact supports the widespread assumption that IQ test scores are heritable?"[53]

Next came a discussion of the Burt studies which were so widely cited by modern hereditarians. After fully describing the methodological ambiguities and incredible statistical consistencies he had discovered, Kamin acidly summarized: "The numbers left behind by Professor Burt are simply not worthy of our current scientific attention. We pass on now to more serious work."[54]

Kamin then critically analyzed the three *other* major published studies of separated identical twins. We have already noted that Newman, Freeman, and Holzinger reported an IQ correlation of .67 for nineteen twin pairs in 1937; in addition, James Shields in Britain had reported a value of .77 for thirty-seven pairs in 1962,[55] and Niels Juel-Nielson reported .62 for twelve Danish pairs in 1965.[56] Minutely analyzing the copious raw data which these authors commendably included in their studies, Kamin argued that their final correlations could not avoid being major exaggerations of true IQ heritability. He showed that most of the twin pairs had not been genuinely and completely "separated," and that the relatively more adequately separated pairs showed significantly larger IQ differences than did the less adequately separated pairs. He showed that twin pairs who had been tested by the same examiner in the Shields study had more similar scores than those who had been tested by two different examiners, illustrating the possibility of unconscious examiner bias in favor of enhancing similarity. He showed that *age* was a confounding factor in two studies, with some of the inter-twin similarity being attributable to the simple fact that the twins were identical in age, and measured on tests which had been standardized according to age levels. Following these and some other criticisms, Kamin concluded his discussion of twin studies with a surprisingly bold assertion: "I see no unambiguous evidence whatever in these studies for *any* heritability of IQ test scores."[57]

Kamin next moved on to consider studies of *adopted children,* which had been generally interpreted by Jensen and other hereditarians as offering strong support for their case. Under ideal scientific conditions, the IQ correlation between adopted children and their adoptive parents would represent the total *environmental* contribution to intelligence, a complement to the separated-twin heritability figure. In several studies, this value had been reported at about .20, a figure logically consistent with an assumed heritability of .80. Moreover, a few studies had correlated adopted children's IQ scores with estimated intelligence levels for their *biological* parents as well; several of these values had been higher than .20, suggesting that heredity had been more important than environment in determining the adopted children's IQs.

Kamin argued, however, that the major adoption studies had been fraught with just as many imperfections and ambiguities as the twin studies. Adoptive homes naturally represent a restricted range of environments, since obviously inferior or pathological placements are automatically ruled out by adoption agencies. Further, Kamin showed that adoptive parents tend to be older and wealthier, and to have fewer children in their families than the "control" families normally used for comparison purposes. On an environmentalist hypothesis, one would expect to find higher than average IQs in children adopted into such privileged homes—which in fact is the case. The *correlations,* however, will be reduced because of the restricted range of the adopting parents, and to that degree will underestimate the true importance of the environmental factor.

Kamin observed that the inevitable occurrence of selective placement poses a double-edged sword for adoption studies, capable of artificially inflating either the hereditarian or the environmentalist case. Hereditarians can argue that selective placement artificially increases the correlation between adoptive parents and their adopted children, since the "innately" brighter children—those known to have intelligent or highly educated biological parents—will tend to be placed in the "better" adoptive homes, maintained by highly intelligent parents. Such an effect would counteract, to some degree, the reduction in the correlations due to restricted range. Environmentalists, on the other hand, can argue that selective placement artificially increases the correlation between the adopted children and their *natural* parents, since those with the most intelligent-seeming natural parents get sent to the best homes and thus have their IQs enhanced the most. In sum, Kamin believed that adoption studies were confounded by myriad factors which made any definitive inference about heritability impossible, and once again he boldly concluded: "The adopted child studies, like the separated twin studies, seem to me to offer no evidence sufficient to reject the hypothesis of zero heritability of IQ scores."[58]

Here was a genuine echo of John Stuart Mill's voice, more than a century later. Kamin, like Mill, did not absolutely deny that intelligence is inheritable, but argued that zero or very low heritability cannot be ruled out. In contrast, he saw the reality of a substantial environmental factor as *unquestionably* established by the greater IQ differences between better separated pairs of identical twins, and by the enhanced IQ levels of adopted children in good homes. Also like Mill, Kamin claimed it is both scientifically unwarranted and ethically irresponsible to abandon environmentalistic hypotheses, and the social programs based on them, because of an assumption that most of the variance in human intellectual ability is hereditary or innate.

After his accidental encounter with Herrnstein and Burt, Kamin changed gears altogether in his professional work. He closed down his animal laboratories to become, in his own words, "a professional critic," reviewing "with a kind of niggling detail" works on the genetics of intelligence and other socially charged topics such as the biology of mental illness. This work enables him to continue the "playing with numbers" he so enjoys, and also to deal directly—though in a far different way—with the large social issues and questions which had preoccupied him as a young man.

In his writings on intelligence, Kamin has proceeded much like a lawyer in an adversarial process, primarily emphasizing the weaknesses of the hereditarian and the strength of the environmentalist cases, with little pretense to "objectivity." Unsurprisingly, he has ruffled feathers in the process, and has been denigrated by hereditarians for extremism and fanaticism. At the same time, however, he has unquestionably placed hereditarian theorists on their toes. Thus the most recent phase of the IQ controversy, in which Kamin and Jensen have both continued to play leading roles, has proceeded with a higher degree of caution and methodological sophistication than before. In addition, there has also remained the disturbing aftermath of "The Burt Affair" to be dealt with by psychologists from both sides.

RECENT DEVELOPMENTS

Almost immediately after making his first discovery about Burt's impossibly invariant twin correlations, Kamin wrote about the matter to Jensen. Jensen, having previously lauded Burt as a man, and cited his work as the bulwark of the hereditarian case, was understandably disturbed. He quickly surveyed Burt's writings systematically, and discovered a total of *twenty* instances where reported correlations remained invariant over changing numbers of subjects. Jensen published these findings in early 1974, now observing that "[Burt's] correlations are useless for hypothesis testing. . . . 20 such instances strain the laws of chance and can only mean error."[59] Since Jensen's paper appeared slightly before Kamin's book, and since Kamin's revelations had heretofore been presented only in talks and mimeographed papers, Jensen's was the first *published* report of Burt's numerical anomalies.

This circumstance produced a bizarre argument, in spite of

the fact that Jensen, in a footnote to his article, credited Kamin with uncovering the first invariant correlations. Jensen's hereditarian ally, Eysenck, published a letter claiming that *Jensen* deserved *priority* for the exposure of Burt, because of his earlier publication in a refereed journal. Kamin, understandably enough, responded testily to Eysenck's "harping" on the priority issue by publishing the date of his first letter to Jensen, and adding: "to squabble about 'priority' is unseemly, especially when no intellectual accomplishment is involved."[60] This brief dispute was symptomatic of the contentious atmosphere which surrounded the IQ controversy during the late 1970s; for while all parties now agreed that Burt's studies should be discounted scientifically, two further questions remained to arouse furious debate.

One, of more human and personal than strictly scientific interest, concerned whether Burt's faulty data had been the result of reasonably honest error, or of deliberate fraud. The second and more scientifically significant question concerned the status of the nature-nurture balance following the removal of Burt's data. The first question has by now been answered more definitively than the second, and we shall turn to it first.

The Burt Scandal

Neither Kamin nor Jensen openly accused Burt of deliberate fraud when they first exposed his faulty statistics, though Kamin privately believed he was guilty of such. When contacted in 1976 by Oliver Gillie, a correspondent for London's *Sunday Times* who had become interested in the Burt case, Kamin still did not use the word fraud, but, Gillie recalls, "went as far towards saying it as is usually regarded decent in academic circles."[61] In the meantime, Gillie had independently learned about Burt's apparently fictitious collaborators, and when one of Burt's former students told him in an interview that "scientifically Burt's results are a fraud," he felt justified in going to press with the story. It was he who first raised the issue of fraud publicly, in a spectacular front-page *Sunday Times* story on October 24, 1976, bearing the headline, "Crucial Data Was Faked by Eminent Scientist."

With the fraud issue now in the open, Kamin became more outspoken. When interviewed by Nicholas Wade for *Science* magazine he now said, "The immediate conclusion I reached after 10 minutes of reading was that Burt was a fraud," and "I suspect that everything the man did from 1909 is wholly fraudulent."[62]

Jensen and Eysenck immediately responded with defenses of Burt's character (though not his research), and attacks on his accusers. Jensen wrote to the London *Times:*

> The charges, as they presently stand, must be judged as the sheer surmise and conjecture, and perhaps wishful thinking, of a few intensely ideological psychologists. Professor Leon Kamin, who apparently spearheaded the attack, has been trying for several years now . . . to wholly discredit the large body of research on the genetics of human mental abilities. The desperate scorched-earth style of criticism . . . has finally gone the limit, with charges of "fraud" and "fakery" now that Burt is no longer here to answer for himself or take warranted legal action against such unfounded defamation.[63]

Eysenck echoed the point shortly thereafter, with a perhaps unintentionally ironic reference to Kamin's old nemesis McCarthy: "One gets a whiff of McCarthyism, or notorious smear campaigns, and of what used to be known as character assassination. . . . It is disappointing to find journals of quality repute like the *Sunday Times* ready and willing to make such forays of witch-hunting."[64]

Perhaps the most balanced comment on the Burt case at this point was made by Wade at the conclusion of his *Science* article, when he said it was then impossible to say whether Burt's flaws "resulted from systematic fraud, mere carelessness, or something in between."[65]

A definitive answer was on the way, however, for the British psychologist Leslie Hearnshaw had been commissioned by Burt's sister to write his biography, with full access to his extant private papers. Originally an admirer of Burt, Hearnshaw had largely changed his opinion by the time his book was published in 1979.

Among Burt's papers, Hearnshaw found no raw IQ data from twins or any other kinship groups, though it remained possible that some had been destroyed during the war, or burned in a general housecleaning shortly after Burt's death. Hearnshaw thought it *possible* that Burt had actually collected some twin data during his early days with the London school system, but there was no hard evidence to prove it. One clear fact, however, was that during Burt's retirement, when his reported twin samples were increasing so dramatically, neither was he testing any new twins himself nor was he in contact with a "Miss Conway" or anyone else who was testing twins. His private letters, papers, and diaries recorded his daily activities in substantial detail, and made absolutely no reference to the subject. The school agencies and granting institutions he would have had to have worked with reported that neither he nor "Miss Conway" had had any contact with them whatsoever.

Perhaps most telling of all were Burt's diaries for the period immediately following Christopher Jencks's request for the raw IQ scores and occupational level ratings of his fifty-three twin pairs—the first such request Burt ever acceded to. When Burt finally sent the scores to Jencks after several weeks he apologized for his tardiness by explaining, "I was away for the Christmas vacation, and college (where the data are stored) was closed until the opening of the term." Hearnshaw learned, however, that Burt had not been away that Christmas and had no data stored at the college, which in any case had been closed for only a short time over the holidays. Further, Hearnshaw reported:

> According to his diary Burt spent the whole of the week from 2 January onwards "calculating data on twins for Jencks." On January 11th he "finished checking the tables for Jencks." Had the I.Q. scores and social class gradings been available they could have been copied out in half an hour at the most. So quite clearly the Table of I.Q. scores and class gradings was an elabo-

rately constructed piece of work, and we are forced to the conclusion that he simply did not possess detailed data.[66]

Hearnshaw's biography also provided the first detailed account of Burt's self-serving "rewriting of the history" of factor analysis, and of his tendency to pack his journal with his own articles under fictitious names. Generally compassionate in tone, the biography also praised Burt's genuine contributions to psychology, and noted mitigating factors such as ill health and marital crises which may have caused Burt to become mentally unbalanced during the last part of his life. In general, however, Hearnshaw settled the basic issue: *much* if not all of Burt's empirical genetic work, including the enormously influential twin studies, had unquestionably been deliberately falsified.

Among the major innocent victims of Burt's malfeasance, of course, were Jensen and Eysenck, who had gone out on a limb to support him, only to be embarrassed by Hearnshaw's shocking revelations. Both now agreed that Burt had in fact perpetrated deliberate fraud. Even so, however, they have continued to argue that the strong scientific case for IQ heritability is *not* significantly altered by the loss of Burt's data. Unsurprisingly, Kamin has vigorously disagreed. We turn first to Jensen's recent statements on the matter.

Jensen's Recent View

Jensen's 1981 book, *Straight Talk about Mental Tests,* was written explicitly for the layman because, he asserts, "the public today is witnessing a war against psychological tests." This war is misguided, he argues, because "I have come to believe that well constructed tests, properly used, provide objective standards for evaluation in education and employment, and that they can contribute substantially to human welfare and social justice."[67] Much of Jensen's case is a reaffirmation of the high heritability of IQ, suggesting that the tests measure something at once real and biologically determined. Dismissing the Burt case as "fascinating but sad—the story of a genius gone awry," Jensen claims that "the total deletion of Burt's empirical legacy would scarcely make an iota of difference to any general conclusions regarding the heritability of intelligence, so much greater is the body of more recent and better evidence."[68]

As primary evidence, Jensen cites a series of median IQ correlations for different kinship pairs, derived from some fifty-one separate studies (and obviously not including Burt's). These median values, reproduced below, seem to Jensen to indicate remarkably consistent and sizable heritability estimates.[69]

MZ twins, reared together	.88
MZ twins, reared apart	.74
DZ twins, reared together	.53
DZ twins, opposite sex	.53
Siblings, reared together	.49
Parent–Child	.52
Foster parent–Adopted child	.19
Unrelated children, reared together	.16

Jensen first considers the direct heritability estimate of .74, provided by the separated MZ twins.* Acknowledging that this may overestimate true heritability to some degree because of correlated environments, Jensen proposes to check it by comparing it with heritability estimates derived from other kinship relations.

A comparison between MZ and DZ twins, all reared *together*, provides one such check. Assuming that both MZ and DZ twins grow up in equally similar environments, the difference between their two correlations (.88 and .53, respectively) must be attributable to the difference in their genetic resemblance. Since DZ twins, like ordinary siblings, share only an average of half their

---

*Jensen's figure of .74 was obtained by pooling all of the subjects from the three major studies and computing a single correlation coefficient, instead of taking the median as he did with other kinship groups. This procedure gave most weight to the study with the most subjects (Shields's), which also happened to produce the highest individual correlation. Had the simple average or median of the three individual correlations (.77, .67, and .62) been taken, a somewhat lower aggregate value of .69 or .67 would have resulted.

genes in common, while MZ twins share them all, the observed difference of .35 should equal one-half of the total genetic variance. The total genetic variance or heritability thus equals $2 \times .35$, or .70. Jensen concedes the possibility that MZ twins might experience somewhat more similar environments than DZs, but doubts that such greater similarity has much effect in view of the fact that opposite-sex DZ twins—who presumably are treated more differently than same-sex DZs—achieve exactly the same IQ correlation of .53. Further, Jensen states:

> It would be difficult to argue that MZ twins reared apart experience more similar environments than DZ twins reared together, and yet the average correlation between MZ twins apart is .74 as compared with .53 for DZ together. ... This fact leaves little doubt of the predominance of genetic over environmental factors in the determination of IQ.[70]

Jensen next considers two other comparisons that theoretically provide estimates of one-half of the genetic variance. Biological parents share approximately half their genes with their children, as do ordinary siblings with each other; the genetic similarities between adoptive parents and their foster children, or between unrelated children reared together, approximate zero. Thus the difference between the ordinary parent-child correlation (.52) and that for foster parent-adopted child (.19) should yield half the genetic variance, as should the difference between correlations for ordinary siblings (.49) and foster siblings (.16). In both cases the difference equals .33, suggesting a heritability of .66.

Finally, Jensen compares the correlation for unrelated children reared together (.16) with that for MZ twins reared together (.88). Since both groups share common environments, but the twins share all of their genes while the foster siblings share none, the straight difference between their two correlations of .72 directly estimates the genetic variance.

Since all of these ways of estimating heritability yield results quite close to .70, this is the figure Jensen now accepts as most probable. Though slightly reduced from the .80 Jensen espoused in 1969, this value still suggests that heredity significantly out-weighs environment in the determination of IQ.

Jensen does add one cautionary note, when he observes that, for unknown reasons, some recent and still ongoing studies seem to be producing higher correlations for DZ twins, and lower ones between full siblings or between parents and their natural children, than the medians he gave in his chart. Substitution of these new values in his equations would produce heritability estimates close to .50, he says. Jensen cannot explain the differences between the newer and older results, but assumes that some large-scale studies currently in progress will soon clarify the picture. And even if the .50 figure is ultimately adopted, he notes, that would still suggest an effect of heredity greater than that demonstrated for any single environmental variable.

Thus Jensen has slightly reduced his "best estimate" of IQ heritability, and may be prepared to go somewhat farther yet. Nevertheless, he remains confident that genetic factors are rel-atively more important than the environment. As we shall see next, Kamin interprets the post-Burtian data rather differently.

Kamin's Rejoinder

Kamin commented acerbically on the hereditar-ians' "incredible claim" that the loss of Burt's data makes little difference to their case, in a published "debate" with Eysenck which appeared in 1981:

> What . . . are we to make of the fact that Burt's trans-parently fraudulent data were accepted for so long, and so unanimously, by the "experts" in the field? When I first criticised Burt's papers, as an outsider to IQ test-ing, Eysenck wrote derisively, in 1974, of my "novitiate status" and my "once-a-year interest" in a subject best left to the experts. The same Burt papers that I first read in 1972 had been read many years earlier by Eysenck, who repeatedly quoted them as gospel. . . .

> To my mind, . . . it is an equally sorry comment on
> the fraternity of IQ testers that, having lost Burt's data,
> they continue to assert that the remaining evidence
> demonstrates the high heritability of IQ.[71]

In his continuing advocacy of the environmentalist position,
Kamin has criticized the lines of evidence now stressed by Jensen
and Eysenck, and cited some new studies of three different types,
which seem to support his case.

MZ versus DZ Twins Reared Together. Recall that
Jensen used twice the difference between the IQ correlations for
these two kinds of twins to estimate heritability at .70, while
admitting that his procedure was justified only on the assumption that both kinds of twins shared environments to approximately the same degree. Kamin holds that this assumption is
demonstrably false, and that MZ twins reared together are in
fact treated much more similarly than DZs reared together. He
cites questionnaire studies showing that MZ twins are much less
likely than DZs to have spent a night apart while growing up,
but much more likely to have had the same friends, to have played
together, to have dressed alike, or to have studied together.
"Obviously, studying the same material at the same time would
tend to produce similar test scores in MZ pairs," he observes;
"there can be no question that, in general, MZs share more similar environments than DZs."[72]

Next, Kamin tries to show that environmental similarities can
and do increase the IQ correlations of twins who have been reared
together. He disagrees with the figures in Jensen's table indicating that opposite-sex DZs have just as high an IQ correlation as
like-sex ones. Locating just four studies in the literature which
provide comparative correlations, Kamin notes that three give
significantly higher values for the like-sex twins. The fourth, which
gives a marginally *lower* correlation for the same-sex twins, and
which is the one most strongly emphasized by the hereditarians,
Kamin believes to be seriously marred by a sampling procedure

which systematically ruled out the most similar same-sex pairs. The bulk of the evidence, in Kamin's view, suggests that the more equal treatment accorded same-sex DZ twins produces greater similarity in their IQs than is found for opposite-sex DZs.

In a related vein, Kamin cites studies indicating that, among same-sex DZs reared together, female pairs tend to be treated more similarly than males (a sex difference which does *not* hold true for MZ pairs). Consistent with the environmentalist hypothesis, one large study gave a significantly higher IQ correlation for female DZs (.70) than for males (.51). Kamin observes that the .70 figure is not too far from the .83 reported in the same study for the genetically identical female *MZs*. Thus Kamin concludes:

> From either [genetic or environmental] viewpoint, one expects the correlation of MZs to be higher than that of DZs. . . . The environmentalist view, however, . . . correctly predicts sex differences observed among DZ twins. . . . These findings cannot disprove the possibility that some part of the MZ-DZ difference in IQ correlation is a genetic effect—but they do show, at the very least, that any estimates of heritability derived from twin studies are inflated.[73]

Adoption Studies. Turning his attention to recent adoption studies, Kamin has stressed two which have solved the methodological problem of matching adoptive and biological families for comparative purposes (recall his earlier finding that adoptive families tended to be smaller and more well off than average families). They did this by investigating only families which contained *both* adopted and biological children. Comparing IQ similarities for adoptive and biological relatives within just these families, the matching was perfect since each family served as its own control. The first of these studies was conducted in Minnesota by Sandra Scarr and Richard Weinberg,[74] and the second in Texas by Joseph Horn, John Loehlin, and Lee

Willerman.[75] The IQ correlations from these studies which seem particularly important to Kamin are the following:

	Minnesota Study	Texas Study
Mother × Biological child	.34	.20
Mother × Adopted child	.29	.22
Father × Biological child	.34	.28
Father × Adopted child	.07	.12
Biological sibling pairs	.37	.35
Biological–Adopted sibling pairs	.30	.29
Adopted–Adopted sibling pairs	.49	—

Observation shows that only the correlations involving fathers were notably larger for biological than for adoptive relations. The lack of significant differences among correlations for mothers and siblings suggests extremely low, possibly zero-order, heritabilities.

Further evidence against a strong genetic effect emerges from an analysis of the *levels* of IQ scores achieved by the adopted and biological children in these families. In both studies the adopting parents had higher than average IQs—almost certainly higher than those of the biological parents of the adopted children. Nevertheless, in the Texas study the adopted and biological children *both* had average IQs of about 112, suggesting that the presumably superior genetic endowment of the biological children made absolutely no difference at all. In Minnesota, the biological children's average IQ was some 6 or 7 points higher than the 109 of the adopted children, indicating the possibility of some genetic effect in addition to the environmental boosting. Kamin observes, however, that the Minnesota adoptees had been placed in homes at significantly older ages than those in Texas, and thus perhaps missed out on some crucial early environmental stimulation that could have raised their IQs further.

The overall results of these two studies are thus somewhat ambiguous, and have been interpreted somewhat differently by

Kamin and their respective authors. The Minnesota authors acknowledge their results indicate that "IQ scores are more malleable than previously thought," but they also believe that the genetic factor may have been artificially minimized in their study by the tendency of parents to lend *extra* support and coaching to their adopted children—working extra hard to make them equal their biological children, as it were. These authors also believe that the parent-child correlations in their study gave "reasonably coherent support for the moderate heritability of IQ scores,"[76] though the sibling correlations gave no evidence of heritability at all. In Texas, the authors repeated the extra-attention argument in accounting for the identical IQs of the adopted and biological children. Further, they applied a mathematically complex "path model analysis" to their overall pattern of correlations, and arrived at a range of heritability estimates centering near .40—"moderate heritabilities," in the words of Horn, Loehlin, and Willerman.

Unsurprisingly, Kamin has chosen to emphasize the positive evidence in these studies for a strong *environmental* effect on IQ, and to deemphasize the positive genetic implications. The "path model" employed by the Texas authors requires several unwarranted assumptions favorable to heredity, he believes, and other inevitable design problems may have inflated the heritability estimates even further. Even so, Kamin observes with satisfaction that the previously *unthinkable* phrase "zero heritability" now begins to crop up from time to time in the work of behavior geneticists, and that the "moderate heritabilities" now being suggested by the Minnesota and Texas authors are "a far cry from the 80 per cent figure so confidently put about by authorities such as Eysenck and Jensen."[77]

Recent Kinship Correlations. Kamin has not failed to exploit the trend which was tentatively acknowledged by Jensen, toward a reduction in the IQ correlations found in recent studies between full biological siblings, or between parents and their biological children. He has cited a particularly large Hawaiian study in which more than 6,000 members from 1,816 different families were given 15 different kinds of intelligence tests.[78] The intelligence correlations between full siblings, and between parents and their biological children, averaged only in the mid .20s and low .30s. Tracking down all of the other post-1963 studies he could find which reported parent-child IQ correlations, Kamin found a total of 16 individual correlations which ranged from .08 to .41, with a median of .33. These values are all lower than the medians around .50 reported in the older literature, and used by Jensen in his latest heritability estimates.* Kamin cannot definitively account for the drop in the correlations, though he believes the new figures are more accurate, emerging from larger and better-controlled studies, using better-validated IQ tests. As he acidly commented in a 1979 address to the Eastern Psychological Association: "For some reason, about one-third of the total resemblance between parent and child has slipped away since 1963. The only place where it can still be found is in the most recent textbooks of psychology and genetics."[79]

Obviously, the highly sophisticated statistical techniques and vast accumulations of kinship correlations which are available today have produced scarcely more agreement on the nature-nurture question than the much more impressionistic evidence cited by Mill and Galton. The hard evidence remains ambiguous, and it is still possible for intelligent and reasonable people to interpret it differently. Nevertheless, there have been a *few* recent signs of growing consensus, and a few important lessons may be drawn from the past century's research on the IQ controversy. We shall consider these in the Conclusion.

SUGGESTED READINGS

The case histories of Ed and Fred, along with those of eighteen other separated identical twin pairs, are given in Horatio Newman, Frank Freeman, and Karl Holzinger's classic study, *Twins: A Study of Heredity and Environment* (Chicago: University of Chicago Press,

---

*If correlations of .33 are substituted for the .52 and .49 employed by Jensen in his calculations reported on page 218, the heritability estimates drop from .66 to .28 or .34.

1937). This book still gives an excellent picture of the fascination as well as the difficulty of doing separated-twin research.

Leslie Hearnshaw's *Cyril Burt: Psychologist* (Ithaca, NY: Cornell University Press, 1979) provides a probing but compassionate account of Burt's life and career, as well as of the scandal which surrounded him after his death. Arthur Jensen's autobiography, entitled "What Is the Question? What Is the Evidence?" appears in Volume 2 of *The Psychologists*, edited by T. S. Krawiec (New York: Oxford, 1974). His explosive article, "How Much Can We Boost IQ and Scholastic Achievement?", together with the original responses to it solicited by the *HER* editors, is in *Environment, Heredity, and Intelligence* (Cambridge, MA: Harvard Educational Review, 1969). For an exposition of Jensen's views following the Burt scandal, see his *Straight Talk about Mental Tests* (New York: Free Press, 1981).

Leon Kamin's early critique of the genetic case, including his exposure of Burt's twin studies, appears in his *The Science and Politics of IQ* (Potomac, MD: Erlbaum, 1974). For his more recent critiques see H. J. Eysenck versus Leon Kamin, *The Intelligence Controversy* (New York: Wiley, 1981).

6 | Conclusion

> Group-administered tests of IQ or scholastic aptitude are probably overused in schools. . . . Teachers need to know how well their pupils have learned what they have been taught in school; they do not need to know their pupils' IQs. . . . Ability grouping [by IQ] at the elementary school level is more a convenience for teachers than a benefit to pupils. . . . The value of the information gained from mass IQ testing cannot justify the sheer monetary cost, even ignoring for the moment the possible abuses of this practice.

Readers might be excused for thinking that the author of the above comments was a foe of IQ testing. Such a supposition would be wrong, however, for the author was Arthur Jensen, in a book written to support the general validity of intelligence testing.[1] The fact that even a supporter of testing like Jensen now expresses reservations about some of the traditional uses of IQ tests shows that at least on certain *practical* issues, the disparate parties to the IQ controversy have drawn closer together in recent years.

CURRENT USES OF IQ TESTS

After the successful introduction of mass intelligence testing by Yerkes, Terman, and followers, IQ tests came to be almost universally administered in American schools. Results were widely used for purposes such as the "streaming" or "tracking" of pupils into faster or slower classes, or designating individuals as "underachievers" or "overachievers" when their IQs surpassed or lagged behind their levels of academic performance. The whole notion of IQ took on a sort of mystique, as scores were guarded in confidential files, unavailable either to the students themselves or to their parents. Those few people who "knew their own IQs" often felt they had privileged information regarding one of the most important facts there was to know about themselves.

The public mystique surrounding IQ tests began to fade seriously with the American civil rights movements of the 1960s and 1970s. While black and other minority students were no longer legally segregated anywhere on purely racial lines, their lower average test scores still relegated them in disproportionate numbers to the slower streams, or to schools for the retarded. This seemed like de facto segregation to many black parents, who began to mount legal challenges to the use of standard IQ tests in classifying their children. As evidence like that reviewed in this book, regarding the standard tests' culturally loaded content and less than perfect validity was read into the court records, several of these challenges were successful. The state of California legally prohibited the use of standard IQ tests on black children in the schools, for example, and school boards elsewhere began voluntarily to curtail their use of tests, to avoid parental complaints and law suits of their own. Equally important, IQ tests began to get a bad public press. When a CBS television documentary entitled "The IQ Myth" severely attacked them in 1975, its very title symbolized the demystification of intelligence testing which was then under way. Publicity surrounding the Burt scandal accelerated the trend.

In response, some thoughtful supporters of testing agreed that some of the complaints about past misuse of IQ tests were valid, but also feared that the reaction against them might go too far. They argued that IQ tests still have substantial if imperfect validity, and so long as they are used sensibly and with adequate safeguards against abuse they can be useful socially. Jensen has been prominent among this group of psychologists, and we shall take his current views as illustrative.

As the quotation at the beginning of this chapter suggests, Jensen now opposes the routine, mass IQ testing of all children in school. This is not because he thinks IQ is uncorrelated with academic achievement, but because he feels IQ is basically beside the point for a teacher. "Achievement itself is the school's main concern," he notes, and "I see no need to measure anything other than achievement itself."[2] Standardized, group-administered *achievement tests,* which measure the extent to which children have mastered the actual *contents* of their subjects, are perfectly appropriate and desirable. But measures of intelligence, aptitude, or potential ought now to be avoided in the vast majority of cases, according to Jensen.

The common practice of "streaming" schoolchildren into homogeneous IQ groups was convenient for teachers and administrators, Jensen adds, but his review of the relevant research indicated that this practice produced negative or at best ambiguous overall results for the children. Pupils in the fast streams occasionally fared slightly better on achievement tests than comparable children left in ordinary, "mixed" classes, but this gain was more than offset by *un*favorable effects on children in the slower streams. Jensen concludes: "There is no compelling evidence that would justify ability grouping in the elementary grades. I believe that schools should aim to keep pupils of as wide a range of abilities as is feasible in regular classes."[3] Grouping by ability or expertise is of course necessary in advanced subjects taught in high school and beyond, but here entrance can be determined by performance in prerequisite courses, achievement tests, or other concrete demonstrations of adequate preparation. IQ scores per se are once again beside the point.

The same basic points hold true for choosing job applicants. Jensen now urges that IQ tests be used cautiously, and only when there is a high demonstrated correlation between IQ and the *post-training* performance on the job in question. The list of such jobs is smaller than might be expected, because while IQ frequently correlates with quickness to learn, or with performance during a training period, it often bears little relationship at all to how well the job is performed *after* training. For occupations which require substantial prior academic training, performance in that training itself will be a more valid predictor than IQ.[4]

Granting these major limitations on the use of intelligence tests, Jensen believes there are three remaining important situations in which they *can* be highly beneficial. First, he argues that *individual* intelligence tests can be invaluable in diagnosing many problem cases, and developing remedial programs for them. The child who persistently makes abnormally slow progress or shows deviant behavior in class, for example, may profitably be referred for testing by a trained expert, on an instrument like the WISC. As was seen in Chapter 4, Wechsler tests go considerably beyond the mere assigning of global IQ scores, but allow for differentiated assessments of strengths and weaknesses in several different aspects of mental functioning. This is testing in the original, "clinical" tradition of Binet, and Jensen believes it should continue.[5]

For *group* IQ tests, Jensen sees two major remaining positive uses. One is for research, both into the theory of intelligence itself, and also into certain applied matters such as the comparative effectiveness of different educational practices. If one wants to know whether Teaching Method A produces better achievement test results than Method B, for example, one must be sure that the groups of students exposed to both methods are similar in original ability. Group-administered IQ tests can provide a handy means for selecting comparable samples for exposure to the two methods. Jensen emphasizes, however, that any IQ scores obtained for research purposes must be kept anonymous, and never entered in the students' official school records.[6]

For Jensen, "the most compelling reason for not doing away with [group] IQ tests completely" is one of the classic defenses of tests, namely, that they can be used to identify unsuspected or hidden academic talent in disadvantaged segments of the population.[7] For a variety of reasons, including the inability to adopt a middle-class style, talented but disadvantaged children may be especially likely to strike their teachers as less able than they really are. Jensen argues that IQ tests, particularly those with many "nonverbal, culture-reduced" items, are often able to penetrate the veneer of cultural disadvantage better than teachers' unaided judgments. Thus IQ tests ought to be given routinely to groups of disadvantaged students—but only for the purpose of identifying *strength*, and never for revealing intellectual weakness. Accordingly, Jensen suggests that the tests be given and scored by people formally unconnected with the children's schools, who will send back information only about those children who do unusually well. Thus alerted, the school can make sure that these children are given every opportunity to develop their abilities. The unmentioned majority of children should all be considered as average by the school, until their actual academic work suggests otherwise. Thus no one needs to be stigmatized by negative results.

Jensen's first two positive suggestions for IQ testing are unlikely to arouse much opposition. Individual clinical testing has been widely endorsed, even by many of those who most strenuously oppose group testing. Jensen's suggestion to use IQ tests for research purposes is also noncontroversial, and unlikely to meet serious challenge from educators or psychologists.

The use of IQ tests to identify unsuspected talent among the disadvantaged may raise a few more questions from critics of testing. How can one ensure that the process does not merely identify those students already most acculturated to middle-class values, for example, or that the failure to be singled out is not interpreted as a stigma? Might not the special attention afforded the designated students sometimes amount to the very kind of streaming that Jensen himself discourages in other contexts? Can Jensen square this suggestion with his other stated belief that school achievement alone, untrammeled by considerations of aptitude or potential, ought to be the primary concern of educators? Even granting these considerations, however, Jensen is surely right in asserting that the discovery of hidden talent in our disadvantaged populations would be of great general benefit. Programs such as he suggests, administered with appropriate caution, certainly seem worth serious consideration.

In sum, there is now a growing consensus that IQ tests have been overused and misused in the past, but that there still may remain for them a useful if more modest place in our society. With respect to the *uses* of tests, then, the IQ controversy has recently become less contentious. On *theoretical* issues, however, more disagreement remains. We saw in Chapter 4 that psychologists are still unable to agree whether "intelligence" is dominated by a unitary general factor, like Spearman's *g*, or is the complex product of many different and largely independent factors. And the unsettled issue which still dwarfs all others in public interest and importance is the nature-nurture question. Let us now consider this aspect of the IQ controversy, as it stands today.

The Nature-Nurture Controversy Today

After the historical survey contained in this book, one question on many minds must be whether the past century of research has produced any real "progress" on the nature-nurture controversy at all. With articulate psychologists like Jensen and Kamin still differing over points identical to those which separated Galton and Mill, and in very similar language, there are evidently many ways in which the basic issues are as unresolved as ever.

Nevertheless, there have been a number of important lessons learned over the past century. Foremost among them, perhaps, is an enhanced appreciation of the complexity of the nature-nurture controversy. Everyone now recognizes that heredity and environment never work in isolation, but only in *interaction* with each other. From the moment of birth onwards, each child's real or presumed "nature" helps *determine* its nurture—though in ways not always easily predictable in advance. For example, a child who is assumed to be inherently "bright"—on the basis of hereditary background, alert demeanor, or any other kind of early sign—may be presented with special advantages on that account. Such children's parents may go out of their way to encourage their budding genuises, for example, or adoption agencies may try particularly hard to place such children in the best foster homes. Dull-seeming children may sometimes elicit the opposite responses—though there may also be situations where extra effort and privilege are provided for children believed to be disadvantaged, as was presumed to have been the case by the authors of the Texas and Minnesota adoption studies described in Chapter 5. Many other plausible kinds of nature-nurture interactions can also be hypothesized—a fact which has led some psychologists to believe that interactions are so variable and ubiquitous as to make futile *any* discussion of heredity and environment as separate factors. One need not go quite so far, perhaps, but still the great importance of interaction as a complicating factor must be acknowledged by all participants in the IQ controversy.

A second tempering realization now shared by all serious investigators concerns the necessarily limited generalizability of any particular research finding. Even if a perfectly valid test of innate intelligence could be developed, and given to a sample of truly separated and randomly placed identical twins in a scientifically ideal experiment, the inter-twin correlation would express the true heritability only for the particular population sampled, within the particular range of environments to which they had been sent. Change the range of environments to which the same population is exposed, or change the makeup of a population exposed to the same range of environments, and the heritability figure would probably change. Richard Herrnstein's controversial *Atlantic Monthly* article on IQ, discussed in the Preface, made essentially this point. Herrnstein argued that if environments could be made more equal for all, then hereditary factors would loom relatively larger in producing the residual differences in their intelligence. In other words, the heritability of intelligence would increase, for that specific situation.

Thus most investigators now recognize that there is not, and never can be, any universal or final answer to the nature-nurture question with respect to intelligence. All that can be hoped for, even under the most ideal of scientific conditions, is an approximate appreciation of the relative strengths of the two factors, within specified populations and ranges of environment.

Granting these limitations, however, there still remain several points which can be made regarding the influences of nature and nurture in those populations and environments which have been most extensively studied so far. We shall consider the current cases for nature and nurture separately, bearing in mind the necessarily limited generalizability of any conclusions.

The Case for Nature

As John Stuart Mill pointed out long ago, any argument in favor of original or ultimate factors logically entails the systematic ruling out of all other possible explanations. Thus the person who wishes to argue in favor of "nature" inevitably faces some challenges which the proponent of "nurture" does not. On the specific issue of IQ, the challenges are compounded by three further facts. First, the best available intelligence tests are patently loaded with items requiring at least some degree of acculturation and education. Second, everyone—even the most enthusiastic hereditarian—agrees that environment plays *some* role in the development of intelligence. And third, everyone also agrees that hereditary and environmental factors are often intercorrelated, and can interact with each other in many different ways. These facts make it relatively easy to construct alternative explanations for research findings which are merely *consistent with* the genetic case. Putting aside the Burt studies— which turned out literally too good to be true for the genetic arguments—all of the major legitimate findings so far have been subject to alternative environmentalistic explanations of one kind or another.

In the absence of the scientifically ideal experiment, the problem for a "neutral" observer of the controversy becomes one of weighing the plausibility of various alternative explanations which have been proferred for essentially ambiguous data. Does there in fact seem to remain any significant residuum of genetic or innate influence, after all plausible environmentalistic factors have been considered? Here subjectivity inevitably enters, and conclusions must necessarily be tentative. It seems to me, however, that several things point to a genuine if not overwhelmingly large role for nature.

One nonstatistical line of evidence derives from individual cases of "prodigies of genius." We have noted that prodigies such as Mozart, Wiener, and Mill were all exposed to unusually stimulating early environments which clearly shaped their talents. But there have unquestionably been *other* children born to parents just as ambitious for them, and just as pedagogically capable as the *pères* Mozart, Wiener, and Mill. Subjected to outstanding early environments, many such children nevertheless turned out to be quite ordinary in their talents and achievements. Extraordinary environments, it seems, do not *always* produce extraordinary intellects. Thus it seems likely that certain intellectual predispositions and limitations are innate, as Galton inferred from his personal experience in 1869. A stimulating environment is certainly *necessary* for the blossoming of intellectual talent, and undoubtedly can do *some* good in all cases; but it also seems that an outstanding final result requires the presence of some appropriate original material for the environment to work on.

With respect to the voluminous experimental and statistical data around which so much of the recent IQ controversy has centered, it is important to note that a substantial hereditary component has yet to be ruled out. Given the logic of the nature-nurture question, it *could have been* ruled out by certain patterns of results: the failure of talent or IQ to run in families, for example. These results did not occur, however, and the avoidance of elimination is not the trivial success for nature that it might at first appear. Even a staunch environmentalist like Leon Kamin, who regards the genetic hypothesis with as much skepticism and hostility as anyone, only goes so far as to say that the possibility of zero IQ heritability has not been eliminated; he concedes that evidence may yet turn up which would offer more convincing proof of a genetic factor. Thus in spite of facing the obstacles that any "ultimate factor theory" is subject to, the genetic hypothesis has managed to remain robustly alive.

Given the logic of the nature-nurture question, the various quantitative results of current heritability studies are probably best interpreted as setting *upper limits* for the influence of genetics. Jensen's current estimate of .70 IQ heritability becomes a "best-case" interpretation of the data, assuming that the many possible experimental artifacts, or correlated environmental effects, did not strongly inflate the final coefficients in the early studies. Jensen now concedes the possibility that newer evidence—still interpreted in this generally best-case manner—may lead him to reduce his estimate to the neighborhood of .50. Thus it seems fair for a "neutral" observer of the IQ controversy to conclude that IQ heritability in our time and society is certainly less than .70, and quite probably less than .50. This still leaves room, of course, for a substantial genetic factor in intelligence.

The Case for Nurture

Turning now to the environment side of the controversy, we find a different sort of situation. Virtually everyone, even the strongest proponent of heredity, agrees that nurture plays *some* role in the determination of intelligence as measured by the standard tests. Positive evidence of this comes from findings such as the greater IQ disparities observed between the more completely separated identical twins, or the IQ enhancement which occurs when children are adopted into good home environments.

Further—although this point may be obscured by some of the rhetoric employed in the debate—virtually all commentators now agree that the environmental factor is of practically important size. Such was not true during the brief period when the fraudulent Burt studies suggested that heredity was at least four times more important than environment, but with the dismissal of those studies the situation has truly changed. Now, though Jensen *says* the loss of Burt's data makes hardly "an iota of difference to any general conclusions regarding the heritability of intelligence,"[8] his statement must be interpreted rather carefully. As we have seen, he has reduced his estimate of heritability, based on a best-case interpretation of the data, from .80 to at least .70 and possibly to .50. This could still leave heredity as the most important single determiner of IQ differences, of course, but Jensen can no longer suggest, as he did in 1969, that it completely overwhelms the influence of environment. The remaining fraction which even he now allows as probably due to environment is of significant size, by any reasonable consideration.

Accordingly, it no longer seems plausible to blame the relative ineffectiveness of programs like Operation Head Start on the imperviousness of intelligence to nurture. Perhaps it was naively optimistic, however, for the program's originators to have believed that just a few hours of "enrichment" each week, outside a child's home and larger cultural environment, could have had many major and permanent effects.* Indeed, the bulk of evidence indicates that environmental influences act most powerfully only when they are prolonged over many years, and involve the broadest aspects of home and culture.

Consider the changes which seem to have occurred in the level of "national intelligence" in the United States. We saw in Chapter 1 that Galton rather sarcastically commented on the lack of high intellectual achievements by Americans in 1865, and blamed it on their inherited limitations of intelligence and character. Today, however, the range and extent of American intellectual contributions would unquestionably yield a more favorable comparative estimate of intellectual capacity. While the genetic makeup of the American population has changed somewhat because of immigration patterns over the past century, few would deny that the upsurge in intellectual creativity has been primarily attributable to a gradual change in the whole culture, with more and better institutions and opportunities for intellectual achievement being made available to ever-increasing numbers of the population.

A recent study of American IQ test scores by James Flynn, a political scientist from New Zealand, has produced some interesting related evidence.[10] Flynn reviewed all the published studies he could find in which the same samples of American subjects took two different Wechsler or Stanford-Binet IQ tests. He discovered a surprising regularity: in almost every case, the subjects

---

*A recent follow-up survey of the major compensatory education programs from the 1960s suggests that they *were* effective in keeping their graduates out of special education classes, and in fostering positive, long-term attitudes toward intellectual activity and achievement. Any significant gains in average IQ, however, disappeared within a few years of the children's leaving the program. Thus the programs were perhaps not as totally ineffective as Jensen suggested in 1969, but neither were they as successful as their originators had hoped they would be.[9]

received higher average IQ scores on the *older* of the two tests they took—the one which had been standardized earlier. Moreover, the differences between their two average scores were closely proportional to the number of years separating the tests' standardizations, with approximately one-third of a point's difference appearing for each year's separation. Though no sample Flynn examined took both the oldest (the 1932 Stanford-Binet) and the newest (the 1978 WAIS) of the many possible tests, Flynn calculated that if they did, a subject who received an IQ of 100 on the 1978 WAIS would have got 114 on the 1932 Stanford-Binet.

This suggests that it takes a better absolute level of performance to obtain any given IQ today than it did fifty years ago; indeed, an average performance of today would have stood at about the 70th percentile of performances then. The tests' standardization samples—and presumably the general populations of which they were representative—have become progressively more "intelligent," and have set increasingly difficult standards. Some of this improvement may have been due merely to an increasing general "test sophistication" among Americans, as they have become increasingly familiar with the type of questions asked in the tests. But it also seems likely that much of the improvement is "real"—that is, that Americans give better test responses today because they are better prepared to act and think in ways defined as "intelligent" by the test constructors.

Genetic explanations cannot easily account for these findings, for there is no reason to believe that the genetic stock of the United States has changed or improved sufficiently over the past two generations. In fact, the classic eugenicist's argument has been that genetic potential is *worsening,* because of differentially high birth rates among the less able segments of the population. Thus average Americans are apparently getting more intelligent, as measured by the tests, in spite of having no better genetic makeup than in the past. This improvement is undoubtedly due to the same sorts of factors which helped raise the frequency of significant American contributions to world science and culture over the past century: namely, the gradually increasing opportunities for the exercise and development of "intelligent" behavior throughout the entire society and culture.

Thus there is no doubt that environment plays a large role in determining both average levels and individual differences in intelligence within our society. Its influence tends to be exerted gradually and cumulatively, however, through the pervasive effects of home and culture acting over years and decades.

For this reason, the attribution of black-white or other racial differences in IQ to genetic factors is not justified, even though one may believe that heredity plays some role in determining individual intelligence levels. There is no question but that black Americans have typically been reared in environments less likely than those of whites to foster success on tasks like intelligence tests. Adoption studies have shown that black children, like all others, benefit intellectually from being reared in stimulating and prosperous home environments. There is no question but that systematic improvement of the conditions under which black children are reared will reduce the deficit in their average IQs. Indeed, there is no reason to think that the attainment of genuine environmental equality, sustained over a generation or two, would not reduce that deficit to zero.

A FINAL WORD

Much of the heat and bitterness surrounding the IQ controversy have arisen because of its involvement with the racial issue. Both in the 1920s and again more recently, the results of intelligence tests were used by some to call into question the innate abilities of minority groups who were struggling to make a better life for themselves in America. The middle-European immigrants of the 1920s and the American blacks of the 1960s both already confronted a great deal of prejudice from many different sources. Thus, whatever the private beliefs of the intelligence testers regarding minority rights, or their warnings that statistical group differences should not influence judgments about individuals, their views inevitably played into the hands of the prejudiced. As Mill warned long ago, the assumption of innate inferiority ill disposes one even to try to improve the conditions of those deemed inferior. Immigrants and blacks naturally felt attacked, and that their legitimate aspirations were being thwarted, by the psychologists' "scientific" analyses of their average intelligence levels.

Moreover, crucial aspects of these "scientific" analyses turned out to be very wrong. In the 1920s, Yerkes, Brigham, and followers grossly exaggerated the validity of the army tests as measures of innate intelligence, independent of cultural factors. In 1969, Jensen's case for black genetic inferiority rested on a presumed IQ heritability of .80—a figure derived from the fraudulent Burt studies and now exposed as a major exaggeration. Thus history has shown that invidious racial comparisons are only too easily constructed out of misleading or tainted "scientific" evidence. Such travesties inevitably produced anger and suspicion, and while that cannot *justify* the excesses perpetrated against Jensen, Herrnstein, and others, it can help explain why they occurred. Had the general hereditarian case not become associated with the racial issue, it would not have aroused such violent opposition. Now, we can perhaps hope that the growing consensus as to the limited (though real) validity of intelligence tests, and the recognition that nurture is vital even if there remains a genetic component to intelligence, will enable this most virulent, racial aspect of the IQ controversy to quiet down.

Even if it does, however, *other* aspects will certainly continue to be warmly, if less violently, debated. The ambiguity of the available scientific data leaves ample room for honest differences of emphasis regarding both the nature and structure of "intelligence" itself, and the relative contributions to it of nature and nurture. But further, and undoubtedly much more important, the IQ controversy is unusual among scientific problems for the degree to which it interacts with the extra-scientific and sometimes even non-rational concerns of its investigators. The biographies in this book suggest how early life experiences, shaping the protagonists' most basic conceptions of themselves, may often have predisposed them toward their scientific positions and interests in adulthood. Mill, Galton, Terman, and

Kamin, for example, were all "prodigies" of one kind or another, and their early experiences can only have sensitized them, in their own different ways, to the vagaries of intellectual development in different people. Galton, Binet, Spearman, and Burt all competed aggressively for schoolboy academic prizes, and this experience must have enhanced the importance of intellectual comparison and measurement in their eyes. In a different vein, Wechsler and Kamin both grew up as sons of middle-European immigrants, and thus could witness firsthand the influence of atypical cultural factors in the shaping of character and ability.

Perhaps because they so often derive from early and fundamental life experiences, scientific positions on the IQ controversy often become highly supercharged with ethical, philosophical, or religious feelings. For Mill and Kamin, the enhancement of ability through environmental reform is a matter of the highest moral urgency, while for Galton the eugenic betterment of the race is literally a religious duty. Spearman was impelled toward his conception of intelligence by an admittedly non-rational loathing of the ethical implications of associationism, and Jensen's adolescent fascination with the philosophy of Gandhi apparently steered him toward his life work.

More mundane but still powerful economic factors have undoubtedly played roles as well. Yerkes and Burt not only placed professional psychology "on the map," but also created whole new professions for psychometricians and educational psychologists in their respective countries, through their championing of intelligence tests. Terman's and Wechsler's commitment to testing was undoubtedly enhanced by the fact that they made a great deal of money through the sale of their successful tests. In short, the IQ controversy has touched on a host of diverse issues—personal, social, philosophical, and economic, as well as purely scientific. From this complex assortment of factors has arisen its peculiar fascination and heat.

The controversy will certainly continue, because we can still all legitimately wonder how our particular abilities would have turned out had we different parents and heredity on the one hand, or different education and culture on the other. We can be certain that we would be different people if any of these were so, but the kind and degree of differences remain unpredictable. Each of us, like the protagonists in this book, will have had experiences to make us wonder about some sorts of influence more than others, and to believe that some are more important than others. More powerful than any available scientific data, these different experiences will continue to produce a wide variety of views—both in the scientists who will continue actually to debate the IQ controversy, and in the public who will continue to observe it with interest.

 Notes

PREFACE

1. Richard Herrnstein, "IQ," *Atlantic Monthly* (*228*:43–64, September 1971).
2. A long collection of these letters was published in *Atlantic Monthly* (*228*:101–110, December 1971).
3. This account is based on the Appendix to Richard Herrnstein, *I.Q. in the Meritocracy* (Boston: Little, Brown, 1973).

⑴ THE NATURE-NURTURE CONTROVERSY

1. Norbert Wiener, *Ex-Prodigy: My Childhood and Youth* (Cambridge, MA: M.I.T. Press, 1953), p. 158.
2. Ibid., p. 159.
3. T. Cohen and R. Donkin, "The Genius Kids: Born or Made?" *The Sunday Times* (London), 23 August 1981, p. 5.
4. John Stuart Mill, *Principles of Political Economy* (Toronto: University of Toronto Press, 1978; originally published 1848), p. 319.
5. Francis Galton, *Hereditary Genius* (Gloucester, MA: Peter Smith, 1972; originally published 1869), p. 56.
6. Michael Packe, *The Life of John Stuart Mill* (New York: Macmillan, 1954), p. 34.
7. John Stuart Mill, *Autobiography* (London: Oxford University Press, 1971), p. 11.
8. Ibid., p. 18.

9. Ibid., p. 20.
10. Ibid., p. 23.
11. Reported in Anna Mill, *John Mill's Boyhood Visit to France* (Toronto: University of Toronto Press, 1960), p. xii.
12. Mill, *Autobiography*, pp. 21–22.
13. Ibid., pp. 19–20.
14. A variorum edition of the *Logic* is given in John Stuart Mill, *A System of Logic, Ratiocinative and Inductive* (Toronto: University of Toronto Press, 1973). Mill's other important psychological expositions are found in his *An Examination of Sir William Hamilton's Philosophy* (Toronto: University of Toronto Press, 1979; originally published 1865); his article, "Bain's Psychology," in John Stuart Mill, *Essays on Philosophy and the Classics* (Toronto: University of Toronto Press, 1978; originally published 1859); and in his editor's annotations to James Mill, *Analysis of the Phenomena of the Human Mind* (London, 1869).
15. Mill, *Logic*, p. 825.
16. Ibid.
17. Ibid., p. 853.
18. Mill, "Bain's Psychology," p. 346.
19. Mill, *Logic*, p. 859.
20. Mill, "Bain's Psychology," pp. 349–350.
21. Mill, *Logic*, p. 856.
22. Ibid., p. 873.
23. Ibid., p. 859.
24. Ibid., pp. 867–868.
25. Mill, *Autobiography*, p. 162.
26. See E. R. August (ed.), Thomas Carlyle: *The Nigger Question* and John Stuart Mill: *The Negro Question* (New York: Appleton-Century-Crofts, 1971).
27. Karl Pearson, *The Life, Letters and Labours of Francis Galton*, 3 vols. (Cambridge, England: The University Press, 1914–1930), Vol. 1, p. 66.
28. The original letters, with their annotations, are currently housed in the Galton Archives in the Manuscripts Room of the Library at University College London.
29. Pearson, *Life of Galton*, Vol. 1, p. 69n.
30. Francis Galton, *Memories of My Life* (London: Methuen, 1908), p. 13.
31. Letter from Francis Galton to S. T. Galton, 26 March 1837, in File 108C of the Galton Archives.
32. Pearson, *Life of Galton*, Vol. 1, pp. 127–128.

33. Letter from Emma Galton to Francis Galton, 23 Oct. 1840, in File 105 of the Galton Archives.
34. Pearson, *Life of Galton,* Vol. 1, pp. 164–165.
35. The complete phrenologist's report is in File 81 of the Galton Archives. Portions of it have been published in D. W. Forrest, *Francis Galton: The Life and Work of a Victorian Genius* (London: Elek, 1974), p. 37.
36. Galton, *Hereditary Genius,* pp. 56–57.
37. Francis Galton, "Zanzibar," *The Mission Field* (*6;*121–130, 1861). Also see Raymond E. Fancher, "Francis Galton's African Ethnography and Its Role in the Development of His Psychology," *British Journal for the History of Science* (*16:*67–79, 1983).
38. Francis Galton, *Inquiries into Human Faculty and Its Development* (New York: Dutton, 1907), p. 17*n.*
39. Galton, *Hereditary Genius,* p. 23.
40. Francis Galton, "Hereditary Talent and Character," *Macmillan's Magazine* (*12:*157–166, 318–327, 1865), p. 321.
41. Ibid., p. 320.
42. Galton, *Hereditary Genius,* p. 79.
43. Ibid., p. 23.
44. Galton, "Hereditary Talent and Character," p. 161.
45. Galton, *Hereditary Genius,* pp. 81–82.
46. Galton, *Inquiries,* p. 172.
47. Galton, "Hereditary Talent and Character," p. 165.
48. Francis Galton, "Hereditary Improvement," *Fraser's Magazine* (*7:*116–130, 1873), p. 126.

[2] THE INVENTION OF INTELLIGENCE TESTS

1. Francis Galton, *Inquiries into Human Faculty and Its Development* (New York: Dutton, 1907), p. 19.
2. Ibid., p. 21.
3. Ibid., pp. 19–20.
4. J. M. Cattell, "Mental Tests and Measurement," *Mind* (*15:*373–381, 1890), p. 374.
5. C. Wissler, "The Correlation of Mental and Physical Tests," *The Psychological Review,* Series of Monograph Supplements (*3*[6], 1901).
6. Quoted in T. Wolf, *Alfred Binet* (Chicago: University of Chicago Press, 1973), p. 3.

7. A. Binet, "De la Fusion des Sensations Semblables," *Revue Philosophique* (*10*:284–294, 1880).

8. J. Delboeuf, Note in *Revue Philosophique* (*10*:644–648, 1880).

9. A. Binet, *L'Étude Experimentale de l'Intelligence* (Paris: Schleicher, 1903), p. 68.

10. Translated from A. Binet, "Le Raisonnement dans les Perceptions," *Revue Philosophique* (*15*:406–432, 1883), p. 412.

11. Quoted in Wolf, *Alfred Binet*, p. 47.

12. Quoted in T. Wolf, "Alfred Binet: A Time of Crisis," *American Psychologist* (*19*:762–771, 1964), p. 764.

13. Quoted in Wolf, *Alfred Binet*, p. 50.

14. A. Binet, *Alterations of Personality* (originally published 1896). In D. W. Robinson, ed., *Significant Contributions to the History of Psychology*, Series C, Volume V (Washington, D.C.: University Publications of America, 1977), p. 76.

15. Quoted in Wolf, *Alfred Binet*, p. 158.

16. A. Binet, "Le Fétichisme dans l'Amour," *Revue Philosophique* (*24*:142–167, 1887).

17. Quoted in Wolf, *Alfred Binet*, p. 67.

18. These three papers appear in English translation in R. H. Pollack and M. W. Brenner, eds., *The Experimental Psychology of Alfred Binet: Selected Papers* (New York: Springer, 1969), under the titles "The Perception of Lengths and Numbers in Some Small Children" (pp. 79–92), "Children's Perceptions" (pp. 93–126), and "Studies of Movements of Some Young Children" (pp. 156–167).

19. A. Binet, "Children's Perceptions," p. 120.

20. A. Binet, "Studies of Movements," p. 157.

21. These studies of memory appear in English translation in Pollack and Brenner, *Psychology of Binet*, pp. 127–130.

22. Translated from A. Binet, *La Suggestibilité* (Paris: Schleicher, 1900), pp. 119–120.

23. A. Binet and L. Henneguy, *La Psychologie des Grands Calculateurs et Joueurs d'Échecs* (Paris: Hachette, 1894).

24. A. Binet and J. Passy, "Notes Psychologiques sur les Auteurs Dramatiques," *L'Année Psychologique* (*1*:60–118, 1895); A. Binet, "M. François de Curel (Notes Psychologiques)," *L'Année Psychologique* (*1*;119–173, 1895).

25. Translated from Binet, *Étude Experimentale de l'Intelligence*, pp. 218–219.

26. Translated from A. Binet and V. Henri, "La Psychologie Individuelle," *L'Année Psychologique* (*2*:411–465, 1896), p. 411.

27. Ibid., p. 417.
28. S. E. Sharp, "Individual Psychology: A Study in Psychological Method," *The American Journal of Psychology* (*10*:329–391, 1899).
29. Quoted in Wolf, *Alfred Binet*, p. 140.
30. "La Création Littéraire: Portrait Psychologique de M. Paul Hervieu," *L'Année Psychologique* (*10*:1–62, 1904).
31. Translated from A. Binet and T. Simon, "Sur la Necessité d'établir un Diagnostic Scientifique des États Inférieurs de l'Intelligence," *L'Année Psychologique* (*11*:161–190, 1905), p. 164.
32. Translated from A. Binet and T. Simon, "Applications des Méthodes Nouvelles au Diognostic du Niveau Intellectuel chez des Enfants Normaux et Anormaux d'Hospice et d'École Primaire," *L'Année Psychologique* (*11*:245–336, 1905), pp. 320–321.
33. Their work on the test was presented in three consecutive articles in the same issue of *L'Année Psychologique*—the two cited in Notes 31 and 32 above, and A. Binet and T. Simon, "Méthodes Nouvelles pour le Diagnostic du Niveau Intellectuel des Anormaux," *L'Année Psychologique* (*11*:191–244, 1905).
34. Translated from Binet and Simon, "Méthodes Nouvelles," pp. 196–197.
35. The 1908 revision appeared in A. Binet and T. Simon, "Le Développement de l'Intelligence chez les Enfants," *L'Année Psychologique* (*14*:1–94, 1908); that of 1911 in A. Binet, "Nouvelles Recherches sur la Mésure du Niveau Intellectuel chez des Enfants d'École," *L'Année Psychologique* (*17*:145–201, 1911).
36. Translated from Binet, "Nouvelles Recherches," p. 149.
37. Ibid., p. 157.
38. Translated from A. Binet, *Les Idées Modernes sur les Enfants* (Paris: Flammarion, 1973), p. 101.
39. Ibid., p. 102.
40. Ibid., p. 107.
41. Ibid., p. 109.
42. Translated from Binet and Simon, "Méthodes Nouvelles," p. 223.
43. Translated from Binet and Simon, "Le Développement de l'Intelligence," p. 85.

3 INTELLIGENCE REDEFINED

1. Charles Spearman, Autobiography, in C. Murchison, ed., *A History of Psychology in Autobiography*, Vol. 1 (Worcester, MA: Clark University Press, 1930), pp. 299–334; see pp. 300–301.

2. Ibid., p. 322.

3. Ibid.

4. Charles Spearman, " 'General Intelligence,' Objectively Determined and Measured," *American Journal of Psychology* (*15*:201–293, 1904), p. 283.

5. Ibid., p. 269.

6. Ibid., p. 270.

7. Ibid., p. 272.

8. Reproduced from Ibid., p. 275.

9. Charles Spearman, *The Nature of "Intelligence" and the Principles of Cognition* (London: Macmillan, 1923), p. 10.

10. Ibid., p. 5.

11. Ibid., pp. 5–6.

12. Bernard Hart and Charles Spearman, "General Ability, Its Existence and Nature," *British Journal of Psychology* (*5*:51–84, 1912), p. 79.

13. Alfred Binet, "Analyse de C. E. Spearman, 'The Proof and Measurement of Association between Two Things' and 'General Intelligence Objectively Determined and Measured,' " *L'Année Psychologique* (*11*:623–624, 1905).

14. For details see Bernard Norton, "Charles Spearman and the General Factor in Intelligence: Genesis and Interpretation in the Light of Sociopersonal Considerations," *Journal of the History of the Behavioral Sciences* (*15*:142–154, 1979); and Raymond E. Fancher, "Spearman's Original Computation of g: A Model for Burt?" *British Journal of Psychology*, 1985 (in press).

15. For a short account of this argument see Godfrey Thomson, Autobiography, in E. G. Boring et al., eds., *A History of Psychology in Autobiography*, Vol. 4 (Worcester, MA: Clark University Press, 1952), pp. 279–294, see pp. 282–283; for more extensive treatment see William Brown and Godfrey Thomson, *Essentials of Mental Measurement*, 4th ed. (Cambridge, England: The University Press, 1940), especially Chapter 9.

16. Stephen Jay Gould, *The Mismeasure of Man* (New York: Norton, 1981), especially Chapter 6.

17. William Stern, Autobiography, in Murchison, *History in Autobiography*, Vol. 1, pp. 335–388, p. 347.

18. Ibid.

19. William Stern, *The Psychological Methods of Intelligence Testing*, translated by G. M. Whipple (Baltimore: Warwick and York, 1914), p. 21.

20. Ibid., pp. 38–39.
21. Ibid., p. 3.
22. Ibid., p. 79.
23. See Theta H. Wolf, *Alfred Binet* (Chicago: University of Chicago Press, 1973), p. 203.
24. Gordon W. Allport, "The Personalistic Psychology of William Stern," in Gordon W. Allport, *The Person in Psychology: Selected Essays* (Boston: Beacon Press, 1968), pp. 271–297, see p. 276.
25. Quoted from the Henry H. Goddard papers, File M33.1, entries for March 31 and April 1, 1908; housed in the Archives of the History of American Psychology at the University of Akron, Ohio.
26. Henry H. Goddard, *Human Efficiency and Levels of Intelligence* (Princeton, NJ: Princeton University Press, 1920), p. 1.
27. Henry H. Goddard, *The Kallikak Family: A Study in the Heredity of Feeble-mindedness* (New York: Macmillan, 1912), p. x.
28. Ibid., pp. 11–12.
29. Ibid., p. 16.
30. Ibid., pp. 29–31.
31. Ibid., pp. 50–51.
32. Ibid., pp. 103 and 29.
33. Henry H. Goddard, "Mental Tests and the Immigrant," *The Journal of Delinquency* (2:243–277, 1917).
34. Gould, *Mismeasure of Man*, p. 171.
35. E.g., see John Higham, *Strangers in the Land: Patterns of American Nativism, 1860–1925* (New Brunswick, N.J.: Rutgers University Press, 1955).
36. Gould, *Mismeasure of Man*, pp. 335–336.
37. Henry H. Goddard, "Feeblemindedness: A Question of Definition," *Journal of Psycho-Asthenics* (33:219–227, 1928), p. 224.

4   THE RISE OF INTELLIGENCE TESTING

1. Quoted in Daniel J. Kevles, "Testing the Army's Intelligence: Psychologists and the Military in World War I," *Journal of American History* (55:565–581, 1968), p. 567.
2. Ibid., p. 571.
3. Robert M. Yerkes, Autobiography, in C. Murchison, ed., *A History of Psychology in Autobiography*, Vol. 2 (Worcester, MA: Clark University Press, 1930), pp. 381–407, p. 384.

4. Ibid., p. 386.
5. Ibid., pp. 390–391.
6. Robert M. Yerkes, "The Binet versus the Point Scale Method of Measuring Intelligence," *Journal of Applied Psychology* (*1:*111–122, 1917), p. 114.
7. Ibid., p. 115.
8. Ibid., p. 114.
9. Robert M. Yerkes, "Psychological Examining in the United States Army," *Memoirs of the National Academy of Sciences* (*15:*890 pp. entire, 1921), see p. 424.
10. See Stephen Jay Gould, *The Mismeasure of Man* (New York: Norton, 1981), pp. 204–214.
11. Yerkes, "Psychological Examining."
12. Kevles, "Testing Army's Intelligence," p. 574.
13. Quoted in Gould, *Mismeasure of Man,* p. 199.
14. Ibid., p. 221.
15. Lippmann's critical articles have been collected together in N. J. Block and G. Dworkin, eds., *The IQ Controversy* (New York: Pantheon Books, 1976).
16. For a summary of these critical reviews see Mark Snyderman and Richard Herrnstein, "Intelligence Tests and the Immigration Act of 1924," *American Psychologist* (*38:*986–995, 1983).
17. Otto Klineberg, Autobiography, in G. Lindzey, ed., *A History of Psychology in Autobiography,* Vol. 6 (Englewood Cliffs, NJ: Prentice Hall, 1974), pp. 163–182, see p. 167.
18. Otto Klineberg, "An Experimental Study of Speed and Other Factors in 'Racial' Differences," *Archives of Psychology,* No. 93, 1928.
19. Otto Klineberg, *Negro Intelligence and Selective Migration* (New York: Columbia University Press, 1935).
20. Carl C. Brigham, "Intelligence Tests of Immigrant Groups," *Psychological Review* (*37:*158–165, 1930).
21. The arguments on both sides appeared in G. M. Whipple, ed., *The Thirty-ninth Yearbook of the National Society for the Study of Education—Intelligence: Its Nature and Nurture* (Bloomington, IL: Public School Publishing Co., 1940). Also see H. L. Minton, "The Iowa Child Welfare Station and the 1940 Debate on Intelligence: Carrying on the Legacy of a Concerned Mother," *Journal of the History of the Behavioral Sciences* (*20:*160–176, 1984).
22. Lewis M. Terman, Autobiography, in Murchison, *History of Psychology in Autobiography,* Vol. 2, pp. 297–331, p. 302.

23. Ibid.
24. Ibid., p. 311.
25. Ibid., p. 331.
26. Ibid., p. 310.
27. Ibid., p. 316.
28. Lewis M. Terman, "A Preliminary Study of the Psychology and Pedagogy of Leadership," *Pedagogical Seminary* (*11*:413–451, 1904), and "A Study in Precocity and Prematuration," *American Journal of Psychology* (*16*:145–183, 1905).
29. Lewis M. Terman, "Genius and Stupidity: A Study of Some of the Intellectual Processes of Seven 'Bright' and Seven 'Stupid' Boys," *Pedagogical Seminary* (*13*:307–373, 1906), p. 329.
30. Ibid., p. 372.
31. Terman, Autobiography, p. 322.
32. Ibid., p. 323.
33. Lewis M. Terman and H. G. Childs, "A Tentative Revision and Extension of the Binet-Simon Measuring Scale of Intelligence," *The Journal of Educational Psychology* (*3*:61–74, 133–143, 199–208, and 277–289, 1912).
34. Lewis M. Terman, The Intelligence Quotient of Francis Galton in Childhood," *American Journal of Psychology* (*28*:209–215, 1917).
35. Catherine Cox, *The Early Mental Traits of Three Hundred Geniuses* (Stanford, CA: Stanford University Press, 1926).
36. Lewis M. Terman, "Human Intelligence and Achievement," reprinted in May V. Seagoe, *Terman and the Gifted* (Los Altos, CA: William Kaufmann, 1975), pp. 216–228, see p. 219.
37. For summaries of the longitudinal study see Ibid., and also Daniel Goleman, "1,528 Little Geniuses and How They Grew," *Psychology Today* (*13*:28–43, February 1980).
38. Arthur Jensen, *Straight Talk about Mental Tests* (New York: Methuen, 1981), pp. 30–31.
39. Richard J. Herrnstein, *I.Q. in the Meritocracy* (London: Allen Lane, 1973), p. 50.
40. Christopher Jencks et al., *Inequality: A Reassessment of the Effect of Family and Schooling in America* (New York: Basic Books, 1972).
41. Roger Brown and Richard J. Herrnstein, *Psychology* (Boston: Little, Brown, 1975), pp. 519–520.
42. Biographical details on Wechsler are taken from his obituary by Joseph Matarazzo, *American Psychologist* (*36*:1542–1543, 1981).
43. David Wechsler, "On the Influence of Education on Intelligence as

Measured by the Binet-Simon Tests," *Journal of Educational Psychology* (*17*:248–257, 1926).

44. David Wechsler, "Analytic Use of the Army Alpha Examination," *Journal of Applied Psychology* (*16*:254–256, 1932).

45. David Wechsler, *The Measurement and Appraisal of Adult Intelligence*, 4th ed. (Baltimore: Williams & Wilkins, 1958), p. 160.

46. Jensen, *Straight Talk*, pp. 54–55.

47. L. L. Thurstone, *Primary Mental Abilities* (Chicago: University of Chicago Press, 1937).

48. J. P. Guilford, "Three Faces of Intellect," *American Psychologist* (*14*:469–479, 1959).

49. See Gould, *Mismeasure of Man*, Chapter 6, for an elaboration of this point.

5 TWINS AND THE GENETICS OF IQ

1. For the full story of Ed and Fred see Horatio Newman, Frank Freeman, and Karl Holzinger, *Twins: A Study of Heredity and Environment* (Chicago: University of Chicago Press, 1937).

2. See Susan L. Farber, *Identical Twins Reared Apart: A Reanalysis* (New York: Basic Books, 1981), Chapter 3.

3. Newman et al., *Twins*, p. 362.

4. This notion is stressed by Burt's biographer, Leslie S. Hearnshaw, in his *Cyril Burt: Psychologist* (Ithaca, NY: Cornell University Press, 1979), pp. 270–274.

5. Cyril Burt, Autobiography, in E. G. Boring and H. S. Langfeld, eds., *A History of Psychology in Autobiography*, Vol. 4 (Worcester, MA: Clark University Press, 1951), pp. 53–73, p. 59.

6. Ibid., p. 56.

7. Ibid., p. 59.

8. Cyril Burt, "Experimental Tests of General Intelligence," *British Journal of Psychology* (*3*:94–177, 1909).

9. Ibid., p. 100.

10. Ibid., p. 176.

11. Quoted in Hearnshaw, *Cyril Burt*, p. 28.

12. Cyril Burt, "The Inheritance of Mental Characteristics," *Eugenics Review* (*4*:168–200, 1912), pp. 193, 200.

13. Cyril Burt, *The Young Delinquent* (London: University of London Press, 1925), p. 57.

14. Burt, Autobiography, pp. 71, 70.
15. Quoted in Hearnshaw, *Cyril Burt,* p. 285.
16. Cyril Burt, "Ability and Income," *British Journal of Educational Psychology (13:*83–98, 1943), p. 91.
17. See Brian Simon, *Intelligence Testing and the Comprehensive School* (London: Lawrence and Wishart, 1953); and Alice Heim, *The Appraisal of Intelligence* (London: Methuen, 1954).
18. Cyril Burt, "The Evidence for the Concept of Intelligence," *British Journal of Educational Psychology (25:*158–177, 1955), p. 158.
19. Ibid., p. 167.
20. Cyril Burt, "The Inheritance of Mental Ability," *American Psychologist (13:*1–15, 1958), pp. 6–7.
21. J. Conway, "The Inheritance of Intelligence and Its Social Implications," *The British Journal of Statistical Psychology (11:*171–190, 1958), p. 186.
22. John McLeish, *The Science of Behaviour* (London: Barrie and Rockliffe, 1963), p. 77.
23. Hearnshaw, *Cyril Burt,* pp. 205, 228.
24. M. Howard, Review of McLeish's *The Science of Behaviour, British Journal of Statistical Psychology (16:*129–135, 1963).
25. Cyril Burt, "The Genetic Determination of Differences in Intelligence: A Study of Monozygotic Twins Reared Together and Apart," *British Journal of Psychology (57:*137–153, 1966), p. 146.
26. Arthur R. Jensen, Obituary of Sir Cyril Burt, *Psychometrika (37:*115–117, 1972).
27. Arthur R. Jensen, "What Is the Question? What Is the Evidence?" in T. S. Krawiec, ed., *The Psychologists,* Vol. 2 (New York: Oxford, 1974), pp. 206–207.
28. Ibid., p. 207.
29. Ibid., p. 208.
30. Ibid., p. 217.
31. Ibid., pp. 233–234.
32. Ibid., p. 219.
33. Ibid., p. 222.
34. Ibid., p. 233.
35. Ibid., p. 234.
36. Arthur R. Jensen, *Genetics and Education* (London: Methuen, 1973), p. 9.
37. Ibid., pp. 10–11.
38. Arthur R. Jensen, "How Much Can We Boost IQ and Scholastic

Achievement?" in *Environment, Heredity, and Intelligence* (Cambridge, MA: Harvard Educational Review, 1969), pp. 1–123, see p. 2.

39. Ibid., p. 9.
40. Ibid., p. 16.
41. Ibid., pp. 28–29.
42. Ibid., pp. 33, 52.
43. Ibid., p. 88.
44. Ibid., p. 82.
45. This account of Jensen's dealings with the *HER* is taken from his *Genetics and Education*, pp. 23–28.
46. James F. Crow, "Genetic Theories and Influences: Comments on the Value of Diversity," in *Environment, Heredity, and Intelligence*, pp. 153–161, see p. 154.
47. J. McV. Hunt, "Has Compensatory Education Failed? Has It Been Attempted?" in *Environment, Heredity, and Intelligence*, pp. 130–152, see pp. 131–132.
48. Arthur R. Jensen, "Reducing the Heredity-Environment Uncertainty," in *Environment, Heredity, and Intelligence*, pp. 209–243, see p. 210.
49. See Jensen, *Genetics and Education*, pp. 31 ff.
50. Most of the personal and biographical information about Leon Kamin, and all of the unreferenced quotations, were obtained during an interview with the author on December 9, 1982.
51. An account of the hearing is in the *New York Times* of January 16, 1954, pp. 1, 6.
52. The story of Kamin's acquittal is in the *New York Times* of January 6, 1956, p. 6.
53. Leon Kamin, *The Science and Politics of I.Q.* (Harmondsworth, England: Penguin Books, 1977), p. 50.
54. Ibid., p. 71.
55. James Shields, *Monozygotic Twins Brought Up Apart and Brought Up Together* (London: Oxford, 1962).
56. Niels Juel-Nielson, "Individual and Environment: A Psychiatric-Psychological Investigation of Monozygotic Twins Reared Apart," *Acta Psychiatrica et Neurologica Scandinavica,* Monographic Supplement, 1965.
57. Leon Kamin, "Heredity, Intelligence, Politics, and Psychology." Dittoed copy of address given to the Eastern Psychological Association and at various other places throughout the U.S. in 1972, pp. 11–15.

58. Ibid., p. 18.
59. Arthur R. Jensen, "Kinship Correlations Reported by Sir Cyril Burt," *Behavior Genetics* (*4*:1–28, 1974), p. 24.
60. See letters from H. J. Eysenck and Leon Kamin in the *Bulletin of the British Psychological Society* (*30*:257–259, 1977).
61. Oliver Gillie, "Burt: The Scandal and the Cover-Up," *Supplement to the Bulletin of the British Psychological Society* (*33*:9–16, 1980), p. 9.
62. Quoted in Nicholas Wade, "IQ and Heredity: Suspicion of Fraud Beclouds Classic Experiment," *Science* (*194*:916–919, 1976), pp. 916, 918.
63. Arthur R. Jensen, Letter to *The Times* of London, December 9, 1976.
64. H. J. Eysenck, "The Case of Sir Cyril Burt: On Fraud and Prejudice in a Scientific Controversy," *Encounter* (*48*:19–24, 1977), pp. 19, 24.
65. Wade, "IQ and Heredity," p. 919.
66. Hearnshaw, *Cyril Burt*, pp. 246–247.
67. Arthur R. Jensen, *Straight Talk about Mental Tests* (New York: The Free Press, 1981), pp. ix, xii.
68. Ibid., pp. 125, 126.
69. Reported in Ibid., p. 92.
70. Ibid., p. 100.
71. Quoted from Kamin's section in H. J. Eysenck versus Leon Kamin, *The Intelligence Controversy* (New York: Wiley, 1981), pp. 105–106.
72. Ibid., p. 127.
73. Ibid., p. 133.
74. Sandra Scarr and Richard A. Weinberg, "Intellectual Similarities within Families of Both Adopted and Biological Children," *Intelligence* (*1*:170–191, 1977).
75. Joseph M. Horn, John C. Loehlin, and Lee Willerman, "Intellectual Resemblances among Adoptive and Biological Relatives: The Texas Adoption Project," *Behavior Genetics* (*9*:177–207, 1979).
76. Scarr and Weinberg, "Intellectual Similarities," p. 190.
77. Kamin in Eysenck-Kamin, *The Intelligence Controversy*, p. 125.
78. J. C. DeFries, R. C. Johnson, A. R. Kuse, G. E. McClearn, J. Polovina, S. G. Vandenberg, and J. R. Wilson, "Familial Resemblance for Specific Cognitive Abilities," *Behavior Genetics* (*9*:23–43, 1979).
79. Leon Kamin, "Psychology as Social Science: The Jensen Affair, Ten Years Later." Dittoed copy of Presidential Address delivered to the Eastern Psychological Association in April 1979, p. 14.

6 CONCLUSION

1. Arthur R. Jensen, *Bias in Mental Testing* (New York: The Free Press, 1980), pp. 738, 717.
2. Ibid., p. 717.
3. Ibid., p. 719.
4. Ibid., pp. 727–729.
5. Ibid., pp. 720–721.
6. Ibid., p. 721.
7. Ibid., pp. 721–722.
8. Arthur R. Jensen, *Straight Talk about Mental Tests* (New York: The Free Press, 1981), p. 126.
9. Irving Lazar and Richard Darlington, "Lasting Effects of Early Education: A Report from the Consortium for Longitudinal Studies," *Monographs of the Society for Research in Child Development* (47, Nos. 2–3, 1982).
10. James R. Flynn, "The Mean IQ of Americans: Massive Gains 1932 to 1978," *Psychological Bulletin* (95:29–51, 1984).

Index

intelligence tests (*continued*)
  origin of idea of, xv, 4, 35–36, 37
  point-scale, 122–23, 124, 151, 153, 154
  research use of, 229, 230
  rise of, 117–61
  suggested readings on, 83, 161
  U.S. popularization of, 119, 126
  validity of, xiii–xiv, 227–31
  WAIS, 153–57, 158–59, 236–37
  WISC, 157, 229
  WPPSI, 157
  of Yakima Indians, 130–31
  Yerkes's ideal, 123
  see also. mental tests
Intelligenzalter, 102
intensity, association by, 12
International Health Exhibition (1884), 41
Iowa, University of, xii, 131–32
"IQ Myth, The," 227
Irish peasants, degradation of, 18

Jamaica, blacks in, 18
James, William, 106
Jencks, Christopher, 184, 215
Jensen, Arthur, xv, 116, 145–46, 148, 159, 161, 184–201, 209, 240
  autobiography of, 186, 225
  background and education of, 185–88
  Burt defended by, 214, 216
  Burt exposed by, 212–13
  as Burt's eulogist, 184–85
  Burt's influence on, 168, 184–85, 188, 192–93, 195
  critics of, 197–201
  current IQ test views of, 228–30
  Direct Learning tests of, 189–91
  Eysenck's influence on, 186–88
  genetics of racial differences and, 168, 191–200, 206, 239
  high heritability of IQ reaffirmed by, 216–19
  Kamin's correspondence with, 212
  Kamin's rejoinder to, 219–24
  racism attributed to, 197–98, 199
  recent views held by, 216–19
  reservations about IQ tests, 226, 228–29

Jensenism controversy, 197–201
job applicants, IQ tests in selection of, 228–29
Johnson, Lyndon B., 191–92
judgment, 74
  social, 75
Juel-Nielson, Niels, 209
juvenile delinquency, Burt's interest in, 173

Kallikak Family, The (Goddard), 108–12, 113–14, 116
  doctored evidence and, 114
  environmental factors and, 113–14
  as propaganda, 114
Kamin, Leon, xv, 169, 200–213, 225, 234, 240
  background and education of, 201–7
  Burt exposed by, 207–9, 212
  current rejoinder of, 219–24
  in Communist party, 203, 204–5
Kevles, Daniel J., 161
King, Martin Luther, Jr., 191
kinship correlations, 183–85, 193, 223–24
Kite, Elizabeth, 110–11, 113
Klineberg, Otto, 130–31, 151
Krawiec, T. S., 225

land reform, 18
language, mental testing and, 60
Lawrence, Ruth, 2–3
Leipzig University, Wundt's Institute at, 44
lethargic stage, 54
letter repetition, as mental test, 47
Life, Letters and Labours of Francis Galton, The (Pearson), 40
Life of John Stuart Mill, The (Packe), 40
Lippmann, Walter, 130
literary creativity, Binet's investigation of, 64
Locke, John, 11
Loehlin, John, 221–23
London County Council, 174–75, 180
London Day Training College, 175
Lorde Andre de, 80
Los Angeles State Normal School, 138